Sustainable Urban Development

CW00551504

Sustainable Urban Development V   ! explores
how the professions responsible for making the built envi̇ṛoṇṃ̇ẹ̇ṇ̇ṭ̇ ......   ̇ịnable are
seeking to respond to this new agenda.

This book is about the transition to sustainability, offering a multi-perspective
debate and case studies concerned with the 'new professionalism' of sustainable
approaches to development and design. To support the discussion, the book looks at
examples of the changes taking place in the professional practice of architecture, town
planning and construction to meet the challenges of sustainable development. The book
covers:

- the challenges faced in the professions
- changes in design and construction processes
- institutional constraints and the need to change governance of the built
environment
- at what level we can expect to see a wider agenda for sustainability emerge, rather
than a series of local and national experiments
- how new knowledge about the impact of changing the built environment can be
transformed into practical action.

With an international perspective, written by academics and practitioners with direct
experience of managing change in Britain, France, Italy, the Netherlands and the Czech
Republic, the examples are drawn from a number of European States. Original research
presented explores the variety of ways in which professional practice is changing in
response to new criteria and new methodologies. Overall, this volume indicates that
sustainable urban development can no longer be treated as an exception to the rules
and regulations which govern the planning, development and design of construction
projects.

This is the fourth volume in the research and debate of the BEQUEST (Building,
Environmental Quality Evaluation for Sustainability) network funded by the European
Commission. The first three books provide a framework, set of protocols, environmental
assessment methods and toolkit for policy makers, academics, professionals and
advanced-level students in Urban Planning, Urban Property Development, Urban Design,
Architecture, Construction and related areas of the Built Environment.

Ian Cooper is a partner at Eclipse Research Consultants, Cambridge, UK.

Martin Symes is Professor Emeritus of Architecture and Planning, University of the
West of England, UK.

Sustainable Urban Development
Editors:
Steven Curwell, Salford University, UK
Mark Deakin, Napier University, UK
Martin Symes, University of the West of England, UK

Sustainable Urban Development Volume 1
The Framework and Protocols for Environmental Assessment
Steven Curwell, Mark Deakin and Martin Symes (eds)

Sustainable Urban Development Volume 2
The Environmental Assessment Methods
Mark Deakin, Peter Nijkamp, Gordon Mitchell and Ron Vreeker (eds)

Sustainable Urban Development Volume 3
A Toolkit for Assessment
Steven Curwell, Mark Deakin, Patrizia Lombardi, Gordon Mitchell and Ron Vreeker (eds)

Sustainable Urban Development Volume 4
Changing Professional Practice
Ian Cooper and Martin Symes (eds)

These volumes are based on the research and debate of the European BEQUEST network (**B**uilding **E**nvironmental **Qu**ality **E**valuation for **S**us**T**ainability). Together the books provide a toolkit of interest and value to policy-makers, professionals and advanced-level students in a variety of disciplines.

Sustainable Urban Development

Volume 4: Changing Professional Practice

Edited by Ian Cooper and Martin Symes

Routledge
Taylor & Francis Group

LONDON AND NEW YORK

First published 2009
by Routledge
2 Park Square, Milton Park, Abingdon, Oxon OX14 4RN

Simultaneously published in the USA and Canada
by Routledge
270 Madison Avenue, New York: NY 10016, USA

Routledge is an imprint of the Taylor and Francis Group, an informa business

© 2009 Ian Cooper and Martin Symes for selection and editorial
material; individual chapters, the contributors.

Typeset in Akzidenz Grotesk by
Keystroke, 28 High Street, Tettenhall, Wolverhampton
Printed and bound in Great Britain by
The Cromwell Press, Trowbridge, Wiltshire

British Library Cataloguing in Publication Data
A catalogue record for this book is available from the British Library

Library of Congress Cataloging in Publication Data
A catalog record for this book has been requested

ISBN10: 0–415–43821–7 (hbk)
ISBN10: 0–415–43822–5 (pbk)
ISBN10: 0–203–89218–6 (ebk)

ISBN13: 978–0–415–43821–6 (hbk)
ISBN13: 978–0–415–43822–3 (pbk)
ISBN13: 978–0–203–89218–6 (ebk)

Contents

Contributors

Stéphanie Abrial: Research Associate, PACTE-CNRS Institut des Etudes Politiques, Université Pierre Mendès-France, Grenoble. She has contributed to the comparative research on new expertise in sustainable building in the United Kingdom and France financed by the French government, with a special interest in methodology for the analysis of open-ended interviews.

Christopher Boyko: Research Fellow, Lancaster Institute for Contemporary Arts, Lancaster University. He is currently examining the urban design decision-making process and its relationship to sustainability on the Engineering and Physical Sciences Research Council (EPSRC) funded research project, VivaCity2020: Urban Sustainability for the 24-Hour City. Other areas of research and teaching interest include tourism, place meaning and identity, multiculturalism and technology and public space. He is a member of the Environmental Design Research Association and the British Urban Regeneration Association.

Ian Cooper: Partner, Eclipse Research Consultants, and Visiting Professor, School of the Built Environment, University of Salford. He has held a watching brief on the development of sustainable development and its impact on the demand and supply sides of the construction sector in the UK since the late 1980s. Since the mid-1990s he has worked extensively on stakeholder engagement in the delivery of a more sustainable built environment, both in the UK, for central government departments and regional government agencies, and through a series of EU-funded projects.

Rachel Cooper: Professor of Design Management and Director, Lancaster Institute for Contemporary Arts, Lancaster University. She publishes widely on Design Management, Design Policy, New Product Development, Design in the Built Environment, Urban Regeneration, Design Against Crime and Socially Responsible Design. She leads the EPSRC project, VivaCity2020: Urban Sustainability for the 24-Hour City. President of the European Academy of Design, and Editor of *The Design Journal*, she is currently a member of the EPSRC Infrastructure and Environment Strategic Advisory Team, and of the advisory panel on the AHRC/ESRC Cultures of Consumption programme as well as Chair of the advisory panel for the Designing for the 21st Century initiative. She is panel convenor for visual arts and media practice, history, theory postgraduate awards and sits on the Council of the AHRC.

Gilles Debizet: Maître de Conférences in Building Management and Planning, the University of Grenoble Joseph Fourier and Laboratoire PACTE-Territoires (CNRS-UJF-UPMF), Grenoble. He studies innovation in public expertise and policies in relation to sustainable development. His latest publications concern Metropolitan Transport, Urban Planning and Building. He is director of the Masters in Maîtrise d'Ouvrage et Management de Patrimoine Bâti run jointly by Grenoble University and the Ecole Nationale Supérieure d'Architecture de Grenoble.

Ivan Dejmal: Dipl. Ing. and Consultant in Prague. Editors' note: We have been very sad to learn that Ivan Dejmal, who was a distinguished practitioner, a leader of his profession in his country, and a former Czech environment minister, died after an intensive illness in February 2008, shortly after completing his contribution to Chapter 7.

Enrico Fabrizio: Architect, PhD student in Energy Technologies at the Politecnico di Torino and at the INSA de Lyon. At Polytechnico di Torino he is a member of the TEBE research group and gives lectures on Sustainable Building at the Faculty of Architecture. At present he works and publishes on modelling and optimisation of multi-energy source systems in sustainable building.

Marco Filippi: Professor of Building Physics and Building Services at the Faculty of Architecture in the Politechnico di Torino, he is director of the PhD course in Technological Innovation for the Built Environment and leader of the TEBE research team (www.polito.it/tebe). He has published widely on thermal building physics, innovative HVAC systems, lighting, applied acoustics and sustainable building. At present he is Vice-Rector for Academic Strategies.

Colin Fudge: Pro-Vice-Chancellor, Executive Dean of the Faculty of Environment and Technology and Director of the WHO Collaborative Research Centre at the University of the West of England as well as Royal Professor of the Swedish Academy of Sciences. He has published extensively on urban regeneration, sustainability and environmental policy. He is Chair of the European Expert Group, Chair of the European Sustainable Cities and Towns Campaign, Visiting Professor at the European University Institute, a member of the Anglo-Swedish Round Table on climate change and adaptation, member of the Scientific Board at Chalmers University and Chair of the South West Regional Centre of Excellence. He is Member of the Royal Town Planning Institute, Honorary Fellow RIBA, and Fellow of the Royal Society of Arts.

Robert Grimshaw: Professor of Facilities Innovation at the University of the West of England, Bristol. He researches and publishes widely on the implication of flexible working for workplace infrastructure and the professional development of Facilities Management. He is a member of the British Institute of Facilities Management, a former Chair of its Professional Standards and Education Committee and the current Chair of its Academic Sub-Committee.

Eric Henry: Research Engineer and Sociologist, CNRS, attached to CRISTO (1992–2006) and PACTE 'Politics and Organisation' (2007+) research centres at the Université Pierre Mendès-France, Grenoble and to the Ministère de l'Equipement. Specialises in the sociology of changes in the firm and in the social-economics of construction. Major interests are organisational innovations, quality management and participatory evaluation. Contributed to the revision of ISO 9000 norms for the Commissariat General du Plan. Continuing links with the Ecole Polytechnique de l'Université de São Paulo and l'Université Flumineuse de Rio de Janeiro.

David Ludlow: Senior Research Fellow, the University of the West of England, Bristol. Member of the EU Expert Group on the Urban Environment, the EU Expert Group on Thematic Strategy on Sustainable Urban Management and of the Royal Town Planning Institute. Consultant to European Commission and European Environment Agency on the development of urban and regional planning in a Pan-European context, and on the development of urban management systems supporting policy integration.

Susan Moore: Lecturer in Planning, Housing, Land and Property, School of City and Regional Planning, Cardiff University, Wales. She has academic and professional backgrounds in planning, human geography and environmental policy in Britain and Canada. Her research interests focus on the intersection of innovation, best practice and strategic policy in the delivery of sustainable residential development. She was post-doctoral research officer on the *SusCon Project* at the Centre for Environmental Policy and Governance, London School of Economics and Political Science.

Magali Paris: Research Assistant, CNRS Sound Space and Urban Environment Research Centre and Associate of CNRS Laboratoire Politiques Publiques, Action Politique, Territoires, Grenoble. She contributed to the implementation of the research 'new expertises in sustainable building' financed by the French government. While completing her PhD in sociology and architecture, she leads and participates in research on the links between dwelling and the urban environment.

Peter Roberts: Chair of the Academy for Sustainable Communities – the UK government agency responsible for skills and knowledge for sustainable communities, professionals and others – and Professor of Sustainable Spatial Development at the University of Leeds. He has researched and published widely on Spatial Planning, Management and Governance, Sustainable Communities and Regeneration Theory, Policy, and Practice, and the Spatial Dimension of Sustainable Development. He is Vice-President of the Town and Country Planning Association, Hon. Vice-Chair of the Regional Studies Association, a member of the Royal Town Planning Institute, an Academician of the Academy of Learned Societies for the Social Sciences and was awarded an OBE for services to Planning and Regeneration.

Yvonne Rydin: Professor of Planning, Environment and Public Policy and Co-Director of the Environment Institute, University College London. She has published widely on planning, urban governance and sustainable development. Since 2004, sustainable construction and design have been a particular focus. She is currently a lead expert on the UK government's Foresight project on Sustainable Energy Management and the Built Environment.

Thomas Scheck: Managing Director of Profile, a European Project Management Consultancy firm based in Paris, Lyon, Rotterdam and Prague with international practice and networks. Dutch of Czech origin, he is Associate Professor in the Master-programme MOBAT, University of Grenoble and EMO – Ecole de Maîtrise d'Ouvrage ('formation continue Ecole Nationale des Ponts et Chaussées et BTP Services'). He is involved in conferences and training for sustainable and energy saving concepts, research programmes and consulting for both public and private sectors. He was a correspondent to the building and architectural professional press.

Martin Symes: Professor Emeritus of Architecture and Planning, University of the West of England and Associate of the CNRS Laboratoire des Organisations Urbaines, Paris. He publishes widely on Urban Renewal, the Architectural Profession and Architectural Education, was Chairman of the Architectural Research Forum and Secretary to the International Association for People-Environment Studies. He is a member of the Royal Institute of British Architects and Fellow of the Royal Society of Arts.

Ger de Vries: Managing director, researcher, and consultant at V & L Consultants in Rotterdam. He is involved in research and consultancy in the field of sustainable and energy-efficient building and living, the sustainable development of the built environment and trends in environmentally aware innovations in housing, buildings, and the construction industry. He is editor of the building journal *bouwIQ* (formerly Duurzaam/Puur Bouwen) and a research associate in Environmental Design at Delft University of Technology, Faculty of Architecture.

Foreword
Colin Fudge

In 1996, the European Union's Expert Group on the Urban Environment had this to say on the move towards sustainability in urban development:

> Whatever the priorities, emphasis must be placed on the 'sustainability transition'. In general it is easier both to diagnose what is wrong with present ways of doing things and to describe desired future states than to establish how to move from the current position to the desired future. The 'sustainability transition' – how to make this step – should be emphasised in policy development, research and practice.
>
> (Expert Group on the Urban Environment 1996: 267)

This notion came from our lengthy discussions in the Expert Group and from practitioner colleagues in cities.

In a Europe of Nations, this transition is proving far from simple. Many changes have taken place, at all levels of policy and practice, and communities are at different stages of progress towards sustainable urban development, but it is not yet clear how effectively this transition can be accomplished. Partly this is because it is unclear whether there is a pan-European view on:

- who should make decisions at each spatial scale, given the different traditions of professional decision-making and governance in the (now greater number of) Member States
- how these decisions can be effectively integrated under the variety of institutional and regulatory structures which operate in different parts of the Union.

These are uncertainties which are accentuated by the fact that competence for urban affairs has not been vested in the European Council, the central body, and by the desire of (most) members to devolve such decision-making to the lowest reasonable level in the hierarchy following the principle of subsidiarity.

The question of the transition seems still to be 'below the parapet' and to bring it 'above the parapet' is not considered easy. To make matters worse, we still have remarkably little comprehensive knowledge about what is currently happening in different nations, regions and localities. Yet if a transition process is to be effectively supported, centrally and locally, we surely need first to understand as fully as possible the recent history of attempts to change older procedures and to understand the barriers to change. This is a central point of this new book.

This is the fourth volume in a series dealing with ways of putting sustainable development into practice, through city building and construction, in Member States of the European Union (EU). It is grounded in the work of the imaginative BEQUEST network – a concerted action originally funded by the European Commission (EC). Volume 1 established a framework for analysis, Volumes 2 and 3 discussed the structure and use of decision-support systems (specifically: evaluation assessment methods) and a toolkit for their use, and this volume reports on the changes in professional practice which provide a context for the introduction of these and other similar methods.

It is argued throughout the series that the requirements of sustainable development pose very special problems for the conventional processes of development, design, construction and use of buildings. Volume 1 suggested the need for new protocols of action for all the professional groups involved and gave exemplars for the form of such protocols. These were phrased in general terms and did not take national legal, economic and cultural traditions into account.

The principal purpose of this fourth volume is to investigate these differences and to show exactly how far the introduction of what may be thought of as a 'new paradigm' for development, design and construction has been achieved in a cross-section of Member States.

The series is one of the main outputs of an EC-funded Concerted Action Programme (ENV4-CT07-0607 Research Directorate of the European Commission), known as **B**uilding **E**nvironmental **Qu**ality **E**valuation for **S**us**T**ainability (BEQUEST). This brought together an 'Intranet' of 24 academics and consultants from 14 partner organisations in 6 Member States, who organised a series of conferences in different cities of the EU in the period 1998–2001. A further 120 representatives of property and construction sector organisations were invited to these meetings and have formed an 'Extranet' for continuing Web-based interactive networking and debate.

Such a widespread and structured discussion group was unprecedented at the time and contacts pursued within it have enabled the editors of the present volume to find a wide range of contributors to this book representing both public and private sector interests from different European Member States.

It can also be noted that members of the BEQUEST team have since worked on two further EC projects under the Information Society Technologies Programme (INTELCITY: IST-2001-37373 and INTELCITIES: IST-2002-507860). These have allowed them to study, among other topics, the adoption of new forms of communication between government organisations at different levels, property and construction professionals, and user groups which is becoming fundamental to thinking about sustainable development.

The relationship between structures of governance and professional bodies is currently a field of considerable interest to national and international research communities. This is partly because policies for an international response to problems of globalisation (including global warming and other environmental issues) depend for their implementation on the expertise and capacity for innovation available at national levels.

Many of these problems, and much of this capacity, are focused on the management of urban and regional development, and therefore on the relationships with the property and construction sectors.

The research reported here has not been published in this form before, nor have discussions of this topic been brought together in a single volume. The book throws new light therefore on the process by which sustainable development is becoming institutionalised in the advanced societies of Europe, and on the ways in which barriers between expert groups are being broken down, altered, rethought and reconstructed to take account of new requirements and new policies and of the entry of new actors into the city development process.

Finally I would like to express my thanks as Chair of the Expert Group on the Urban Environment to the editors, authors and publisher for bringing this work to fruition and indeed for the commitment to the whole series. This fourth volume is to be welcomed as one of the first serious attempts to answer this most important question: how is the 'sustainability transition' actually taking place?

In this sense this book continues the work of the Expert Group on the Urban Envrionment and the development of more sustainable cities in Europe.

REFERENCE

Expert Group on the Urban Environment (1996) *European Sustainable Cities*. Luxembourg: Office for Official Publications of the European Communities.

Preface
A European Perspective
Ian Cooper and Martin Symes

THE BEQUEST NETWORK AND ITS TRAJECTORY

This volume is the fourth in a series stimulated by the work of the BEQUEST Network, a 'concerted action' originally funded by the European Commission. In the mid-1990s, the BEQUEST network saw its mission as being to identify common issues underlying the growing interest in sustainable development expressed by representatives of both the demand and supply sides of the property and infrastructure industries. The project suggested structuring them in such a way as to provide a framework for analysis, evaluation and subsequent action on the construction of urban developments (Bentivegna et al. 2002).

This exercise in structuring and framing was begun by discussing the PICABUE representation of sustainable development (itself an abstraction of the ten principles of Agenda 21 which were seen as most relevant to urban redevelopment): see Figure 0.1.

The working method adopted for conceptualising and concretising the meaning of sustainable urban development (SUD) for construction professionals was an integrated, iterative process of discussion and consensus building across the range of disciplines involved in the production and operation of the built environment, and in defining its spatial context. A principal outcome of this approach was the BEQUEST Framework (see Figure 0.2). This was constructed to act as a collaborative platform for building a consensus about the constituent components of SUD. The Framework was to be supported by a set of protocols and assessment methods which together would form a tool kit for evaluating the sustainability of proposed urban (re-)developments.

The BEQUEST Framework was also intended to provide opportunities for fruitful dialogue and debate about SUD between stakeholders – especially between planners, property developers, designers, constructors, operators and users of the built environment. Such debate was seen by members of the BEQUEST network as one of the gateways through which stakeholders needed to pass in their journey towards sustainable urban development. BEQUEST has conceived of such gateways as either 'hard' (usually explicit and regulatory) or 'soft' (that is to say informal, centred on emergent accepted practice or based on tacit understandings). These gateways

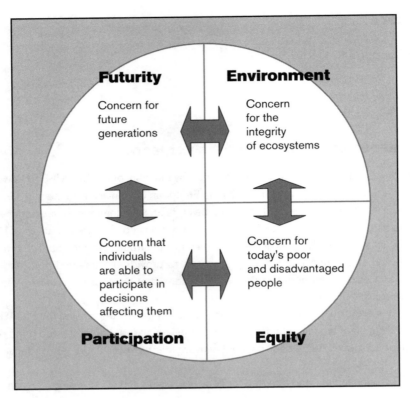

0.1 The PICABUE definition of principles underpinning sustainable development
Source: Cooper 1997

include the points where stakeholders find themselves crossing over from the comfort of operating within the boundaries of their own knowledge domain and embarking on a journey that takes them into engagement with other domains. In this process of crossing boundaries, stakeholders would be seen as beating a path towards SUD, using the BEQUEST Framework and protocols as guides to staying on track. In this way, BEQUEST was seen as offering both a vision of and a methodology for evaluating sustainable urban development from within a shared, cross-disciplinary, collaborative platform. The notion of sustainable urban development as 'a journey to be shared' – with interim staging posts, pivotal crossings to be negotiated, and (multiple) pathways between which choices have to be made – echoes the EC Expert Group on the Urban Environment's 1996 call for a focus on the 'transition' to sustainability. This call is repeated in the Foreword to this volume and usefully updated in Chapter 6, which deals with recent EU-wide agreements made in Bristol and Leipzig (see pp. 127–143).

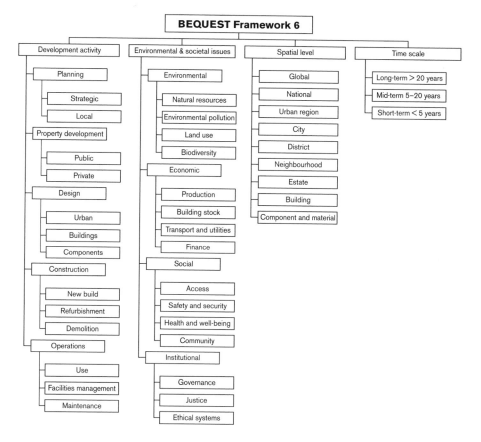

0.2 The BEQUEST Framework
Source: Curwell et al. 2005

Bentivegna et al. (2002: 83) made clear that the BEQUEST Network saw Sustainable Development as a relative rather than an absolute concept and as a process not a product or fixed destination concerned with very long time frames. The progress in understanding this process which BEQUEST has made so far is set out in the volumes in this series.

Volume 1 set out the BEQUEST Framework and a set of protocols for assessing the environmental impact of urban development proposals. Volume 2 offered a detailed account of both the simple and advanced environmental assessment methods that are currently being used. As well as outlining the statutory instruments then in place by the European Commission for assessing the environmental impact of urban development, Volume 2 also examined the systems thinking lying behind assessment methods and looked at how well they accommodate public participation in future urban development. Volume 3 progressed the BEQUEST trajectory by bringing together 13 case studies on the use of the Framework, protocols and assessment methods as a system for supporting decision-making about how to make urban developments more sustainable. Volume 3 focused on diagnosing the challenges that land use planning now faces and on investigating whether it is possible to meet these challenges by using (very) advanced assessment methods to evaluate some of the leading visions and scenarios that are being proposed.

A continuous thread running through the first three volumes in the series has been the provision of information, examples and methods for supporting built environment and construction professionals in the decisions they have to take about how to make the production and operation of the built environment more sustainable.

In this volume an additional dimension is added with the focus of debate being reversed. Instead of seeking to analyse, or theorise about, possible decision-making systems, this volume attempts to review the present context of actions aimed at sustainable development: to understand the present state of the art in the *transition to sustainability* in urban planning, development and design. It aims to ask questions about the process of moving towards sustainability in urban development, and is based on studies undertaken across a selection of Member States of the European Union, about:

- the level of consensus which is emerging about what new information to use
- what legislative and professional frameworks are proving most appropriate
- how adopting the goals of sustainability in urban development projects affects what it means to be a built environment professional.

REFERENCES

Bentivegna, V., Curwell, S., Deakin, M., Lombardi, P., Mitchell, G. and Nijkamp, P. (2002) A vision and methodology for integrated sustainable urban development: BEQUEST. *Building Research and Information* **30**(2): 83–94.

Cooper, I. (1997) Environmental assessment methods for use at the building and city scale: Constructing bridges or building common ground. In P. Brandon, P. Lombardi and V. Bentivegna (eds) *Evaluation of the Built Environment for Sustainability*. London: E.&F.N. Spon.

Curwell, S., Deakin, M. and Symes, M. (eds) (2005) *Sustainable Urban Development: Volume 1, The Framework and Protocols for Environmental Assessment*. London: Routledge.

Acknowledgements

The editors owe a substantial debt of gratitude to the authors of the chapters which comprise this volume. They have taken part in a peer reviewing process in which many individuals have contributed to improving the quality of the whole publication. The editors also thank the series editors for their rapid and enthusiastic response to the proposal that the series, on sustainable urban development, should include a special volume on the professionalisation process we have observed.

Chapters in this volume report on research projects funded by a number of British, French, Dutch and Italian government and local government agencies as well as the European Commission.

Contributions have been made by key individuals in private sector organisations (Eclipse Research Consultants, Profile Consulting, Johnson Controls International) with expertise in this field, and staff of a number of universities (University College London, London School of Economics, Lancaster University, University of Leeds, University of Salford, University of the West of England, Cardiff University, Université Pierre Mendès-France Grenoble, Université Joseph Fourier Grenoble, Delft University of Technology, Politecnico di Torino).

The authors and editors would like to express their deepest gratitude to Caroline Mallinder and her team at Taylor & Francis for the high quality support offered throughout the complex process of writing and publishing this volume. The series editors echo this sentiment for the complete Sustainable Urban Development Series which has appeared under the Routledge imprint.

1

Introduction
Ian Cooper and Martin Symes

This book is about the transition to sustainability. Specifically, it discusses ways in which professionals responsible for the production and operation of the built environment are responding to the pressure to make urban development more sustainable. At the heart of this process lies an ability to transform new knowledge about the impact of changing the built environment into practical action. The expertise required is largely in the hands of professionals and, although there is a market for this service, government is responsible for promoting its use and effective application. The general population, present and future, will feel the impact of its quality. The relationships between the market, government, the professions and the public are crucial and need to be rethought carefully – not least because of the new forms of governance that sustainable development may require.

This is the fourth volume in a series on sustainable urban development. The series is based on experience in the European Union and has been stimulated by BEQUEST, a research network funded by the European Commission to build a common assessment framework and vocabulary for professionals involved in the production of the built environment. Earlier volumes in the series have emphasised the *urban* environmental, economic and social objectives of sustainable development, published detailed critiques of assessment methods which may be used in *spatial* planning and *construction* project implementation. They have also provided case study descriptions of a number of major developments in which sustainability has been sought. This new volume focuses on a multidisciplinary debate about the *continuing process* of professionalising the relevant knowledge. It is critical that the information required for designing for sustainable development is fully absorbed into everyday practice. To support discussion of what is required, examples of changes which have occurred so far are drawn from a number of European countries.

This volume includes reports of original research which explores the variety of ways in which professional practice is changing in response to new criteria and new methodologies. It points to a 'new professionalism' that is becoming established. It asks whether this will emerge simply by incorporating new ideas within existing professions or through the rise of new professional identities to challenge existing ones. For, as this volume indicates, sustainable urban development can no longer be treated as an exception to the rules and regulations which govern the planning, development and design of construction projects: just a response that requires additions to existing professional agendas. Rather, new norms are emerging with variations in the way they are developing in different parts of the European Union. Much of the new form of practice is held in common. And this newly emerging consensus will have implications beyond just adding a few extra criteria to an already extensive list of project requirements.

A SOCIAL SCIENCE PERSPECTIVE

One of the main arguments of this book is that the problems raised by transforming knowledge into action are not only technical but also economic and social, hence making new demands on professional culture. Of course, there is new information to be absorbed, but even this can founder on traditional approaches to knowledge management, which often involve combining a loose understanding of the relevant science with an emphasis on the use of tacit knowledge. The working methods used in a development process by its client and design team are also frequently unclear. For example, a rift can emerge between participants whose aim is to find new solutions to a given task and those who limit themselves to modifying a tried and tested approach.

One basic problem is that of aiming for sustainable development while adhering to a traditional view of professional behaviour and decision-making, since these are based on service to a particular client, with only a very general sense of responsibility for the economic and social impact on a wider community. For development to be sustainable the reverse must become the case. Broad impacts must come first, and individual benefits follow. Unfortunately this sense of priorities usually cuts across the reward structure of the development and construction industries, with their traditional professional territories and current division of labour. The status quo is being questioned by the new actors emerging, especially those from the voluntary sector, with different expectations of who should do what and how the costs and benefits should be distributed. The established professions must respond.

A number of difficult questions need to be raised about the attempt to define the knowledge which is relevant to sustainable development. There are also interesting questions to be considered about the forms of professionalism in current practice. After addressing these questions, this introduction lists a selection of probable technical and socio-economic barriers to the professionalisation of the knowledge required for sustainable development. There then follows a series of questions about the processes of change which may be required. Since local detail is added and discussed in the case-based chapters (Parts I and II of the book), a brief description of each of these is then included. An attempt to draw the multifaceted strands of theory and practice explored throughout the book together is made in the concluding chapter.

QUESTIONS CONCERNING SUSTAINABLE DEVELOPMENT

A major challenge for redefining professionalism in this field is that knowledge about sustainable development remains contested. Hence the discussion in the first of the volumes in this series bears summarising here.

The foundations of concern for the impact of science and technology on the environment were laid by Rachel Carson (1965). Her work focused on problems of the natural environment but introduced many of the solutions which are promoted today in the broader context of concern for the human-made environment. These include: the need to conserve species variety, the need to approach changing natural processes with caution, the need to avoid taking calculated risks and the need to consider who has the right to make decisions which affect the future. The term *sustainable development*, which refocused the debate on the economic and social purposes of applying science to environmental problems, was coined by Barbara Ward in the mid-1970s (Holmberg and Sandbrook 1992). It has rapidly gained currency in governmental and non-governmental circles concerned with the changing quality of life. Dickens (2004) shows many more recent examples of the way in which our species is now considered to be a part of – rather than outside or above – nature, and how, as society transforms its environment, people's own natures are being transformed as well. But both the terminology of science and its application can be contested in relation to the production of the built environment, as elsewhere. Of course all science is contested, as the case study by Latour and Woolgar (1986) shows only too clearly. But the situation with the science underlying calls for sustainable development is especially complex.

Pearce et al. (1989) listed more than 60 detailed definitions of the term sustainable development. In an important discussion Beckerman (1994) argued that the technical issues addressed and the value judgements made by proponents of sustainable development are frequently confused with each other. He called for greater clarity in the analysis. Contributing to this latter process, Mitchell (2000: 68, drawing on Mitchell 1999), argued that in practice the various definitions can be summarised with reference to two well-known statements. One is from the World Conservation Union (IUCN), United Nations Environment Programme (UNEP) and World Wide Fund for Nature (WWF), that sustainable development 'improves the quality of life while living within the carrying capacity of supporting ecosystems' (IUCN-UNEP-WWF 1991); the other is that sustainable development is 'development that meets the needs of current generations without compromising the ability of future generations to meet their needs and aspirations' (World Commission on Environment and Development (WCED) 1987). This point is also made in Cooper (1997) and Deakin et al. (2001).

The United Nations Earth Summit, held in Rio de Janeiro in 1992, developed a programme of action, Local Agenda 21 (United Nations 1993). This was followed up with a Habitat Conference in 1996, in which special emphasis fell on the consequences of urban development, both because urban development aims to change the quality of life and because it has environmental impact. The European Council held a major conference of cities and towns in Europe at which the Aalborg Charter (1994) was adopted. This referred among other topics to the need for establishing a strongly participatory process. The European Commission DG XI set up an expert group on the urban environment and this first reported in 1996 (Commission of the European Communities (CEC) 1996). Its conclusions then included the need to integrate economic, social and environmental policy objectives, and stressed the importance of developing an approach to urban management which would emphasis integration and partnership mechanisms.

The decade since 1996 has demonstrated that the broad approach to sustainable development advocated by EU expert group is not easy to implement in everyday political decision-making at any scale. This has often resulted in retreats to addressing specific issues, often a particular scale. For instance, at a national level, the attraction of seeking a focus on the manipulation of one particular indicator can be seen in the British government's Stern Review (Stern 2006).[1] This focuses on the impact of carbon dioxide emissions on climate change, arguing for an urgent international effort to reduce emissions by

- emissions trading
- technology cooperation
- adaptation of development policy.

This review suggested that the main scientific issues are settled and that we can safely predict rises in temperature (with consequent effects on sea water levels) and urban consequences on this basis. But such information is not always accepted without question. For example Stern (2006) gives the proportions of global emissions which underlie this scenario and appear to have direct impact on town planning as 40 per cent divided as follows:

Land Use	18 per cent
Buildings	8 per cent
Transport	14 per cent

One major criticism that can be made of this influential report recalls Beckermann's (1994) comments:

> in their treatment of climate science the Oxonia papers contain serious gaps and errors; . . . the science of climate change is still in its infancy and the account given is . . . questionable, misleading and biased.
>
> (Lavoisier Group, cited by Byatt et al. 2006: 146)

continuing

> the treatment extends to economic and statistical aspects [and] presents as valid and authoritative twin sets of results which have been subjected to damaging . . . criticism . . . a reconstruction of Northern Hemisphere mean temperature 'anomalies' over the period from AD 1000 [and] projections of greenhouse gas emissions [which are] in large part based on economic analysis [which] there is good reason to query.
>
> (Byatt et al. 2006: 147)

As these comments illustrate, it is important to understand that even at the global scale there is disagreement even about single factor issues such as carbon emissions. In the case of a multi-factor issue like sustainable development, especially when framed at lower (national, regional, local and construction project) scales, disagreements are therefore to be expected. Such disagreement has to be seen, not as an anomaly to be explained away but as an integral part of the 'picture' with which professionals are being asked to deal when seeking to adapt their working practices to the new set of challenges.

At the local government scale, the emergence of much stronger levels of concern about environmental quality has already had some impact in most European countries. Following the Rio conference in 1992, local authorities introduced Agenda 21 initiatives, and, depending on national administrative systems, revised their town planning and building control regulations. This has led to the increased use of environmental assessment methods to evaluate the sustainability of urban development (see Volume 3 of this series). Any attempt at configuring a new professionalism in response to sustainable development must take account of the part played by these methodologies in new forms of decision-making and governance. Oestreicher (1995) suggested that this trend will continue, arguing that:

> From time immemorial, local communities have been concerned with shaping the . . . environment . . . But in view of the threatened balance between the human and the non-human on our planet, we have to . . . reconsider the foundations of local government.
>
> (Ostreicher 1995: 35)

Mitchell (1999, 2000) sought to address the problems currently experienced by present-day local government officers and others in making the concepts of sustainable development more operational. He showed that measurement issues are significant when debate moves on from scientific discussion to the possibility of corrective action. There has been a rapid expansion in the volume of data available on the performance of 'human-environment systems' and the emergence of indicator systems has been extensively discussed, for example, by Bell and Morse (1999). Many of these features were considered in detail in Volume 2 of this series.

In an important review of the literature, Hatfield Dodds (2000) examined the scientific debate over the development of sustainability indicators and identified five different 'approaches' which are used to build support for corrective action on matters concerning, for example, environmental quality and ecological integrity. The first approach identified by Hatfield Dodds (2000) is 'sustainable income'. This is the most common and starts from the position that past practice has taken insufficient account of environmental resources and the damage which can be imposed upon them. The second approach is 'maintaining ecological integrity'. This argues that it is not enough to take account of environmental costs and that consideration should be given to the capital stock of resources consumed, special measures being taken to maintain 'natural capital'. The third approach is concerned with 'inequality, institutions and environmental impact'. This derives from the observation that the distribution of income and power shape environmental impacts for a given level of resource use. The fourth approach is focused on 'participation and sustainable well-being'. This is a demand-side approach and draws attention to non-economic needs, biological requirements and social norms. The fifth and final approach in this classification is that which seeks 'alternative ethical approaches'. At their most extreme, those expressing this point of view trace the difficulty of achieving sustainability to 'mainstream ethics and religious traditions, which treat the environment as a commodity which exists only for human benefit'.

A similar classification of 'approaches' to achieving sustainability in architectural practice can be found in Guy and Farmer (2001). Referring also to work by Hannigan (1995) they wrote:

> The premise is that individuals, groups and institutions embody widely different perceptions of what environmental innovation is about. Each of these actors may share a commitment to sustainable development but are likely to differ greatly in their interpretation of the causes of and hence the solution to unsustainability.
>
> (Guy and Farmer 2001: 140)

Guy and Farmer identified designers as adopting six different approaches – 'eco-technic, eco-centric, eco-aesthetic, eco-cultural, eco-medical and eco-social' – calling these 'competing logics of sustainable architecture'. Their typology is elaborated further according to: sources of environmental knowledge, technologies, idealised concept of place, image of space and building image.

When the BEQUEST network members originally met in the 1990s they were mainly interested by Hatfield Dodds' second, third and fourth approaches. They chose not to duplicate ongoing investigations into indicators but proceeded at a more basic level, clarifying issues and seeking to understand their implications for sustainability evaluation processes. Their conclusions were founded on an application of the PICABUE analysis (Mitchell et al. 1995) which condenses the complex and lengthy Agenda 21 documentation and the goals of the Aalborg Charter into a 'shorthand form'. It lays its emphasis on the need for:

- ecological integrity
- equity
- public participation
- futurity (consideration of future generations).

Guy and Farmer (2001) included BEQUEST in their 'ecocentric logic', whose proponents are concerned with buildings and their place in nature. Indeed, this integration of ecological integrity, equality of resource consumption and participation in decision-making, was seen by some network members as providing an ethical basis for considering the future of urban development (Brandon and Lombardi 2005).

Another of the arguments in this volume is that there is a tension in practice between broad international or national aims for sustainable development and local, negotiated, agreements on what professionals are being asked to deliver. In practice, as Guy and Moore (2005) suggested, 'the challenge of sustainability is more a matter of local interpretation than of setting universal or objective goals'.

Volume 1 of this series (Curwell et al. 2005) sets out a set of protocols for assessing the sustainability of development by professional groups, suggesting that developers, planners, designers, the construction industry and building managers should all approach this task in the following broad sequence of actions:

- preliminary activities
- planning of assessment activity
- what to do in assessing
- carrying out the environmental assessment
- carrying out consultations
- taking into account the environmental report and consultations

- providing information on the decisions
- monitoring.

That volume treats the activities of each profession as relatively independent and bases its recommendations on traditional definitions of the structure of professional activities. But these are simplifications which need to be investigated further in two particular ways. In the first case multidisciplinarity, or at the very least, close cooperation between professions, is essential for the full achievement of the broader goals of sustainable development. Second, it is very probable that division of labour between professionals, and between them and other actors in the development process, is undergoing substantial change as sustainable development becomes the norm.

Thus when the authors contributing chapters to this fourth volume indicate that action over a broad front is required, the cases recounted in their chapters not only identify numerous barriers to transforming the knowledge available into a form in which it can be used by professionals, but also show how some of these barriers are being overcome by those who hope that sustainable urban development can be achieved. Some of these aspects are outlined in the sections which follow.

QUESTIONS CONCERNING PROFESSIONALISM

The growth of professionalism is argued by the historian Perkin (1989) to have been one of the main social and economic trends of the twentieth century. He described processes of growth in the application of expertise to increasing living standards in the West (where market economies have been developed to the full) and to political integration in the former Soviet bloc (where state organisation was much more significant). Until the latter part of that century, Perkin suggested, the British 'mixed economy' provided an important example of a society in which professional experts, although divided between state and private sector employment, worked in a balanced way to support both types of socio-economic development. Much of the academic literature on the activities and behaviour of specific professional groups has been published in the United States, where a 'Chicago School' dominated debate (Dingwall and Lewis 1983). Their point of view seems to be that professional groups are generated when new forms of knowledge which are seen to have practical potential begin to command a market, in business, becoming, at a later stage, subject like other forms of economic activity, to regulation by the state. Special forms of education and training are established, emphasising practical experience as well as theoretical understanding, and institutes are established which claim authority over qualifications required for newcomers to enter the market. Classic examples are the professions of law and medicine, for which all members of a well-ordered society have, arguably, a common need. Such professions are recognised by the political system, and legitimised. There is general agreement on what a doctor can and should be able to do, for example: rewards are standardised as far as possible and special measures are taken to ensure that disadvantaged members of society have access to their services in cases of need.

Knowledge about the development, design, construction and maintenance of the built environment has also led to professionalisation. But most observers agree that the process as described above is incomplete. For instance, there is no general agreement that a society *must* have architects (and so on) if it is to provide adequate shelter for everyone. As Duffy and Hutton (1998) demonstrated, architects (and others) have to struggle to make the case that they need the protection from market forces (and unscrupulous businesses) which is enjoyed by doctors and lawyers.

The extent to which the general public needs protection is also debated: in different states of the European Union the extent to which this is considered necessary varies a good deal. As in the more general case of professions described by Perkin (1989), the United Kingdom provides an example of a middle way, somewhere between the United States, where, as Gutman (1988) showed, architects have to compete with engineers for the work of designing most building types, and that of the former Soviet bloc, in which all major projects were controlled by the state. Nor is there agreement in Europe about the dividing lines between different types of profession. Although all states have engineers, some have more divisions of engineering than others. The UK, again for example, has a whole set of professional groups (the surveyors) which does not exist in France. To make matters more confused, the extent to which professionalisation of building design is incomplete has varied over the years (see McEwen 1974), and will no doubt continue to do so. This is partly because, as Gutman (1988) described for facilities management, new forms of knowledge relevant to construction require different levels of specialist understanding.

Thus a major issue for this volume is the extent to which the uncertainty of definition associated with the 'science' of sustainable development is beginning to interact with the confusion surrounding professional structures and behaviour among those responsible for the built environment, creating constraints to the implementation of sustainable development. A first overview suggests that these constraints may fall into two groups, technical and socio-economic.

Technical constraints on professionalising sustainable development

New information

Building lasts a very long time, materials are usually durable and conventional methods of assembly tried and tested. But there have been a number of recent examples of spectacular failures when new and untried materials have been used. There should be little difficulty in finding information concerning construction possibilities, but much of that which can be found is about feasibility at the assembly stage: information about the performance of new materials in prolonged use or about long-term changes in behaviour can be hard to come by. Sustainability is about the long-term effects of the use of resources and this is only now becoming the focus of some of the databases which are available. More of this kind of information is urgently required.

Understanding of relevant science versus the use of tacit knowledge

This is a particular problem for the design process since, as Schön (1983) argued, decision-making is often a matter of informed judgement, rather than fine calculation. Even in engineering decision-making, practice is usually dependent on rules of thumb or on generous safety factors, so that the limiting conditions which have to be defined by scientific experiment are never fully tested. Yet sustainability requires sound knowledge on the performance of buildings, and of the impact of user behaviour in the long run and clients have a need for performance guarantees. So, in future, for designers just to have a wide experience may no longer be enough.

Emphasis on innovation versus refinement of existing solutions

Professionals often build their reputations on work which has been undertaken over a period of time and gives an impression of long-term achievement even though many apparently new solutions are developed from implicitly understood or tacitly known precedents (see, for example, Alexander 1979). Sustainability frequently calls into question the repeated use of known solutions, these often being 'part of the problem'. But Kohler (2003) argued that it should also take the form of calls to re-evaluate past 'vernacular' solutions – incuding building materials that have, in developed countries, fallen from the conventional palette – and with them much of the skill and understanding that accompanied their use.

Emphasis on evidence-based decision-making

Pressures to deliver sustainability coincide with increasing emphasis, particularly within the public sector, on aligning procurement practices with a robust, transparent and seemingly auditable evidence-base. But it can be argued that buildings should not only be fit for purpose: they should also expand our perceptions of the possible and add value to the activities they house. They should help school children learn better, hospital patients to recover more quickly, office workers to perform more productively, occupants of houses to live a better quality of life. Similarly, the design of neighbourhoods should increase health and well-being and help augment local social capital, while reducing (fear of) crime and the need to use (private) transport. And urban design should increase social cohesion and promote the economic competitiveness not only of individual cities but also of whole city-regions and their hinterlands. These are not just rhetorical EU and national government policies: they are implementation imperatives against which local professionals are now being expected to deliver. There are crucial questions to answer – about the quality of the evidence base available to designers, about what is meant by evidence-based design (widely advocated in the design of commercial and health-care buildings) (Wikipedia 2007) and about the strengths and limitations of its application to other types of construction. Leaman (2003), for instance, suggested that

> building performance studies do not thrive well in a 'normal science' research framework as *inter alia* hypothesis testing usually fails in the face of multivariate complexity (where it is hard to pin down cause and effect and contexts change from case to case).
>
> (Leaman 2003: 173)

Social and economic constraints on professionalising sustainable development

Service to the client versus impact on the wider community
In order to claim protection from market forces, built environment professionals have traditionally claimed concern for the wider community even when working on specific projects for particular clients (see Willis 1981, for architects). Such claims have been contested by anti-professionalism movements (see Crinson and Lubbock 1994, again on architecture). One of the issues raised by this book is whether the trends to legitimise sustainability as a focus for professionalism (e.g. by licensing BREEAM consultants or even by redefining the mission statement of particular professional institutions) is either technically possible or ethically appropriate. Even when professionals claim a higher social purpose, they are not normally able to resolve conflicts of interest between the work a client is prepared to pay for and socially orientated work which is done for the public good, or included in development proposals as part of a professional response. Decision-making about *design choices* is often inevitably biased towards the interest of those who foot the bill. One of the problems of designing with sustainability in mind is that, beyond the immediate client,

those whose interest lie outside immediate return on investment or are only played out in the longer term, such as future generations, have no voice or resources to make themselves heard.

Professional territories and traditional divisions of labour

That the division of knowledge is reflected in the division of labour may seem self-evident – but it may also be a historical product of the impact of the Enlightenment and so subject to considerable variation between national cultures. The continued relevance or utility of such divisions may need re-evaluating in the face of sustainability which respects neither discipline nor domain boundaries. At a global level, there may be no agreed division of knowledge and no shared tradition of a division of labour, although Symes et al. (1995) suggested ways in which the market for construction services can influence changes in the division of labour. But Young (1993) has shown how the breaking down of such divisions has already been helpful at a local (and local government) level and professional networking fulfils important functions in the coordination of environmental improvement programmes. Sustainability requires local needs to be coordinated with global problems: if this is impossible, and, as Gutman (1988) showed, it often is, conflicts between professions will undoubtedly arise.

New actors and their expectations

Early pressures for taking issues of sustainability to the top of the international agenda have frequently been driven by non-governmental organisations (NGOs) and activists from the voluntary sector. Their role in urban and building design and development is increasingly important but yet to be fully established, let alone regularised in a way professionals can feel comfortable with. Many existing actors may be relocated, marginalised or even displaced when or as this does occur. Clearly the sooner their roles become regularised, the easier it will be for governments and others to formalise the new structures of decision-making which are required. There has been some discussion of the ways in which general environmental activists have joined existing pressure groups, set up their own 'sects' or influenced government priorities (see Douglas and Wildavsky 1982) but this thinking does not yet appear to have been applied to practices adopted in the built environment. Perhaps this book is the place to begin to do so.

QUESTIONS CONCERNING THE TRANSITION

Overcoming constraints

Addressing the changing aspirations of urban development policy may require not just a change of professional methods but a change in professional values as well. Given the pressures, barriers and constraints described above, it is important to review the principal ways in which these changes may occur. A number of types of event need to be considered. A brief inspection of the literature would suggest that the situation is complicated by the fact that professional work is based on the application in practice of changes in science itself. Thus it appears we have to consider not only whether, and how, the science is changing, and how far this is being adopted by practice (both a technical and an economic process: often known as innovation), but also the extent to which these developments are being legitimised or professionalised (through socio-political processes).

In science, the most radical changes have been called the paradigm shift. This term is drawn from studies by Kuhn (1962) and others on the social history of science. Kuhn wrote about 'normal science' and 'revolutionary science', the latter becoming possible, or even necessary, at the moment when the former can no longer solve satisfactorily the problems which it is posed. Results given by parameters of the normal paradigm begin to seem aberrant or just plain useless. Then it is seen that another parameter gives results which are unexpected or even interesting. After some hesitation, these results are then accepted by the scientific community: the problematic to which they are linked is redefined, and another methodology (a new paradigm and a new normal science) becomes established. A new set of problems, which *can* be solved, is the focus of research, and work in the laboratory continues anew. But the leaders of the former scientific community have to accept that their way of doing things has too many limitations and that new leaders must emerge. A scientific revolution has occurred, but through a (partly) social process. Some of the changes which can be seen in urban development and which are aimed at increasing sustainability may be based on the absorption of just such types of change in the science-base into the currency of professional practice.

Certainly new performance parameters have to be measured, new design solutions have to be synthesised. Kohler (2003) explicitly discussed 'new planning paradigms' suggesting that 'sustainability certainly marks a turning point in the planning discussion after the second world war'. If and when such a fundamental change does occur, it will have implications for all aspects of urban development. This may call into question, for instance, the primacy given to aesthetic values by architects. Ideas about what constitutes efficiency in construction trades and processes may need redefinition. Problems which were difficult to solve using the international style of modernism, such as contextual design, or teamwork in building, may all appear suddenly as much easier to resolve using more regionally and locally sensitive approaches (Cole and Lorch 2003). If the latter changes occur, then a revolution in development methods may be underway. If so, changes taking place in professionalism may perhaps be understood as being partly a consequence of a scientific revolution (see a discussion by Symes 2001).

We must beware of thinking that professional practice is only science based: it can also be based on (often tacit) knowledge derived from other sources, including ethical systems and personal values. Simple reference to a new 'science of sustainability' is also problematic. First of all, there would have to be many 'sciences', because sustainability transcends many (hard/soft) science disciplines and domains. Second, many of the scientific concepts/principles of sustainability are (ultimately and probably illegitimately) borrowed from ecology and then applied (like ecosystems) to human-made artefacts. Third, much of the argument in sustainable development that is made by analogy (and/or illegitimate borrowings) is not evidence based. For example, compaction, densification, mixed use, are often identified as key components of sustainable urban development. But it is hard to find an evidence-base demonstrating that these choices are more 'sustainable' than others. As Breheny (1996) said in the mid-1990s, urban sustainability is an area where policy imperatives may be running on ahead of research evidence. If appropriate research does not exist, and therefore cannot be absorbed into practice, the rhetoric of sustainable development may simply be applied within 'business as usual'. Then there would be an opposite situation which it would be important to identify, namely that sometimes nothing happens other than that people start using new or different words to describe what they have always done before but called something else. Larson (1977) in the United States has called this 'merely ideological' change in professional practice.

A second type of change discussed in the literature is about innovation, and, as a subset of this, its diffusion. In a paper which discusses the role of research in engineering and design organisations in terms of their 'capacity to learn', Gann (2003) (drawing on Cohen and Levinthal 1990) wrote:

> R&D has two faces: one side is the development of new ideas for innovation and problem-solving, the other is the capability that allows organisations to absorb ideas from elsewhere.
>
> (Gann 2003: 47)

Innovations are often described as of greater or lesser degree: incremental change, step change, composite change and hybrid change are terms which apply here (see, for example, Slaughter 1998). Presumably organisations can also have differential abilities to absorb such innovations. Professional groups – Gann (2003) called them 'communities of practice' – and professional firms are surely no exception to this. In a wider discussion of innovation methods, Dodgson et al. (2005) gave telling examples from the construction services industry (the case of Arup, multidisciplinary engineers, and the case of Gehry, an architect whose practice has adopted computer-aided design on an extensive scale). Neither of these examples deal with innovation concerning sustainable development, but they suggest that the object of discussion in this book is ripe for investigation.

In this case of the diffusion of innovations, we can refer to the work of Rogers (1995), who observed the process of change in many industrial situations. A study by Symes and Pauwels (1999) adapted his observations as follows:

> It is a mistake to think of the spread of a new idea (or any other innovation) as taking place in a linear way, simply from one person who knows, to another who does not, but then just learns it. Innovations are diffused by exchange, in which people interact with each other . . . each transmitter or receiver [not being] of equal value . . . Rogers suggests that in the very first stages of innovation – diffusion, interpersonal channels of communication have a particularly strong effect . . . Early adopters . . . rely on the more cosmopolitan channels, whereas late adopters, often the majority, rely on observing the results of early applications . . . Over a period of time, innovations will be modified, through 'reinvention' . . . and sometimes experience 'early rejection'. Persons who influence the transmission process can be considered 'change-agents' and the system of which they form a part can be considered a 'diffusion network'.
>
> (Symes and Pauwels 1999: 100)

Symes and Pauwels (1999) continued by applying this concept of a network, helping to spread ideas, to a case study of guidance on sustainability in urban design, in which it emerged that when a

> series of specific innovations was identified . . . some conflicted with current bureaucratic standards, others with perceptions of market acceptability. Some seem to have been readily introduced, others resisted or modified in the urban design process. Importantly . . . a set of different actors . . . was identified. They played different roles, worked on the project at different stages, had different concerns about the innovations proposed and had different levels of enthusiasm for their introduction.
>
> (Symes and Pauwels 1999: 115)

The case studies in this book go some way towards showing how far the *sustainability transition* has yet led to a reorganisation of practice and its governance, that is at the levels of the process of development decision-making and of the adoption of new forms of institution.

A variety of changing practices will be illustrated in these chapters. The cases are written from a number of different perspectives, and bring in different types of evidence. They should indicate that both professional knowledge and professional behaviour are being adapted in a wide variety of ways to the needs of the new goals and that this is beginning to be recognised in changes to the governance of the built environment. In different parts of the United Kingdom, Building Regulations and Planning Guidance are undergoing radical revision. In France the author of a government research report discussed in Chapter 10 of this book, Henry et al. (2006: 38) (quoting Haumont 1999) stated: 'architects find themselves condemned to continuously relegitimate themselves, socially and culturally' and asks whether this process will 'take another turn with the introduction of the requirement for sustainability' (trans. M. Symes). Professional life will surely have to adapt.

SUMMARIES OF CASE-BASED CHAPTERS

These chapters are divided into Parts I and II of this volume. Both parts report empirical studies of recent attempts to create more sustainable developments and draw on a number of theories of professionalism currently in use, allowing reflection upon their value as explanations of the process of change which is being experienced.

Part I includes a group of five chapters reporting on research which has dealt with the basic policy-making and decision-making *processes* which are applied to sustainable urban development, emphasising pan-European issues. In order, the chapters are concerned with

- networks
- policy interaction
- decision-making
- professional conflicts
- coordination skills.

Chapter 2, by Rydin and Moore, reports on a research project undertaken at the London School of Economics in 2004–2006. This examined how *policy learning* about sustainable construction is being spread across Europe and reflects upon lessons for understanding governance. In particular it questions the common assumption that effective knowledge transfer is dependent upon a successful 'cascade effect'. This chapter draws on a programme of interviews with decision-makers at various levels and relates the findings to models of multilevel governance.

Chapter 3, by Ludlow, a member of the Eurocities consortium, addresses policy implementation and skills development studied in research undertaken for the Commission on a Europe-wide issue, *urban sprawl*. This is a problem for all parts of the EU and is exacerbated both by the different recent histories of older and newer Member States and by great variations in the skills available. Chapter 4, by Boyko and Rachel Cooper, discusses interdisciplinary decision-making in *urban design*, as studied in an applied research project funded by the UK's Engineering and Physical Science Research Council as part of its Sustainable Urban Environment programme. It seeks to model the processes which have taken place over a number of years in a variety of British cities, including a part of Europe's largest, London: and to propose modifications which would allow the consideration of sustainability to be more effective.

Chapter 5, by Ian Cooper, includes two case studies in the United Kingdom where the move to sustainability in urban development has been intertwined with a number of government-supported attempts to improve the effectiveness and efficiency of development and construction processes. It suggests that the very notion of sustainable development – let alone its practical implementation – *confronts the professions with serious challenges*. This chapter is used to explore how these challenges are being played out in the UK in the context of recent changes in two specific examples of regulation and regeneration of the built environment – sustainable construction and neighbourhood renewal. The chapter discusses the value of 'conflict' and 'consensus' theories of professions in order to question whether the changes taking place in the UK will advance the interests of specific professions while undermining others.

The final chapter in Part I, Chapter 6 by Roberts, is based on international studies undertaken by the Academy for Sustainable Communities, an initiative of the UK government. It argues for a need to go beyond token inter-professional collaboration and for the establishment of new methods of *training, research and practice*. There is a skills deficit associated with 'silo working' by the traditional professions. The cross-cutting learning which is required should be extended to local authorities, the voluntary sector and community participants.

Part II consists of six chapters dealing with pressures on, and developments in, the *institutions* which govern professional activity in a number of European states. They offer a detailed understanding of important differences. In order, they are concerned with:

- political history and political goals
- the debate over regulations and markets
- projects which diverge from ideal models

- individuals' interpretations of their new roles
- the influence of cultural context
- the difficulty of reinventing professionalism.

Chapter 7, by Scheck, Dejmal and de Vries, gives an overview of sustainable construction and urbanism in *the Netherlands and the Czech Republic*. It contrasts the experience of two small and highly developed countries and allows discussion of the recent evolution (both positive and negative) of environmental and social practice in the 'old' and the 'new' Europe.

After this are three chapters which draw on a research project financed by the French government. Chapter 8, by Henry and Paris (who refer to experience in the Netherlands, France and Great Britain), contrasts interestingly with the previous one as it uses a theory of *institutionalisation* to explain professional dynamics as well as the barriers to change. The authors show that the three countries have introduced environmental standards and guidelines in different ways, to conserve energy, use more renewables, manage the use of water and reduce air pollution. In the Netherlands, an integrated approach was achieved but is now being questioned, whereas French policy focused on achieving measurable goals over a specific range of criteria and in Britain, although a broader agenda has been pursued, construction industry tendering methods and forms of contract have made this agenda harder to implement. Chapter 9, by Debizet and Symes, takes up these themes, considering *expertise and methodology*, looking at ten case studies, split between France and Britain of the use of the new evaluation methodologies (respectively HQE and BREEAM). They illustrate the stages at which sustainability goals were introduced and discuss the likelihood that these could be carried through the life of a project without serious compromise to meeting the needs of local communities and of local or national politicians. Differences appeared between public and private sector activities, the new roles played by various other professions causing particular difficulties for architects. Readers of the earlier volumes in the BEQUEST series will find these comments enrich the discussion of these assessment methods which were published there.

Next, in Chapter 10, Abrial considers *professional leadership*. Based on interviews carried out in France, the author discusses the major role played by pioneering individuals, whom are termed 'Founders' of the movement towards increasing sustainability. Three broad themes are addressed: the emergence of a conviction that environmental quality mattered, the realisation that new skills not only were required but also could be made available if the disciplinary field were expanded, and the particular experiences of individuals whose efforts were thereby confirmed and reinforced. Non-conventional career pathways have been developed and personal commitments to the newly recognised goals have been established.

Chapter 11, by Filippi and Fabrizio, concerns the Mediterranean edge of the European Union, and is on *rule and the market* in Italy; it includes evidence from a number of case studies. Italian standards (compulsory and voluntary) for rating sustainable building are introduced and compared with those available in other nations. The chapter presents the application of these standards at different phases (design competition, design stage, construction). Potentials and drawbacks of a standard based evaluation of building sustainability are also highlighted, allowing the boundary conditions for sustainable building design and construction to be drawn. The authors suggest that the attitude of building owners and building designers toward an environmental friendly building design and construction is problematic in the Italian situation and that there is a great need for a new professional skill, for design team members able to supply the architect with the most advanced knowledge of building physics, building technologies and equipment.

The final chapter in Part II, Chapter 12 by Grimshaw, is concerned with a profession emerging in the United Kingdom, *facilities management* (FM). The traditional view of professions includes the idea that they have a duty to society over and above that to their employers (the clients). The author argues that FM institutions, which have adopted traditionally conservative definitions of the training and membership requirements of a profession, cannot easily develop the flexibility and innovative capacity which sustainability requires. Contractual responsibilities to clients marry ill with a multidimensional response to the new challenges with which professionals are faced.

CONCLUSIONS

In the final chapter of the book, an overview is attempted which seeks to draw the theory and the practice described together. It argues that the chapters in this book may be seen as suggesting not only that *the transition to sustainable urban development* requires new approaches to professional behaviour but also that this 'new professionalism' is likely to vary in different geographical areas and under different historical and cultural conditions. This final chapter discusses where there appear to be new applications of scientific knowledge, innovations in the behaviour of planning authorities, property developers and the construction industries, and new links between public and private sector organisations. A number of chapter authors have emphasised the need for new forms of integrated and collaborative professional teamwork and for new ways of working with the industry, with government and with the public. Since many of these changes clearly challenge present arrangements and accepted values, the research collected together in this book should help those who find that, being involved in the production of a more sustainable built environment, they must rethink what it means to be 'professional'. The book also reinforces the BEQUEST trajectory, described in the Preface, which defines Sustainable Urban Development as a shared journey, 'a process, not a product or a fixed destination'.

NOTE

1   Readers will be aware that since the research reports which are contained in later chapters of this volume were finalised (in midsummer 2007), the attempt to focus political debate on predictions of global climate change has intensified. The editors suggest that, valid though this effort may be, the problems identified in the discussions which are published here remain both current and significant. An example of the push on climate change is to be found in remarks by Porritt (2007), a seasoned campaigner:

> Listening to government ministers and business leaders over the last few months, even hardened sustainable development practitioners have been known to own up to the odd *My Fair Lady* moment: 'By George, I think they've got it!' and that is not just because the words are coming out in more or less the right order, but because they are increasingly backed by serious action.
>
> (Porritt 2007: 7)

But not all observers take such an optimistic view. Tickell (2007), an equally experienced commentator on these topics, takes a rather more sceptical position, writing:

> There is just one problem. While there is widespread agreement that we need to do 'something', and that this something has to go a great deal further than anything the world has managed before, there is as yet little agreement as to just what that 'something' ought to be.
>
> (Tickell 2007: 46)

So the professional field in Britain, as no doubt elsewhere, remains divided between those who seek a practical consensus, a median approach, and those who still seek to address a broader set of goals. The former include the architects' main institution, the Royal Institute of British Architects (RIBA), which promotes its *Climate Change Toolkit* on the somewhat unambitious grounds that 'we must design and build more energy efficient buildings and learn to improve the existing stock fast' (RIBA 2007: 89). The latter are well represented in the *ZEDbook*, where Dunster et al. (2008) argue that since 'every aspect of our contemporary society runs on cheap fossil fuel . . . the problems caused by over consumption are not just environmental'. According to them: 'Millions worldwide are living in fear and squalor as a direct result [of this]'. As practitioners with social and community projects in old Europe as well as the newly developing areas of China, they maintain that 'though few doubt the severity of the problems faced by humanity, there is still resistance from businesses, developers, planners, architects and government . . . to making . . . our lifestyles sustainable' (Dunster et al. 2008: back cover).

REFERENCES

Aalborg Charter (1994) Aalborg Charter: available at www.iclei.org/la21/echarter.htm.

Alexander, C. (1979) *The Timeless Way of Building*. New York: Oxford University Press.

Beckerman, W. (1994) Sustainable development: Is it a useful concept? *Environmental Values* 3: 191–209.

Bell, S. and Morse, S. (1999) *Sustainability Indicators: Measuring the Immeasurable*. London: Earthscan.

Brandon, P. and Lombardi, P. (2005) *Evaluating Sustainable Development in the Built Environment*. Oxford: Blackwell.

Breheny, M. (1996) Centrists, decentrists and compromisers: Views on the future of urban form. In M. Jenks, E. Burton and K. Williams (eds) *The Compact City: A Sustainable Urban Form?* London: E.&F.N. Spon.

Byatt, I., Castles, I., Henderson, D., Lawson, N., McKitrick, R. et al. (2006) The Stern review 'Oxonia Papers': A critique. *World Economics* 7(2): 145–151.

Carson, R. (1965) *Silent Spring*. Harmondsworth, Penguin.

Cohen, W. and Levinthal, D. (1990) Absorptive capacity: A new perspective on learning and innovation. *Administrative Science Quarterly* 35(2): 128–152.

Cole, R. and Lorch, R. (eds) (2003) *Building Culture and Environment: Informing Local and Global Practices*. Oxford: Blackwell.

Commission of the European Communities (CEC) (1996) *European Sustainable Cities: Report of the Expert Group on the Urban Environment*. Luxembourg: Office for Official Publications of the European Commission.

Cooper, I. (1997) Environmental assessment methods for use at the building and city scale: Constructing bridges or identifying common ground. In P. Brandon, P. Lombardi and V. Bentivenga (eds) *Evaluation of the Built Environment for Sustainability*. London: E.&F.N. Spon.

Crinson, M. and Lubbock, J. (1994) *Architecture, Art or Profession? Three Hundred Years of Architectural Education in Britain*. Manchester: Manchester University Press.

Curwell, S., Deakin, M. and Symes, M. (eds) (2005) *Sustainable Urban Development, Volume 1: The Framework and Protocols for Environmental Assessment*. Abingdon: Routledge.

Deakin, M., Curwell, S. and Lombardi, P. (2001) BEQUEST: The framework and directory of assessment methods. *International Journal of Life Cycle Assessment* 6(6): 373–383.

Dickens, P. (2004) *Society and Nature: Changing our Environment, Changing Ourselves*. Cambridge: Polity.

Dingwall, R. and Lewis, P. (eds) (1983) *The Sociology of the Professions.* London: Macmillan.

Dodgson, M., Gann, D. and Salter, A. (2005) *Think, Play, Do: Technology, Innovation and Organization.* Oxford: Oxford University Press.

Douglas, M. and Wildavsky, A. (1982) *Risk and Culture: An Essay on the Selection of Technological and Environmental Dangers.* Berkeley, CA: University of California Press.

Duffy, F. and Hutton, L. (1998) *Architectural Knowledge: The Idea of a Profession.* London: E.&F.N. Spon.

Dunster, B., Simmons, C. and Gilbert, B. (2008) *The ZEDbook: Solutions for a Shrinking World.* Abingdon: Taylor and Francis.

Gann, D.M. (2003) Trading places: Sharing knowledge about environmental building techniques. In R. Cole and R. Lorch (eds) *Building Culture and Environment: Informing Local and Global Practices.* Oxford: Blackwell.

Gutman, R. (1988) *Architectural Practice: A Critical View.* Princeton, NJ: Princeton Architectural Press.

Guy, S. and Farmer, G. (2001) Reinterpreting sustainable architecture. *Journal of Architectural Education* 54(3): 140–148.

Guy, S. and Moore, S.A. (eds) (2005) *Sustainable Architectures: Cultures and Natures in Europe and North America.* New York: Spon Press.

Hannigan, J. (1995) *Environmental Sociology: A Social Constructivist Perspective.* London: Routledge.

Hatfield Dodds, S. (2000) Pathways and paradigms for sustaining human communities. In R.J. Lawrence (ed.) *Sustaining Human Settlement: A Challenge for the New Millennium.* North Shields: Urban International Press.

Haumont, B. (1999) Etre architecte en Europe. *Les Cahiers de la Recherche Architecturale* 2–3: 75–84.

Henry, E., Abrial, S., Codet-Boisse, J., Debizet, G., Paris, M. and Puybaraud, M. (2006) Expertises, competences et gestion des projets de construction durables. Unpublished report following research financed by Plan Urbanisme, Construction, Architecture, Ministère des Transports, de l'Equipement, du Tourisme et de la Mer, Paris.

Holmberg, J. and Sandbrook, R. (1992) Sustainable development: What is to be done? In J. Holmberg (ed.) *Policies for a Small Planet.* London: IIED/Earthscan.

IUCN-UNEP-WWF (1991) *Caring for the Earth: Second Report on World Conservation and Development.* London: Earthscan.

Kohler, N. (2003) Cultural issues for a sustainable built environment. In R. Cole and R. Lorch (eds) *Building Culture and Environment: Informing Local and Global Practice.* Oxford: Blackwell.

Kuhn, T. (1962) *The Structure of Scientific Revolutions.* Chicago, IL: University of Chicago Press.

Larson, M.S. (1977) *The Rise of the Professions: A Sociological Analysis*. Berkeley, CA: University of California Press.

Latour, B. and Woolgar, S. (1986) *Laboratory Life: The Construction of Scientific Facts*. Princeton, NJ: Princeton University Press.

Leaman, A. (2003) User needs and expectations. In R. Cole and R. Lorch (eds) *Building Culture and Environment: Informing Local and Global Practice*. Oxford: Blackwell.

McEwen, M. (1974) *Crisis in Architecture*. London: RIBA Publications.

Mitchell, G. (1999) Demand forecasting as a tool for the sustainable development of water resources. *International Journal of Sustainable Development and World Ecology* 6: 1–11.

Mitchell, G. (2000) Indicators as tools to guide progress on the sustainable development pathway. In R.J. Lawrence (ed.) *Sustaining Human Settlement: A Challenge for the New Millennium*. North Shields: Urban International Press.

Mitchell, G., May, A. and Macdonald, A. (1995) PICABUE: A methodological framework for the development of indicators of sustainable development. *International Journal of Sustainable Development World Ecology* 2(2): 104–123.

Oestreicher, J. (1995) Governing local communities: A view back and a look forward. *Trialog* 45: 33–35.

Pearce, D.W, Markandya, A. and Barbier, E.B. (1989) *Blueprint for a Green Economy*. London: Earthscan.

Perkin, H. (1989) *The Rise of Professional Society: England since 1880*. London: Routledge.

Porritt, J. (2007) *Sustainability. Duffy Eley Giffone Worthington, 06/07 Annual Review* p. 7.

Rogers, E. (1995) *Diffusion of Innovations*, 4th edn. New York: Free Press.

Royal Institute of British Architects (RIBA) (2007) Climate Change Toolkit now available. *RIBA Journal* November: 89.

Schön, D. (1983) *The Reflective Practitioner: How Professionals Think in Action*. London: Temple Smith.

Stern, N. (2006) *Stern Review on the Economics of Climate Change: Final Report* available at www.hm-treasury.gov.uk/independent_reviews/ (accessed 31/10/06).

Slaughter, E. (1998) Models of construction innovation. *Journal of Construction Engineering and Management* 124(3): 226–231.

Symes, M. (2001) La durabilité: question multidimensionelle traversant toutes les opérations. *Interprofessionalité et action collective dans les metiers de la conception, Cahiers RAMAU* 2: 39–46.

Symes, M. and Pauwels, S. (1999) The diffusion of innovations in urban design: The case of sustainability in the Hulme development guide. *Journal of Urban Design* 4(1): 97–117.

Symes, M., Eley, J. and Seidel, A.D. (1995) *Architects and their Practices: A Changing Profession*. Oxford: Butterworth Architecture.

Tickell, O. (2007) Sensible solutions: Clarifying climate chaos. Kyoto 2: The framework for a second climate change protocol. *Resurgence* 241: 46–47.

United Nations (1993) *Report of the United Nations Conference on Environment and Development, Rio de Janeiro, Volume 1: Resolutions*. New York: United Nations.

Wikipedia (2007) *Evidence-based Design* available at en.wikipedia.org/wiki (accessed 29/01/07).

Willis, A.J. (1981) *The Architect in Practice*. London: Granada.

World Commission on Environment and Development (WCED) (1987) *Our Common Future*. Oxford: Oxford University Press.

Young, S. (1993) *The Politics of the Environment*. Manchester: Baseline Books.

Part I

Changing Processes

2

Sustainable Construction and Policy Learning in Europe
Cascades, Networks or Fragmentation?
Yvonne Rydin and Susan Moore

The mix of design and construction features required to minimise the environmental impact of new buildings and developments can broadly be termed sustainable construction and design. Many of these features require new ways of developing and constructing and a shift away from established decision-making by all those involved in urban development: planners, construction companies, developers, building materials suppliers, etc. The shift towards more sustainable construction and design, therefore, requires innovation and learning – learning to do development differently. This learning process is complicated by the multiple interpretations of what specifically constitute practices of sustainable construction, as this can vary greatly by issue, sector and policy mandate. Proponents of sustainable construction might promote technological shifts in terms of materials, energy use and waste reduction, or they might encourage cultural and behavioural adaptations to how society views, uses and plans its urban built environments. This bifurcation into two arguably complementary but practically disparate agendas – a technological agenda and an urban environment agenda – implicitly suggests to many that 'sustainability' can be reduced to a function of innovation in construction and building technology trends.

Thus learning in the area of sustainable construction is by and large considered to be an arena for applied learning. The technology involved is a mix of high and low tech, existing and cutting-edge; and the actors involved in urban development need to learn how to incorporate sustainable technology within their designs and construction practice. Furthermore, there is applied learning in policy contexts where actors need to understand how to encourage the application of sustainable technologies and modes of construction. The planning system also needs to learn how to promote sustainable urban developments and encourage private sector actors to embed sustainability in their development proposals. This requires the reshaping of policy systems to ensure that technical knowledge penetrates the planning policy process. Moreover, the bifurcated sustainable construction agenda, by inference, implies the necessity for policy learning across multiple levels of urban governance in order to overcome a lack of knowledge and policy co-generation arising from poor communication between industry and policy networks.

This chapter examines how policy learning about sustainable construction is being promoted across European and national levels, and reflects on the lessons for understanding European governance. It focuses on the more technical aspects of constructing new development and leaves aside the spatial planning aspects concerning patterns of land uses and transport infrastructure, for example. It draws on empirical work undertaken within the SusCon Project at the London School of Economics during 2004–2006,[1] which included a phase focused on European and British national policy and knowledge networks. A total of 21 semi-structured face-to-face interviews were conducted as part of this phase with a range of network actors, predominantly in London and Brussels, involved in promoting sustainable construction in policy and practice. The primary aim of the SusCon Project, as a whole, was to address the perceived gaps between knowledge generation, use and learning, and the necessity of bridging such gaps for the successful translation of knowledge into practice. The project sought to examine how knowledge about sustainable construction can become embedded in planning practice and, by implication, how planners and associated practitioners and organisations learn and handle new knowledge in this area.

One of the original themes of the SusCon Project questioned the seemingly common assumption among policy-makers and practitioners alike that effective knowledge transfer and policy learning is reliant upon a successful cascade effect (i.e. from the European level to national to regional and local level, and eventually to the sector, industry or practitioner levels). Evidence from our interviews conducted with a range of policy, research, industry and professional stakeholders within European, British and London-based sustainable construction networks suggested however that this ideal cascade is not occurring. To understand how and why this is the case, we turn first to the nature of policy learning and how this relates to models of European governance, in particular the application of multilevel governance perspectives. This is followed by a discussion of the nature of European networks concerning sustainable construction as identified within the empirical component of the SusCon Project and how these networks relate to the capacity for policy learning across European-national boundaries. The key issues affecting the transfer of sustainable construction policy and knowledge between the different levels of governance (i.e. EU, national, local) are identified and discussed in brief. The chapter concludes on the nature of this transfer process, commenting on the oft-posited notion of the knowledge and policy cascade or trickle-down and its relationship to models of multilevel governance.

POLICY LEARNING AND EUROPEAN MULTILEVEL GOVERNANCE

The idea of policy systems having a cognitive dimension and being centrally concerned with change has received increasing attention over recent years. This has been termed policy learning and Nilsson (2005a: 209–211) identifies three types: technical or instrumental; conceptual; and political. Thus in the case of sustainable construction, policy learning could range from the identification of new technologies to reduce carbon emissions from buildings and, more significantly, their promotion through policy instruments, to the incorporation of sustainability as a relevant goal for construction and development sectors and the development of arguments for the importance of assessing construction and development per se in sustainability terms.

The essence of the policy learning approach is that learning occurs through relationships between policy actors and that mapping the pattern of such relationships can help understand why learning is (or is not) happening and the form that it takes. Nilsson and Persson (2003: 353) argue that environmental concerns will be strongly integrated into policy across domains where new networks are created that break across established linkages. This allows a problem-solving approach to decision-making, which underpins mutual learning, and a new outlook on the problem; in other words, a new policy frame. By contrast, where existing networks and frames are cemented and the policy problem is not mutually shared across policy territories, learning is replaced by bargaining. In such a situation, recourse is to forms of mediation, negotiation and deliberation to handle the conflict over the issue, rather than learning to advance solutions to the issue (Nilsson and Dalkmann 2001: 315).

So this suggests the value of studying the relationships between actors involved in learning about sustainable construction and identifying the orientation towards mutually sharing, reframing and problem solving. These relationships would focus around knowledge acquisition, information distribution, interpretation and organisational memory (Nilsson 2005b). When working across boundaries (whether territorial, organisational or sectoral), interpretation is particularly important; this can also be termed lesson drawing, where knowledge is interpreted to gain new understandings of the cause–effect relations involved in policy problems and how to resolve them, leading to the devising of new lessons for specific goals, strategies and activities.

This sets a particular challenge for learning within Europe and across European-national boundaries. Here learning within policy systems has to interface with the nature of European governance and the role of national and sub-national governmental organisations within that European governance. European governance has been the subject of considerable academic attention and debate (Fairbrass and Jordan 2003;

Jordan 2001; Jordan et al. 2005). While at first conceived by sovereign nation states to serve their economic and political purposes, the European Union has now 'metamorphosed into a much more complex and unpredictable political system' (Jordan 2001: 194). This system is characterised as fractured, decentralised and lacking in spatial and functional lines of authority. In particular, the decentring process has involved the 'relative empowerment of sub-national actors, hence the term multilevel governance' (Jordan 2001: 194). Broadly defined, multilevel governance refers to the 'dispersion of authority away from central government – upwards to the supranational level, downwards to subnational jurisdictions, and sideways to public/private networks' (Hooghe and Marks 2001: 3; see also Peters and Pierre 2001).

Hooghe and Marks (2001) identify two types of multilevel governance. Type I is argued to be 'a hierarchical approach which focuses on the ways in which competences and authority are shaped between different levels of government' (Bulkeley and Betsill 2005: 48). This describes a vertical model wherein there is 'a simultaneous movement of political power . . . up to trans-national levels of government and down to local communities, but in a coordinated manner' (Eckerberg and Joas 2004: 407). Learning within such a model would also be hierarchical, emanating from higher and larger authorities and trickling down to more local contexts, where it can be applied or shaped for local application.

Type II is characterised by Hooghe and Marks (2001: 4) as 'a complex, fluid, patchwork of innumerable, overlapping jurisdictions' which can be functionally split into still other jurisdictions that 'may come and go as demands for governance change'. Bulkely and Betsill (2005: 48) summarise Type II as 'a polycentric model in which multiple overlapping and interconnected horizontal spheres of authority are involved in governing particular issues'. The general thrust of the shift in responsibility is from governmental actors and authorities towards non-governmental actors, and this is significant because it implies that 'both national and local governments' autonomous position is constrained by new political actors participating in the "normal" political process' (Eckerberg and Joas 2004: 407). Learning within Type II multilevel governance would be more fluid, operating across complex networks. Following the policy learning literature (see above) it can be supposed that such learning would be more effective, since it would break down established barriers by building links between actors in different tiers and organisations, while within a trickle-down model the transfer would be from tier to tier in a more structured manner.

EUROPEAN POLICY LEARNING NETWORKS ON SUSTAINABLE CONSTRUCTION

There is general evidence that policy development within Europe goes along with an emphasis on learning, both operating within a fairly fluid network approach. The process of policy coordination, principally within the European Commission (the executive of the EU), follows 'the open method', which Kjer (2004: 113) describes as involving benchmarking and mutual monitoring with an emphasis on mutual learning. This means that the EU places significance on knowledge for strategic policy delivery. It is instructive to highlight a few general characteristics of European networks where knowledge is concerned. Jönsson and Strömvik (2005: 19) point out that participation in EU networks rests on a combination of 'know-how' and 'know-who'. Networks are issue based, and expertise in a particular area is a prerequisite for involvement in networks. At the same time, networks are not limited to accredited experts but connect to a range of actors in heterogeneous organisations. EU networks also tend to transcend organisational boundaries and involve the governmental, non-governmental and private sectors as well as ranging across levels. Thus the EU provides an unusual abundance of access points to the policy-making process for interested actors. However, given the large number of possible actors involved on any issue, there tend to be means of limiting access; prompting some of our interviewees to refer to the EU networks as 'clubs'. Some actors have accumulated considerable political capital through their knowledge and experienced use of these access points. But while EU networks are not hierarchical, neither are they entirely horizontal. There are multiple linking organisations and the role of the Commission itself is predominant within these networks.

To help structure the European system of formal and informal links between bureaucratic and non-bureaucratic contacts (Ruzza 1996), the EU has adopted a thematic approach running across multi-sectoral policy areas. The Thematic Strategy on the Urban Environment (UTS) is one such example. Sustainable construction was included as one of four themes in the consultation draft of the UTS (Commission of the European Communities (CEC) 2004a) alongside urban environmental management, urban transport and urban design. Yet, the final version of the strategy, adopted by the Commission in January 2006 (CEC 2006), was structured rather differently, with more emphasis on process than substantive themes. Under discussion of the synergies with other policies, sustainable construction was specifically mentioned though as a means of addressing climate change. We should note that the research programme within the EU also follows a thematic approach and is set up to favour the funding of projects that foster negotiation, partnership and non-hierarchical exchanges between institutions at different governmental levels and scales in order to implement the Thematic Strategies.

However, there is also a sector-based approach. Under the banner of promoting the competitiveness of the construction sector, a European Working Group for Sustainable Construction produced an agenda report in 2001. This drew on the work of task groups on environmentally friendly construction materials, energy efficiency in buildings, construction and demolition, and construction life cycle costing. This sector-based work has fed into work standardising the assessment of environmental impacts across Europe (see below). It also meshes with sector-based work within nation states. For example, in Britain, the Department of Trade and Industry (DTI) has also developed a sector-based strategy on sustainable construction. A first strategy was published in 2000 (DTI 2000) and a revised version in 2006 as a consultation draft (DTI 2006). This is a broad ranging document that identifies six areas for improvement:

- establishing effective construction programmes
- developing and supporting well-focused and capable public sector clients
- designing and decision-making based on 'whole-life' value
- using the appropriate procurement and contracting strategies
- working collaboratively through fully integrated teams
- evaluating performance and embedding project learning.

The European Construction Technology Platform (ECTP) has also developed a 25-year Strategic Research Agenda that has quickly become the de facto agenda for the future of construction. It comprises a comprehensive wish list of different elements of change in the construction industry. The European Council for Construction Research, Development and Innovation (ECCREDI) and E-Core (a research network) are seeking to create and link national platforms under the ECTP umbrella and use this to influence future EU research funding. Within the UK, the national platform has only recently been established, supported by a £3 million Knowledge Transfer Network under the auspices of the DTI. Information and communication technologies (ICT), off-site methods and modern construction methods are likely to be prioritised by the DTI since the sustainability agenda in Britain is strongly driven by an understanding of construction technology trends.

The reliance on best practice

While these networks exist to foster the transfer of ideas and knowledge, there has been an overwhelming emphasis on best practice as the means of effecting this. There has been a heavy reliance on best practice and voluntary accreditation schemes as a way to encourage change, as regulation in this area is only slowly emerging, compared to some other sectors. For example, the National Focal Points Programme is one such best practice-focused project working across the European Commission and Member States. Within the network each Member State has a national focal point and the network office provides links and support to aid local problem solving, etc. Existing best practices are evaluated against a template that is then used on the national and sub-national/local levels to assess construction and development practices. Other individual examples of best practice on construction and development sites abound; the Constructing Excellence website, for example, emphasises such cases, arguing that they prove sustainable construction is practicable and that the business case can be made (www.constructingexcellence.org.uk); see also Constructing Excellence's website for a profile on the Joint UK–Sweden Initiative on Sustainable Construction (www.constructingexcellence.org.uk/uksweden/default.jsp).

While such best practice examples are laudable and the publicity surrounding them integral to the learning processes of urban planners and the construction industry, the emphasis on them also reinforces a degree of passivity on the part of the planning system and a limited use of the regulatory potential of this system. The reliance on best practice cases also often means that problems of transferability of practice from locality to locality and from context to context are ignored (Bulkeley 2006). Bulkeley (2006) argues that the way that the concept of best practice is used can decontextualise the complex problems of achieving a more sustainable outcome in a specific local site. The adoption of best practice within sustainable construction networks may appear to promote dissemination but it actually constructs a boundary object that may fail to move effectively from the more generalised networks where knowledge is constructed to the local networks of implementation. A boundary object can be understood as a compound of an artefact with associated discourses and processes; it allows the transformation of knowledge generated in academic or regulatory contexts into usable knowledge in a bureaucratic context.

Rather than providing a template that can be adopted in any locality, best practice does not remove the necessity for localised construction of sustainability knowledge. It throws the emphasis back onto the role of local government and local governance. In the European context this also raises the issue of subsidiarity (discussed further below). As one of our interviewees emphasised, the continued attempt to develop generalisable practice guidance at the European level often leads to vacuous statements with little real impact. Referring to the idea of a three-dimensional (3-D) matrix for sustainable construction, which could apply in a variety of contexts (builder, researcher, policy-makers in any locality), he commented:

> When one puts this into the context of the EU level – if you can come to any agreement on anything at all given these three levels (and about something that is inherently local) it is difficult to avoid coming up with a lot of platitudes.

This has not prevented the ongoing search for ways to make generalised European stances and knowledge on sustainable construction more available and relevant to specific local contexts.

Voluntary and regulatory approaches

The reliance on best practice is rooted in the preference for voluntary as opposed to regulatory approaches in this policy area. Several of our EU interviewees pointed to the lack of implementation powers at higher levels to ensure the adoption of research and policies across different governmental levels and across sectoral boundaries. The interviews also pointed to a dearth of knowledge brokers and spanners, that is those who work to improve the handling and circulation of knowledge within policy and research networks. In the UK, Constructing Excellence stood out in this regard as a self-acknowledged 'broker' and was identified as such by other interviewees. There does not seem to be an equivalent organisation taking up the broker role within the European context. Rather, most brokering seems to occur within specific projects and initiatives not across the sustainable construction issue as a whole.

Regulatory measures, however, would be a means of forcing the adoption of new technologies. In the absence of such measures or their limited applicability, the emphasis falls instead on exhortation or a persuasive flow of knowledge and information about new practices. But the lack of regulation can itself inhibit interest in learning. As one interviewee commented:

> [it is] sometimes difficult for federations to get their members interested. It is a matter of nationality as well. We have Dutch and French members that are extremely interested in what is happening, mainly the Netherlands because so much is regulated.

He went on to make the point that 'it is only when it comes to the time when it is transposed into national legislation that they realise in the companies that they will have to do something.' The lack of knowledge brokers able effectively to link the European and national technical and policy networks is critical to the poor dissemination and translation of knowledge into formats appropriate to the various actors involved in promoting sustainable construction in different contexts. The development of checklists, codes and toolkits to prioritise sustainable construction has, in the UK for example, been less effectively devised and used than anticipated. This in part is due to the lack of individuals and agencies championing the transfer of knowledge from the domain of policy learning to the domain of organisational learning within firms, federations, agencies and local authorities.

In Britain, there has been a shift towards more stringent regulation being proposed, at least where housebuilding is concerned. The Building Regulations, which regulate the construction methods used in development, have been upgraded. With effect from 6 April 2006, all new buildings have to comply with revised regulations contained in Part L that increase energy efficiency by at least 20 per cent, a cumulative increase of 40 per cent since 2002. But the draft of *Building a Green Future: towards Zero Carbon Development* promises to ramp up this regulation to the point where all new housing will be carbon-zero by 2016. General planning policy guidance has also been supplemented to try and ensure that this regulation is matched by urban planning practice (www.communities.gov.uk/pub/142/ConsultationPlanningPolicyStatement PlanningandClimateChangeSupplementtoPlanning1_id1505142.pdf). This is an attempt to try to bridge the gap between a largely aspirational planning agenda for local sustainable development and the practices of the development and construction industries in actually delivering this kind of development. However, this has largely happened without reference to European policy frameworks. European regulation in this area has tended to focus on the promotion of standardisation in environmental assessment.

Standardisation of environmental assessment
Conceptually, it can be argued that sustainable construction operates as an *informing ideal*. A type of invisible or even impossible yardstick that has come to be accepted and legitimised as a register enabling a common vocabulary for discussing the interconnectedness of all phases in the design, construction, use and management of buildings across multiple disciplinary and sectoral divisions. The characteristics of how each individual stakeholder conceptualises and prioritises issues, ideas and approaches under the banner of sustainable construction is then understood as the means by which each actor makes use of his/her own repertoire of practices, experiences and conventions to render the invisible yardstick 'real' (cf. Guy and Shove 2000). But the proliferation of definitions that arises can be problematic for practice and so there has been considerable effort going into standardisation of what is meant by more sustainable building materials and a more sustainable (or at least energy efficient) building. While this does not remove the need for tailoring the interpretation of sustainable construction to a specific context, it does represent a European response to the problems of diverse interpretations.

A significant case of standardisation is provided by the Council of European Producers of Materials for Construction (CEPMC), which started work in 1995 on the eventual standardisation of product standards for building products from an environmental perspective (EPDs) and tested it on four major insulation products. A major conference was held in Brussels in 2000–2001 and work moved on to compare the emergent EU scheme with major national schemes. Following arguments made by CEPMC for a European scheme, the Commission provided some funding for a consultant's report undertaken by EcoBalance, part of Price Waterhouse Coopers (PWC). The Directorate General for the Environment within the Commission also did a study on EPDs, followed by another PWC report, this time for the Directorate General for Enterprise. This led to a final recommendation for European standardisation on building products. This is quite a significant move. A federation representative within the construction industry in Europe commented once a performance standard is codified in a formal contract document, a requirement to fulfil the specification is set and a precedent made for further contracts. However, the process of rolling out EPD standardisation is proving a lengthy one and it will take several years to complete the process.

Standardisation work is also being undertaken by the Standing Committee on Construction (CEC 2004b) focused on the standardisation of methods for the assessment of the environmental performance of buildings through life-cycle analysis. The 2002 Directive on the energy performance of buildings (CEC 2002) also required a standard methodology for assessing this performance, alongside setting minimum energy efficiency requirements for all new and larger refurbished buildings, and requiring energy certification on completion, sale or lease. It should be noted however, that the Directive fell short of actually specifying a European methodology that would operate across different countries.

A European construction sector?

The economic context for the difficulties of establishing strong European learning networks is the split within the construction industry between the national/regional and the global contexts. The absence of a European-wide construction industry to match the research and development (R&D) and policy effort at the European scale was noted by several of our interviewees (see also Barr 2004), particularly in relation to housebuilding. As a result European construction industry federations often have limited contact with their local members; 'There is a barrier, because we are a federation of federations or associations, so we don't always know what gets down to the companies themselves unless they come to our meetings.' This can prove problematic when the attempt is made to convey information, ideas and knowledge emanating at the European level to more local contexts. Some organisations, such as the Architects' Council of Europe, operate exclusively on policy-making at the European level obviously limiting the potential for broader network linkages.

There is a particular issue with reaching the smaller firms that actually make up the majority of the industry (although not its workload). One interviewee referred to small firms as being in effect 'off the radar'. Even within the national context, the importance of regional construction firms may mean that national policy and knowledge discussions are not able to engage with commercial actors and their networks. Furthermore, learning within the industry more generally is constrained by the extent to which firms fail to exhibit the characteristics of 'learning organisations' (Easterby-Smith 1997) and the problems of forcing innovation through long supply chains, geographically extended across national, European and global markets, given that existing national networks and frames are cemented and the policy problem is not mutually shared across territories.

The role of European local and regional government

There are similar problems of forcing or promoting a change towards sustainable construction through the sub-national regional and local government networks. There is an underlying basis for this in that urban policy and planning is a slightly problematic area for the EU; the Union has no formal competence here unlike the environmental and economic policy domains. This shapes the way that it can address the issue of sustainable construction and urban development. In part, it has thrown the emphasis back onto policy learning. One tactic that the European level has adopted in response to problems of competence is to use knowledge and learning to seek influence in areas where it does not have formal powers.

But this highlights a problem, in so far as very localised action is needed to achieve the goal of sustainable construction. For example, the anticipated impact of the EU Thematic Strategy on the Urban Environment, from the DG ENV perspective, is said to be at the local and regional level, with the responsibility falling to national Member States to integrate the Strategy into their national plans: in other words, 'success depends on an effective cascade' (Interview 2005, DG ENV). Yet, practitioners in the field suggest that no strategic link exists between construction and planning at the local authority or central government level, let alone the pan-EU level. It was commented that the EU is waiting for service deliverers to operationalise the necessary synthesis.

UK-based consultants in the field indicated that the UK is past the agenda-setting stage on sustainable communities and sustainable construction, and the priorities are now being passed onto the local and regional public sector to implement. But, in practice, sustainable construction is not explicitly or uniformly prioritised. As a result, aspirational policy imperatives continue to be delivered but there is little or no alignment with local and regional delivery mechanisms and best practice is not trickling down from evidence-based demonstration projects. As one interviewee said:

> Success demands trusting regional organisations to deliver EU knowledge, best practice and policy at the local levels. This needs only one connection to fail for a problem to arise. The hope is that the failed connection happens low in the policy and knowledge chain where there are multiple networks or other possible agents to pull up the slack. If it happens

high up, then the information and knowledge never makes it to the networks of knowledge transfer.

Another interviewee commented that these problems of transfer could slow down implementation considerably. The estimated time lag between the announcement of a Thematic Strategy or Directive at the EU level to that of having an impact on local practice in a Member State was identified by interviewees as three to eight years. Simple language translation is also implicated in these problems. Translation is becoming increasingly problematic in the European context given the enlargement of the Union and financial constraints. Documents are now translated into fewer (usually three) languages and are often reduced in length to keep costs of translation down, leading one DG ENV representative to remark on the UTS:

> there was a cap on the number of characters allowed and the technical annexes are only published in English. The final document was boiled down and boiled down to the point where I have to remind myself what stayed v. what was cut.

An inherent lack of information at the European level about what is happening at the level of the locality was consistently highlighted by our interviewees as a cause for concern. Some suggested that the principle of subsidiarity combined with a pan-EU scope will mean a lowest common denominator in policy development. Others noted the very informal network of communication that seems to be operating within local government may also hinder knowledge and policy transfer. It seems that only the largest local authorities are able to engage directly with European initiatives. For example, the Greater London Authority (GLA) is able to employ a European Office that looks two ways, informing the GLA and its funding partners of what the EU is doing and highlighting potential impacts for London, while also informing the EU of what London is doing. The national context also shapes the nature of linkages between Europe, nation state and local/regional government. For example, Germany has construction codes but this is delivered at the tender level, while in Sweden it is carried out at the local level and is a key role for local government.

POLICY LEARNING IN EUROPE: A CASCADE?

Despite the identification of these barriers to successful policy learning, many of our interviewees nevertheless adhered to the notion of a knowledge cascade – that is to say that sustainable construction knowledge (e.g. technologies, methods, practices etc.) are being cascaded from international, to national, to regional, and finally to local scales (Bulkeley 2005). Constructing Excellence defined itself as depending on a trickle-down effect and the Association of London Government European Service also claimed to play a role in trickling down information: 'We help with the information gap between local and EU levels.'

Some interviewees, while espousing the ideal of a cascade or trickle-down effect, were however very clear about the deficiencies of this model. 'We are unaware of how effective this cascade effect is down from Europe'. A prominent sustainable construction analyst claimed that 'trickle down is left to chance, with no flow management in place'. In response to this understanding, Constructing Excellence offered an alternative model of how they actually operate:

> I think it is about connecting circles, because you get that core component that is both learning and disseminating. Then you have got to get someone disseminating beyond those people with direct experience, and you have also got to get the learning to feed into that group so they look more widely than their immediate current experience. Flows in and flows out. They are connected yet separate as well. But it is also a bit like a 3-D matrix.

Adopting a model like this implies abandoning the language of barriers and instead focusing on the nature of relationships between actors, across tiers, across sectors, across nations, that will advance policy learning. As Guy and Marvin (1999) argue:

> Rather than focusing on the notion of barriers, an alternative approach would acknowledge that action is shaped by a multiplicity of factors that cannot be reduced to a simple view of a 'barrier' to change. Instead there is a multiplicity of local contexts within which individual and organizational behaviour is shaped. This way of seeing views social action not in terms of individualized and manageable behaviour, but rather as the capacity of socialized actors to innovate within highly constrained and dynamic contexts of action that may sometimes enable, and sometimes inhibit, environmental innovation.
>
> (Guy and Marvin 1999: 272)

In policy and decision-making terms, Guy and Marvin's logic suggests the need to look more closely at how 'the changing social organization of environmental innovation structures the potential of different coalitions of actors to shape sustainable cities' and to identify 'windows of opportunity arising from the coexistence of different social, political and commercial interests in alternative forms of environmental innovation' (Guy and Marvin 1999: 272). Donovan et al. (2005) likewise argue that the barriers typology generates a tendency for actors to adopt 'tried and tested patterns of behaviour in the face of uncertainties surrounding how to interpret sustainability'. This risk-averse behaviour thus dissuades innovation because it 'pre-figures failure by assuming some ideal end-point for sustainability' (Donovan et al. 2005: 22). The solution according to Donovan et al. (2005) is to reframe the barriers as opportunities, wherein it is explicit that sustainability is not an end-point but a journey. Moving beyond the barriers approach and seeing sustainable construction networks as constrained and dynamic contexts of action offers us a new vantage point to re-engage with the utility of the multilevel governance perspective.

From a policy perspective sustainable construction is viewed as an issue that can be addressed through the channels of a Type I governance arrangement – a normative framework within which 'functions are bundled, and the levels of government are multiple but limited' (Hooghe and Marks 2001: 4). Thus from a DG ENV perspective a successful EU Thematic Strategy or Directive will have its greatest impact at the local level but this is dependent on the intermediate levels of government 'performing' their intended role. However, at the level of practical implementation of sustainable construction knowledge and innovation the technical agenda has advanced further than the policy agenda because of its affinity with a Type II governance model. Again, in Type II

> the number of jurisdictions is vast, rather than limited; in which jurisdictions are not aligned on just a few levels, but operate at diverse territorial scales; in which jurisdictions are functionally specific rather than multi-task; and where jurisdictions are intended to be flexible rather than fixed.
>
> Hooghe and Marks 2001: 6)

In other words, the sustainable construction technical agenda has surpassed that of a multifaceted, yet vertically coordinated policy approach because it is goal-oriented and supported by a strong network of horizontal functional associations.

More specifically, the sustainable construction technological agenda fits succinctly with the policy provision design principles which, according Hooghe and Marks (2001: 14), characterise Type II governance:

- *Functional specificity*: specific competencies are hived off, and insulated, in separate jurisdictions. Jurisdictions are numerous and intersect, but they are relatively inert with respect to each other.
- *Low level of distributional conflict*: the emphasis in each jurisdiction is on Pareto optimality in problem solving rather than distributional bargaining with societal-wide consequences.
- *Ad-hoc, policy-specific architecture*: the unit of political engineering in Type I governance is the jurisdiction; in Type II governance it is the individual policy problem.

Thus the concentration within the technological agenda on specific sector-based deficits in performance of more sustainable construction methods, techniques and approaches fits within the Type II approach to policy solutions targeted at particular problems. These are seen as best addressed by functionally differentiated networks of actors with particular skills and knowledge related to the problems at hand. Again, here we underscore the applicability of the policy emphasis on technical problem solving as opposed to more holistic planning for societal-wide 'sustainability'.

In our particular application to sustainable construction we have found that, within policy arenas, the relatively stable framework of Type I with its dispersion of authority via the rational but simultaneous empowerment of sub-national and supranational institutions has supported the continued relevance of a knowledge and policy 'cascade'. However, at the level of practice, a Type II logic appears to be advancing at the edges of the classical Type I jurisdictions, that is to say where central government still remains accountable, but is not the primary service provider, nor the only source of formal authority. There is a burgeoning industry of issue and task-specific standard-setting jurisdictions that operate at arm's length from traditional government, which are largely autonomous but overlap territorially (Hooghe and Marks 2001: 10). This suggests that policy and research actors are forced to negotiate a much more complex, fluid, transient web of networks with significant barriers to the smooth trickle-down of new knowledge and policy on sustainable construction.

The lack of a common definition of sustainable construction has not constrained development of initiatives on it, both within industry practice and urban planning policy. The expectation of an ideal vertical 'cascade' of sustainable construction knowledge, research and policy is, however, undermined by how little is done to encourage, facilitate and monitor its execution or flow management. This expectation is also undermined by the growth in Type II governance structures which suggests that the hierarchical or vertical path dependency of a cascade is outdated, and moreover, counter-productive to the co-generation of sustainable construction knowledge, policy and practice. The purpose of this chapter has not been to highlight the barriers to a successful cascade in order to reinstate the validity of the cascade as a policy tool or management approach. Nor were we, in the process, attempting to identify the means to overcome said barriers to the transfer of sustainable construction knowledge and hence the improvement of policy. Rather we have attempted to open up a discussion of the nature of multilevel governance networks involved in this particular urban policy issue and how these influence learning and the flow of knowledge aimed at promoting sustainable urban development.

NOTE

1   The full results of this empirical work are reported in a number of publications, including Cooper 2006; Nye and Rydin 2006; Rydin and Burchell 2006; Rydin and Nye 2008; Rydin and Vandergert 2006; Rydin et al. 2006; Rydin et al. 2007; Rydin et al., in press. These are also all available on the LSE website for the Centre for Environmental Policy and Governance: www.lse.ac.uk/collections/geographyAndEnvironment/CEPG/ SustainableConstruction.htm. The SusCon project was funded by the Higher Education Funding Council for England under its Higher Education Initiative Fund Tranche 2.

REFERENCES

Barr, D. (2004) Procurement of construction research: The future. *B4E Building for a European Future: strategies and alliances for construction innovation*. ECCREDI, Maastrict, NL, 14–15 October.

Bulkeley, H. (2005) Reconfiguring environmental governance: Towards a politics of scales and networks. *Political Geography* 24: 875–902.

Bulkeley, H. (2006) Urban sustainability: Learning from Best Practice. *Environment and Planning A* 38(6): 1029–1044.

Bulkeley, H. and Betsill, M. (2005) 'Rethinking sustainable cities: Multi-level governance and the 'Urban' politics of climate change. *Environmental Politics* 14(1): 42–63.

Commission of the European Communities (CEC) (2002) *Directive on the Energy Performance of Buildings*. Directive 2002/91/EC. Brussels: CEC.

Commission of the European Communities (2004a) *Towards a Thematic Strategy on the Urban Environment*. COM(2004)60 final. Brussels: CEC.

Commission of the European Communities (2004b) *Development of Horizontal Standardised Methods for the Assessment of the Integrated Environmental Performance of Buildings*. M/350. Brussels: CEC.

Commission of the European Communities (2006) *Thematic Strategy on the Urban Environment*. COM(2005)718 Final3. Brussels: CEC.

Cooper, I. (2006) *Sustainable Construction and Planning: The Policy Agenda*. London: Centre for Environmental Policy and Governance, London School of Economics.

Department of Communities and Local Government (DCLG) (2006) *Consultation: Planning Policy Statement Planning and Climate Change, Supplement to PPS1*. London: DCLG.

Department of Trade and Industry (DTI) (2000) *Strategy for Sustainable Construction: Building a Better Quality of Life*. London: DTI.

Department of Trade and Industry (2006) *Sustainable Construction Strategy Report 2006*. London: DTI.

Donovan, R., Evans, J., Bryson, J., Porter, L. and Hunt, D. (2005) Large-scale urban regeneration and sustainability: Reflections on the 'barriers' typology. Working Paper 05/01. Birmingham: University of Birmingham.

Easterby-Smith, M. (1997) Disciplines of organisational learning: Contribution and critiques. *Human Relations* 50(9): 1085–1113.

Eckerberg, K. and Joas, M. (2004) Multi-level environmental governance: A concept under stress? *Local Environment* 9(5): 405–412.

Fairbrass, J. and Jordan, A. (2003) EU Environmental Governance: Uncomplicated and predictable policy-making? CSERGE Working Paper EDM 02-03. Norwich: University of East Anglia.

Guy, S. and Marvin, S. (1999) Understanding sustainable cities: Competing urban futures. *European Urban and Regional Studies* 6(3): 268–275.

Guy, S. and Shove, E. (2000) *A Sociology of Energy, Buildings and the Environment: Constructing Knowledge, Designing Practice.* London: Routledge.

Hooghe, L. and Marks, G. (2001) Types of multi-level governance. *European Integration online Papers (EIoP)* 5(11) http://eiop.or.at/eiop/texte/2001-011a.htm.

Jönsson, C. and Strömvik, M. (2005) Chapter 2: Negotiation in networks. In O. Elgstrom and C. Jönsson (eds) *European Union Negotiations: Processes, Networks and Institutions.* London: Routledge.

Jordan, A. (2001) The European Union: An evolving system of multilevel governance . . . or government. *Policy and Politics* 29(2): 193–208.

Jordan, A., Schout, A. and Zito, A. (2005) Coordinating European Union Environmental Policy: Shifting from passive to active coordination? CSERGE Working Paper EDM 04–05. Norwich: University of East Anglia.

Kjer, A. (2004) *Governance.* Cambridge: Polity.

Nilsson, M. (2005a) Learning, frames, and environmental policy integration: The case of energy policy in Sweden. *Environment and Planning C* 23(2): 207–226.

Nilsson, M. (2005b) Connecting reason to power: Assessments, Learning and Environmental Policy Integration in Swedish energy policy. PhD thesis submitted to Technical University of Delft.

Nilsson, M. and Persson, A. (2003) Framework for analysing environmental policy intergration. *Journal of Environmental Policy and Planning* 5(4): 333–359.

Nilsson, M. and Dalkmann, H. (2001) Decision making and strategy environmental assessment. *Journal of Environmental Assessment Policy and Management* 3(3): 305–327.

Nye, M. and Rydin, Y. (2006) *Evaluating Sustainable Housing Construction Standards in London: Report to the GLA.* London: Centre for Environmental Policy and Governance, London School of Economics.

Peters, B.G. and Pierre, J. (2001) Developments in intergovernmental relations: Towards multilevel governance. *Policy and Politics* 29(2): 131–135.

Ruzza, C. (1996) Inter-organisational negotiations in political decision-making: Brussels' EC bureaucrats and the environment. In C. Samson and N. South (eds) *The Social Construction of Social Policy: Methodologies, Racism, Citizenship and the Environment.* London: Macmillan.

Rydin, Y. and Burchell, K. (2006) *Sustainable Construction and Planning: The Conference Report*. London: Centre for Environmental Policy and Governance, London School of Economics.

Rydin, Y. and Nye, M. (2008) The contribution of ecological footprinting to planning policy development: Using REAP to evaluate policies for sustainable housing construction. *Environment and Planning B* 35: 227–247.

Rydin, Y. and Vandergert, P. (2006) *Sustainable Construction and Planning: The Research Agenda*. London: Centre for Environmental Policy and Governance, London School of Economics.

Rydin, Y., Amjad, U., Moore, S., Nye, M. and Whitaker, M. (2006) *Sustainable Construction and Planning: The Academic Report*. London: Centre for Environmental Policy and Governance, London School of Economics.

Rydin, Y., Moore, S. and Nye, M. (2007) Using ecological footprints as a policy driver: The case of sustainable construction planning policy in London. *Local Environment* 12(1): 1–15.

Rydin, Y., Whitaker, M. and Amjad, U. (in press) Environmentally sustainable construction: Knowledge and learning in London planning departments. *Planning Theory and Practice*.

3

Urban Sprawl
New Challenges for City-region Governance
David Ludlow

The urban future of Europe is a matter of great concern. More than a quarter of the European Union's territory has now been directly affected by urban land use; by 2020, approximately 80 per cent of Europeans will be living in urban areas, while in seven countries the proportion will be 90 per cent or more. As a result, the various demands for land in and around cities are becoming increasingly acute. On a daily basis, rapid, visible and conflicting changes in land use are shaping landscapes in cities and around them as never before.

Nowadays, society's collective reliance on land and nature for food, raw materials and waste absorption results in a resource demand without precedent in history. In Europe, consumption patterns are completely different from what they were in the mid-1980s. Transport, new types of housing, communication, tourism and leisure have emerged as major components of household consumption. As most of the population lives in urban areas, agricultural land uses and their functions in the countryside have consequently evolved.

The countryside ensures both the feeding of the city populations and maintenance of a diminishing rural population. Coasts are being urbanised at an accelerating rate, and resident communities are being transformed in order to accommodate these new economies. As a result, coastal areas are becoming increasingly intertwined with the hinterland and more dependent on tourism and secondary homes (European Environment Agency (EEA) 2006a).

In this modified landscape, a powerful force is at work: cities are spreading, minimising the time and distances between and in-and-out of the cities. This expansion occurring in a scattered way throughout Europe's countryside is called urban sprawl, and it is now rightly regarded as one of the major common challenges facing present-day urban Europe.

WHY SPRAWL MATTERS

Sprawl threatens the very culture of Europe, as it creates environmental, social and economic impacts for both the cities and countryside of Europe. Moreover, it seriously undermines efforts to meet the global challenge of climate change. Urban sprawl is synonymous with unplanned incremental urban development, characterised by a low density mix of land uses on the urban fringe (see Box 3.1). Classically, urban sprawl is a US phenomenon associated with the rapid low-density outward expansion of US cities, stemming back to the early part of the twentieth century. It was fuelled by the rapid growth of private car ownership and the preference for detached houses with gardens. In Europe, cities have traditionally been much more compact, developing a dense historical core shaped before the emergence of modern transport systems. Compared to most American cities, their European counterparts still remain in many cases compact. However, European cities were more compact and less sprawled in the mid-1950s than they are today, and urban sprawl is now a common phenomenon throughout Europe. Moreover, there is no apparent slowing in these trends and the urban areas particularly at risk are in the southern, eastern and central parts of Europe.

The sprawling nature of Europe's cities is critically important because of the major impacts that are evident in increased energy, land and soil consumption. These impacts threaten both the natural and rural environments, raising greenhouse gas emissions that cause climate change and elevated air and noise pollution levels which often exceed the agreed human safety limits. Thus, urban sprawl produces many adverse impacts that have direct effects on the quality of life for people living in cities.

BOX 3.1   URBAN SPRAWL DEFINED

Urban sprawl is commonly used to describe physically expanding urban areas. The European Environment Agency (EEA 2006b) has described sprawl as the physical pattern of low-density expansion of large urban areas, under market conditions, mainly into the surrounding agricultural areas. Sprawl is the leading edge of urban growth and implies little planning control of land subdivision. Development is patchy, scattered and strung out, with a tendency for discontinuity. It leapfrogs over areas, leaving agricultural enclaves. Sprawling cities are the opposite of compact cities – full of empty spaces that indicate the inefficiencies in development and highlight the consequences of uncontrolled growth.

Source: European Environment Agency 2006b

Why are cities sprawling?

Historically, the growth of cities has been driven by increasing urban population. However, in Europe, even where there is little or no population pressure, a variety of factors are still driving sprawl.

Global socio-economic forces are interacting with more localised environmental and spatial factors to generate the common characteristic of urban sprawl evident throughout Europe today. The mix of forces include both macro and micro socio-economic trends such as the means of transportation, the price of land, individual housing preferences, demographic trends, cultural traditions and constraints, the attractiveness of existing urban areas, and, not least, the application of land use planning policies at both local and regional scales.

Sprawl has accelerated in response to improved transportation links and enhanced personal mobility. This has made it possible to live increasingly far from city centres, while retaining all the advantages of a city location, or indeed to live in one city and work in another.

Overall, evidence suggests that where unplanned, decentralised development dominates, sprawl will occur in a mechanistic way. Conversely, where growth around the periphery of the city is coordinated by strong urban policy, more compact forms of urban development can be secured.

Policy responses and city-region governance

Europe's cities have a key role and contribution to perform in addressing the problems of urban sprawl as part of their responsibility to deliver social and environmental goals as well as economic growth, jobs and competitiveness. This is fully recognised by the EU institutions together with regional and local authorities (European Commission 2005), and sustainable urban development appears prominently in many European policy commitments, not least EU regional policy.

However, the reality is often that these issues are addressed with isolated, short-term and ineffective policies. There is a need to emphasise the integrated functions of land use, transport and energy as components of a single system in considering the question 'How can the EU support local authorities in this endeavour?'

Ultimately, local and regional authorities are charged with the responsibility of solving the interconnected issues of land use, transport and energy and their implications for urban sprawl. The conclusions here are therefore focused on the role of the EU in supporting the development of local, regional and national policy frameworks.

URBAN SPRAWL: A EUROPEAN OVERVIEW

The process of urbanisation in Europe has evolved as a clear cycle of change during the post-war period from urbanisation to suburbanisation to de-urbanisation and, most recently, to re-urbanisation. At the same time all available evidence demonstrates conclusively that urban sprawl has accompanied the growth of urban areas across Europe since the mid-1950s. Indeed during the ten-year period 1990–2000 the growth of urban areas and associated infrastructure throughout Europe consumed more than 8,000 sq. km of land.

The areas with the most visible impacts of urban sprawl are in countries or regions with high population density and economic activity (Belgium, the Netherlands, southern and western Germany, northern Italy, the Paris region) and/or rapid economic growth (Ireland, Portugal, eastern Germany, the Madrid region). Sprawl is particularly evident where countries or regions have benefited from EU regional policies. New development patterns can also be observed, around smaller towns, along trans- portation corridors, and along many parts of the coast, such as in the case of Spain where the artificial areas may cover up to 50 per cent of the total land area.

Sprawl also follows the expected rapid economic development in many parts of the new Member States, as greater access to EU markets, and Cohesion Fund and Structural Funds investments drive economic development. The 2004 accession is too recent to permit full understanding of the potential impacts of urban sprawl driven by this economic expansion, but some insights can be provided by comparisons between eastern Germany and Poland for the period 1990–2000. East Germany benefited from large monetary transfers from West Germany after unification in 1990, making it one of the most rapidly developing regions in Europe. In contrast, just to the east, in Poland, where EU membership is more recent, there was less development during the period 1990–2000 and the differences in the levels of urban sprawl between Germany and Poland are quite marked.

Overall, since the mid-1950s, European cities have expanded on average by 78 per cent, whereas the population has grown by only 33 per cent (see Figure 3.1). A major consequence of this trend is that European cities have become much less compact. The dense enclosed quarters of the compact city have been replaced by free-standing apartment blocks, semi-detached and detached houses. In half of the urban areas studied in the MOLAND project, more than 90 per cent of all residential areas built after the mid-1950s were low density areas, with less than 80 per cent of the land surface covered by buildings, roads and other structures. Only in 5 of the 24 cities, all in southern or central parts of Europe, were more than 50 per cent of new housing areas, built during the same period, densely built-up.

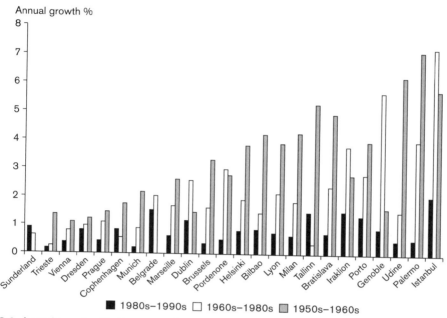

Annual growth %

■ 1980s–1990s ☐ 1960s–1980s ▨ 1950s–1960s

3.1 Annual growth of built-up areas for selected European cities
Source: MOLAND 2002

Clusters of sprawling and compact cities

The MOLAND project has provided an assessment of the most sprawled and most compact urban areas in Europe based on the following indicators:

* growth of built-up areas (1950s–1990s)
* share of dense residential areas of all residential areas (1990s)
* share of low density residential areas of all new residential areas (mid-1950s onwards)
* residential density (1990s)
* the change in growth rates for population and built-up areas (1950s–1990s)
* available built-up area per person (1990s).

This analysis for selected cities in Europe, shows the most compact city, Bilbao, is three times denser than the most sprawled city, Udine. Generally the analysis demonstrates certain clustering of cities according to the degree of sprawl or compactness that appears to be more pronounced in certain regions of Europe than others (see Table 3.1).

Table 3.1 Distribution of Europe's sprawling and compact cities

	Southern European cities	Eastern and central European cities	Northern and western European cities
Sprawled		Udine Pordenone Dresden	
			Helsinki Copenhagen Dublin Brussels Grenoble
	Marseille Porto	Trieste Vienna Bratislava Belgrade	Sunderland Lyon Tallinn
	Iraklion Palermo Milan	Prague Munich	
Compact	Bilbao		

Source: MOLAND 2002

Southern European cities have a long urban tradition in which the urbanisation process has been relatively slow, with fewer periods of rapid growth and the cities developed have accordingly been very compact. In recent decades, however, urban sprawl has started to develop at unprecedented rates, and it is most probable that unless land use planning and zoning restrictions are more rigorously applied the gap between northern and southern cities will rapidly narrow (Blue Plan 2005; Dura-Guimera 2003; Muñoz 2003). Bilbao lies in a class of its own in respect of density and compactness, much of which can be attributed to its geographical location, adjacent to the sea and bordered elsewhere by mountains. Nonetheless it is apparent that physical constraints cannot provide the entire explanation of its success, and credit should also be given to the active local planning regime and its well developed transport system.

Clusters of compact cities are also evident in the former socialist countries of central and eastern Europe. The compact urban form and high densities mainly reflect the strong centralised planning regimes and reliance on public transport that prevailed during the communist era (Couch et al. 2005; Ott 2001). These cities are now facing the same threats of rapid urban sprawl as the cities of southern European as the land market is liberated, housing preferences evolve, improving economic prospects create new pressures for low density urban expansion, and less restrictive planning controls prevail. Dresden is an exception among former socialist cities with a much less compact structure due to the unique circumstances of its wartime experience and subsequent reconstruction.

In northern Italy, small and medium sized cities are also special cases as the whole region has experienced marked urban sprawl in the past decades and the process continues. The most sprawled cities in the study, Udine and Pordenone, are relatively small cities in the Venezia-Friuli-Giulia region. In smaller cities, in general, densities are lower as the population pressure is lower and in many cases the planning regulations are more permissive, allowing more low density building than in large cities.

In general cities in northern and western Europe have less of an urban tradition, and have been more strongly influenced by planning ideologies supporting extensive garden suburbs (Hall 2002). This has resulted in much lower densities and more suburban development, particularly as individual housing preferences in north and west European cities have also favoured semi-detached and detached houses.

Along the coastal regions of Europe major population growth is accommodated by continuous sprawling development. During the period 1990–2000, urbanisation of the coast grew approximately 30 per cent faster than inland areas, with the highest rates of increase (20–35 per cent) in the coastal zones of Portugal, Ireland and Spain.

The new phenomenon of coastal urbanisation and urban sprawl in coastal zones challenges the state of the environment and sustainability of the coastal areas (see Box 3.2). Many of the mountainous regions of Europe are also under threat from urban impacts, especially where transport routes provide good communications with adjacent lowland regional centres.

All the available evidence demonstrates that throughout Europe urban areas have expanded considerably more rapidly than the growth of population during the post-war decades. There is no apparent slowing down in these trends. Particularly at risk are the urban areas of the southern, eastern and central parts of Europe, where the urban structure has historically been very compact, but which in the past few decades have started to grow rapidly outwards.

For these reasons, it is apparent that new policies and tools are necessary to control and channel urban expansion so that urban areas can develop in a more sustainable manner. However, in order to define which sustainable urban planning strategies should be adopted, it is essential to more fully understand the socio-economic drivers that provide the motors of sprawl.

DRIVERS OF URBAN SPRAWL

Deeper understanding of the relationships between the trends that drive urban sprawl, and the specific national, regional and local considerations that fashion the development of the cities and regions of Europe, is essential to redress the adverse effects of sprawl. Sustainable urban planning strategies to combat urban sprawl can be effectively specified only when the forces driving urban sprawl are better understood.

BOX 3.2 PORTUGAL AND SPAIN: THREATS TO THE COASTS OF EUROPE

Coastal urbanisation and urban sprawl in coastal zones is no longer necessarily induced and supported by the main coastal cities. By its nature, urban land use along the coasts has become suburban. This new phenomenon, which challenges the state of the environment and sustainability of the coastal areas, is recognised by coastal managers across Europe (Conference of Peripheral Maritime Regions (CPMR) 2005: 17).

The predominant pattern of residential urbanisation is diffuse settlements adjacent to or disconnected from concentrated urban centres. Residential sprawl is on average responsible for more than 45 per cent of coastal zone land transformation into artificial surfaces. There is an increasing demand for investment in coastal residences due to tourism and leisure from northern Europe. In addition, there is also domestic demand from the inland population, such as retired people. Since the mid-1990s residential expansion has spread to the coasts of other regional seas, for example the Atlantic coast of Portugal.

Portugal has experienced some of the most rapid increases in urban development in the EU, focused around major cities and the coast. Portugal's urban development is concentrated around the two metropolitan areas of Lisbon and Porto, along the coastline from Lisbon/Setubal to Porto/Viana do Castelo, and more recently along the Algarve coast. In 2000, 50 per cent of continental Portugal's urban areas were located within 13 km of the coastline, an area which accounts for only 13 per cent of the total land area. Given the persistently high urban pressures along the coastline, these zones are subject to special development and legal measures.

In Spain, economic growth and tourism has resulted in an increased number of households and second homes particularly along the Mediterranean coast. Illustrative of this phenomenon are the Costa del Sol and Costa Brava, which developed significantly during the 1950s and 1960s due to the demand for high quality holidays. This led to the combined development of accommodation, infrastructure and leisure facilities, such as golf courses and marinas. This development is still very intensive.

Source: European Environment Agency 2006a

Macro-economic factors

Global economic growth is one of the most powerful drivers of urban sprawl. Globalisation of the economy is fundamentally interrelated with the development of information and communication technologies. Both phenomena are beginning to have profound impacts on the spatial distribution of population and employment. Overall, it is likely that ICT will drive urban development towards an even more sprawled future (Audriac 2005).

Global competition is also driving efforts to secure economies of scale in the distribution and consumption of goods transforming the retail sector over the past decades. In the 1950s, most shops were small and located in the middle of residential areas, and the majority of the population did their shopping on foot. Nowadays, major out-of-town shopping centres are the dominant form of retail provision, which together with the surrounding parking areas occupy vast areas of land accessible only by car.

Global forces are reinforced by EU integration which has far-reaching impacts upon the economies of European cities. Barriers to trade between Member States have been substantially removed and an important feature of this trend is the emergence of the 'super regions' which transcend national boundaries. EU Structural and Cohesion Funds investments throughout Europe can either drive sprawl or support its containment. Investment in new motorways including the Trans-European Transport Networks (TEN-T) and other road connections, readily attract new development along the line of the improved transport links, frequently exacerbating urban sprawl. Alternatively, Structural Funds interventions can be channelled to the redevelopment of deteriorating inner cities making them more attractive for housing and other public and private investments, thereby assisting in the development of more compact cities.

New transport investment, in particular motorway construction, can be a powerful stimulant for new development and sprawl, based on the development of both shopping centres and residential areas. Land use and transport are inter-dependent in complex ways as development influences mobility patterns. The rapid development of transport networks since the early 1960s has impacted particularly strongly outside the historic city centres and these new networks today occupy significantly more space than previous networks. Furthermore, industrial, commercial and transport areas occupy between 25 per cent and 50 per cent of all built-up land, and on average one-third of urban land is used for these purposes.

New suburban development without adequate public transportation typically increases the demand for private car use. In contrast the construction of new light rail systems has a tendency to increase housing densities around access points (Handy 2005). Households make choices between residential areas taking into account the price of housing and the price of commuting between the workplace and home. When travel costs fall below a certain threshold and income reaches a certain level the rate of sprawl quickens, and unsurprisingly sprawl is more common in regions where incomes are high and commuting costs are low (Wu 2006).

Micro-economic factors

From the perspective of land economics, high land prices in the core of the city force developers to seek lower prices in the more peripheral areas. The extremely low price of agricultural land, in most cases good agricultural land, compared to already urbanised land such as brownfield sites or former industrial sites, is also an important factor underlying urban sprawl. This factor is particularly important in the economic heart of Europe stretching from the United Kingdom down through the Benelux countries, Germany and France.

Furthermore, the price of agricultural land is universally much lower than the price of land zoned for housing or the development of services. Agricultural land therefore becomes a highly attractive target for investors and developers. Although planning permission for non-agricultural development increases the value of agricultural land substantially, its price still remains at much lower levels than land in the core urban areas. These factors and processes are well illustrated by Dublin, where population growth and economic development, as well as house type and price, are predicted to be the main drivers of land use change in the Greater Dublin area during the coming decades. High house prices in Dublin are a significant push factor driving the population towards the rural fringes of the city where it is cheaper to buy or build a house (see Box 3.3).

BOX 3.3   DUBLIN METROPOLITAN AREA: RAPIDLY GROWING ECONOMY AND POPULATION

Dublin is a relatively small city by European and international standards. However, it dominates the urban pattern of Ireland in terms of demography, employment and enterprise (Bannon et al. 2000). The Greater Dublin metropolitan area population was 1,535,000 in 2002, 40 per cent of the total Irish population. The National Spatial Strategy 2002 suggests that by 2020 the Greater Dublin area population will be in the range of 1.9–2.2 million. The strong growth of Greater Dublin is a result of the region's role, both within Ireland and as a European capital city. Consequently, the Greater Dublin area will need to accommodate 403,000–480,000 additional inhabitants by the year 2020.

Population growth and economic development, as well as house type and price, are predicted to be the main drivers of land use change in the Greater

Dublin area during the coming decades. High house prices in Dublin are a significant push factor, driving the population towards the rural fringes of the city where it is cheaper to buy or build a house. Another push factor is the small size of apartments in the city centre, forcing families with children needing more space to move out of the city where houses prices are lower and housing more affordable. Personal housing preferences also play an important role, as rural living is the Irish housing ideal (Mitchell 2004). This preference is realised in single-family houses in open countryside with the benefits of the proximity to the capital or other urban areas. The realisation of this ideal is greatly facilitated by the planning regime, which imposes few constraints on the conversion of agricultural areas to low-density housing areas.

Urban–rural migration in the Greater Dublin area has led to the growth of rural towns and villages at the expense of the City of Dublin. The growth of residential areas appears to follow the line of road and rail transport, suggesting a preference for rural living but with the benefits of proximity to urban areas including employment. Another push factor is the transport system in Dublin. Commuting times are long and the lack of orbital roads and rail networks means that to get from one side of the city to the other necessitates a journey through the centre. Often it is quicker to commute from outside Dublin to the centre rather than from one side to the other (Gkartzios and Scott 2005).

The regional MOLAND model was applied to the Greater Dublin metropolitan region consisting of the following nine counties: Dublin Co., Kildare, Laois, Longford, Lough, Meath, Offaly, West Meath and Wicklow. According to the 2025 scenario, the outward expansion of residential areas in the Greater Dublin area is estimated to increase by 110 per cent over the forecast period. In the same period commercial areas will more than double while industrial areas will grow slightly more modestly. The main development axis is to the north from the Greater Dublin area along the seashore as well as inland. To the south little new residential, or industrial or commercial development will take place because of the physical constraints of upland areas. The 2025 scenario also suggests the development of Dublin City to the northwest along the line of the Dublin–Belfast corridor. This development will encourage Dublin City to develop from a monocentric to polycentric relationship with the neighbouring cities of Dundalk, Newry and Drogheda. The Greater Dublin Metropolitan area needs land use guidance and zoning as well as new infrastructure if it is going to achieve a more sustainable form of development over the period to 2025.

Source: MOLAND 2002

More and more people in Europe regard a new house, ideally a semi-detached or detached house in the suburban or rural areas outside the city, as the prime investment to be made in their lifetimes. Properties on the peripheries of cities are considered to be better investments because land prices are generally lower than in the core, and the value of property is expected to rise more rapidly outside the urban core (Couch and Karecha 2006; Wu 2006). Similar considerations apply in respect of the purchase of second homes, which are also seen as good investments.

Municipalities and public development agencies have a crucial role in the process of conversion of agricultural or natural land to space for housing or commercial development. Throughout the EU, they have the responsibility for land use zoning. However, competition among municipalities for new income generating jobs and services is great, and many municipalities can be tempted to relax controls on the development of agricultural land and even offer tax benefits to commercial and industrial enterprises to invest in the municipality. Competition of this nature between municipalities fuels urban sprawl.

Social factors

As the evidence above indicates, population growth no longer determines the outward expansion of built-up areas. The persistence of the suburban ideal underpins the apparently ever-increasing demand for houses in the sprawled suburbs and peripheral urban areas, and forms a vital stimulus to urban sprawl.

In contrast to the attractions of the suburbs, the many negative aspects of the inner city cores, including poor environment, social problems and crime, also create powerful drivers of urban sprawl. City cores are perceived by many as more polluted, noisy and unsafe than the suburbs. The built-up environment is also considered unattractive because of poor urban planning, with areas lacking green open space and sports facilities. Unemployment, poverty, single parent households, drug abuse and minorities with integration problems are all identified with inner city areas. These negative environmental factors drive many families with small children out of the city.

Families with small children are most likely to move to suburban areas and to rural areas outside the city, and in contrast elderly and single people are least likely to move out of cities. As the trend towards an increasingly ageing population and smaller households continues, it may be anticipated that some slowing down of the movement from cities to suburbs will occur in the coming decades (Couch and Karecha 2006).

IMPACTS OF URBAN SPRAWL

The drivers of sprawl and their impacts are fully interconnected and underpin the concept of sustainable development and the associated ecosystems' view of the functioning of the city and its surrounding areas. For example, many environmental problems generated by the expansion of cities create economic and social implications for the city. Urban sprawl and the demise of local shopping and social infrastructures affect many cities with negative effects on the urban economy. Furthermore, environmentally degraded urban areas are less likely to attract new enterprise and services, posing a significant impediment to further local investment. This in turn causes reallocation and the further exacerbation of urban sprawl.

Similarly as families move out of the city, social segregation begins to intensify. Municipal tax revenues are lowered, and can become insufficient to maintain services such as schools and hospitals. The quality of schools plays a crucial role as parents try to secure the best education for their children. In the inner city a downward cycle of deprivation can readily become established as more and more of the population attempt to move out, reinforcing the problems of those that must remain (Burton 2000; Couch and Karecha 2006).

Environmental impacts: natural resources and energy

Urban development involves the substantial consumption of various natural resources. The consumption of land and soil are of particular concern as they are mostly non-renewable resources. In contrast to changes in agricultural land use, the development of farmland for new housing or roads tends to be permanent and reversible only at very high costs.

A key consequence of the increasing consumption of land and reductions in population densities as cities sprawl is the growing consumption of energy. Generally, compact urban developments with higher population densities are more energy efficient. Evidence from 17 cities around the world (see Figure 3.2) shows a consistent link between population density and energy consumption. In particular high energy consumption rates are associated with the lower population densities characteristic of sprawling environments, dependent on lengthy distribution systems that undermine efficient energy use.

Urban sprawl inhibits the development of public transport and solutions based on the development of mass transportation systems, and the provision of alternative choices in transportation that are essential to ensure the efficient working of urban environments. Transport-related energy consumption in cities depends on a variety of factors including the nature of the rail and road networks, the extent of the development of mass transportation systems, and the modal split between public and private transport. Evidence shows that there is a significant increase in travel-related

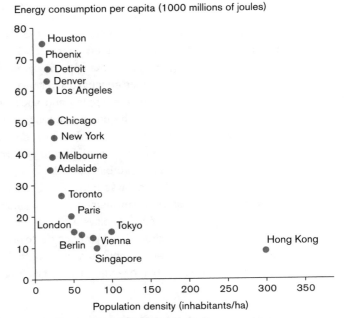

3.2 Population density and energy consumption: selected world cities
Source: Adapted from Newman and Kenworthy 1999

energy consumption in cities as densities fall. Essentially, the sprawling city is dominated by relatively energy inefficient car use, as the car is frequently the only practical alternative to more energy efficient, but typically inadequate and relatively expensive public transportation systems.

Increased transport related energy consumption is in turn leading to an increase in the emission of carbon dioxide to the atmosphere. The relationship between population densities and carbon dioxide emissions (see Figure 3.3) is apparent as emissions increase progressively with falling urban densities. Although there are several factors that may explain differentials in carbon dioxide emissions between cities, including the level of industrial activity and local climatic conditions, again the predominance of car-borne transportation in sprawling cities is clearly a major factor in the growth of urban greenhouse gas emissions. Urban sprawl therefore poses significant threats to the EU Kyoto commitments to reduce greenhouse gas emissions by 2020.

Environmental impacts: natural and protected areas

The impacts of sprawl on natural and protected areas are significant. Land sustains a number of ecosystems functions including the production of food, habitat for natural

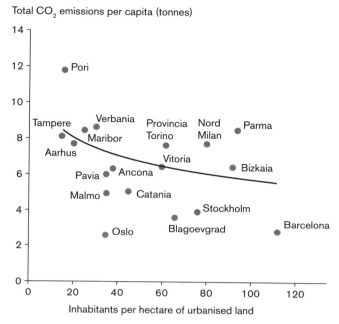

Total CO$_2$ emissions per capita (tonnes)

3.3 Population density and carbon dioxide emissions, selected European cities
Source: Adapted from Ambiente Italia 2003

species, recreation, water retention and storage, that are interconnected with adjacent land uses. The considerable impact of urban sprawl on natural and protected areas is exacerbated by the increased proximity and accessibility of urban activities to natural areas, imposing stress on ecosystems and species through noise and air pollution.

But even where the direct advance of urban land on natural and protected areas is minimised, the indirect fragmentation impacts of transport and other urban-related infrastructure developments create barrier effects that degrade the ecological functions of natural habitats. Immediate impacts such as the loss of agricultural and natural land or the fragmentation of forests, wetlands and other habitats are well-known direct and irreversible impacts.

Urban land fragmentation, with the disruption of migration corridors for wildlife species, isolates these populations and can reduce natural habitats to such an extent that the minimum area required for the viability of species populations is no longer maintained. This process of degradation of ecological networks clearly threatens to undermine the important nature conservation efforts of initiatives such as Natura 2000 (see Box 3.4).

BOX 3.4   URBAN PRESSURE ON NATURA 2000 SITES

Pressures on natural areas are derived not only from new land use change but equally from the cumulative effects of land uses in the past. Impacts are generated not only from major urban areas but also from the combined impacts of several small sources that can have equally severe effects.

Pressures on urban areas are also great on coastal zones, particularly in the western Mediterranean, where there is a clear contrast between the expansion of urban areas on the coast and inland. In the case of Barcelona geographic constraints are driving sprawl to the coast, and as a consequence Natura 2000 sites on the coast are becoming more isolated. Elsewhere new urban development is encroaching on inland protected areas. In some localities urbanisation is occurring within Natura 2000 sites.

Impact of transport infrastructure on protected sites:
Via Baltica road development, southern part in Lithuania
and north-eastern Poland

Via Baltica is one of the routes planned within the TEN networks to connect the Baltic states and Finland with the rest of the EU. The route commences in Helsinki passing through the Baltic states to Warsaw and beyond. Via Baltica crosses the most important environmental zone in Poland. Unique in Europe, it consists of four very important natural forest and marshland sites. The marshes of Biebrza are the only natural wetlands remaining in the whole of Europe, and their protection is a key environmental priority for Poland.

The EU funds have now provided financial aid for the Polish government to commit to the construction of this part of the TEN networks, and despite major protests from ecological groups, as well as questions raised at the EU level, most of the plans for the Via Baltica have been accepted.

The proposal is to build a dual carriageway that connects the border zone with the main cities of the region as an extension to the existing national road. The proposal routes part of the road close to the borders of the Biebrza National Park, and part of the route is directed through one of the Natura 2000 sites. To minimise environmental damage the route will be limited to a dual carriageway, instead of a motorway, and elsewhere the route will be tunnelled or constructed on raised embankments. Clearly, there are many questions raised regarding the environmental impacts of this section of Via Baltica on the Trans-boundary Environmental Protection Zone.

Source: European Environment Agency (2005)

Socio-economic impacts: urban quality of life

Urban sprawl produces many adverse environmental impacts that have direct impacts on the quality of life and human health in cities, such as poor air quality and high noise levels that often exceed the agreed human safety limits. In the period 1996–2002 significant proportions of the urban population were exposed to air pollutant concentrations in excess of the EU limit values (25–50 per cent of the urban population for different pollutants). It is estimated that approximately 20 million Europeans suffer from respiratory problems linked to air pollution. In particular, the societal cost of asthma has been estimated at 3 billion euro per year. Although current legislation restricts the emission of harmful substances, certain extreme events facilitated by climatic conditions, or even accidents, are of concern given the large number of people potentially exposed to these threats.

The level of air pollution exposure in the densely developed centres of cities may often be at higher levels than the suburbs due to the greater concentrations and slower movement of traffic. However, the noise produced by all vehicles, and the rapid growth in transport, particularly air and road transport, is more ubiquitous and has resulted in well over 120 million people throughout the EU being exposed to noise levels affecting their well-being.

From a social perspective urban sprawl generates greater segregation of residential development according to income. Consequently, it can exacerbate urban social and economic divisions. Social polarisation associated with urban sprawl is in some cities so apparent that the concept of the 'divided' or 'dual' city has been applied to describe the divisions between the inner city core and the suburban outskirts. In the inner city, poor quality neighbourhoods often house a mix of unemployed people, the elderly poor, single young people and minority ethnic groups, often suffering from the impacts of the selective nature of migration and employment loss.

These socio-economic problems are not, however, unique to city centres. In many cities similar social and economic problems have increasingly developed in the more peripheral areas where post-war rehousing schemes are now home to some of the most disadvantaged urban groups and the location of the lowest quality environments.

From an economic perspective, urban sprawl is at the very least a more costly form of urban development due to

- increased household spending on commuting from home to work over longer and longer distances
- the cost to business of the congestion in sprawled urban areas with inefficient transportation systems

- the additional costs of the extension of urban infrastructures including utilities and related services, across the urban region.

Overall, the interconnectedness of the impacts of sprawl poses some of the greatest challenges for the design of effective policy solutions to combat the problems of sprawl. Active urban renewal and redevelopment policies in many urban areas are successfully reversing the deconcentration of urban centres and the decay of central city districts (Working Group 2004). These conclusions are reinforced, for example, by experience from both Munich and Stockholm where the efficient control of urban sprawl and resulting increase in population densities fosters the use of public transport and reduces the growth of car use (Cameron et al. 2004; Lyons et al. 2003). Nonetheless the failure to control urban sprawl at the local level despite the policies and tools that are available supports the case for the development of new initiatives and new policy visions to address these policy failures.

POLICY RESPONSES AND CITY-REGION GOVERNANCE

Creating high quality urban areas requires close coordination between different policies and initiatives, and better cooperation between different levels of administration. Member States have a responsibility to help regional and local authorities to improve the environmental performance of the cities of their country.

(Communication from the European Commission to the Council and the European Parliament on Thematic Strategy on the Urban Environment 2006)

Local authority and EU responsibilities

The development of new initiatives and policy visions to address the failure to control urban sprawl at the local level is clearly an urgent priority. In fact policies to address the issue of urban sprawl are operating in many cities as part of a broader initiative to achieve the sustainable development of Europe's city-regions. But in many cases these issues are addressed with isolated, short-term, and ineffective policies. The question remains to be answered: 'How can the EU support local authorities in this endeavour, and what is the appropriate relationship between local and EU initiatives?'

Local and regional authorities have the prime responsibility for solving the interrelated issues of land use, transport and energy and their implications for urban sprawl. At the same time the EU has obligations to act to address the impacts of urban sprawl for a wide variety of policy reasons. These include its commitments under environmental treaties to ensure that these impacts do not seriously undermine EU commitments to the Kyoto Protocol on greenhouse gas emissions. Other legal bases for action originate from the fact that some problems of urban sprawl arise from European intervention in other policy domains.

EU intervention in many policy domains impacts on urban development, including notably, the EU commitment to sustainable development and policies to tackle climate change. Here the growth of urban greenhouse gas emissions due to the dominance of car transport in the EU's sprawling cities threatens to undermine EU Kyoto commitments to reduce greenhouse gas emissions by 2020.

Furthermore the substantial EU Cohesion and Structural Funds budget transfers to Member States providing powerful drivers of macro-economic change to support EU integration, have also put pressure on cities, and have produced inadvertent socio-economic effects that promote sprawl. As outlined above EU Structural and Cohesion Funds investments throughout Europe, such as the Trans-European Transport Networks (TEN-T), can either drive sprawl or support its containment. These are challenges that must be faced at regional, local and European levels, in the framework of the common transport policy and the Trans-European Transport Network. In this respect, it is pertinent that in April 2004 the European Parliament and the Council identified 30 priority projects that represent an investment of 225 billion euro by 2020, involving, for example, the construction of 12,000 km of highways.

The coordination of land use policies and Structural and Cohesion Funds investments remains key to support the containment of urban sprawl. EU regional policy perspectives will play a major role in developing new transport networks during the 2007–2013 period, in accordance with the priority objectives proposed by the Commission, including convergence, regional competitiveness and employment, and territorial cooperation. Impact assessments of the effects on the expansion of city-regions generated by these new transport investments will be critical for the attainment of all these priority objectives. Overall, these various obligations define a clear responsibility and mandate for the EU to take an active lead in the development of new initiatives, including impact assessment, to counter the environmental and socio-economic impacts of sprawl.

Barriers to effective policy delivery

One starting point in response to these issues concerning the most appropriate relationship between local and EU initiatives to combat urban sprawl is a focus on the barriers to more effective policy delivery. Successful execution of strategies and actions requires the identification and mitigation of the many barriers that exist.

Arguably the very complex nature of urban systems should be highlighted as a principal barrier for current administrative and political initiatives tackling the problems of urban sprawl. A fundamental challenge remains understanding, in both functional and operational terms, the unsustainable development patterns of the cities and regions of Europe so that future unsustainable development can be corrected or avoided.

Critically the paradigm of the compact city as an immediate antidote to the sprawling city still cannot be fully substantiated. The effectiveness of compaction, as well as centralisation and concentration, have been thoroughly examined, including the various ways in which compaction can be achieved, such as intensification, new high density development, traditional neighbourhood development etc. However, there are still uncertainties, particularly in the areas of ecological, social and economic impacts (Williams et al. 2000).

Furthermore, the relationship between urban compactness and travel patterns (mobility), which are central to the debate, is not entirely clear (Williams et al. 2000). The simple model of the causal relationship between high-density development and reductions in mobility demand does not hold up in all circumstances and there is a need to improve monitoring and analysis of such links, for example by using employment catchment areas to define functional urban regions (Laconte 2006).

Beyond these issues of complexity and uncertainty, EU-funded reports such as TRANSplus (2003) and SCATTER (2002) have identified a variety of barriers to integrated and sustainable development of the European city. Barriers can be attitudinal, financial, institutional, instrumental, legal, physical, political, procedural, social, and/or technical, and typically will be a mixture of most of these.

The SCATTER project focused on obstacles to addressing urban sprawl, especially organisational issues within and between authorities, such as:

- imbalance between territory or competences, and objectives
- complexity of institutions involved in metropolitan management
- political representation at local and regional levels and other potential conflicts of interest
- shortcomings related to available legal and fiscal tools
- difficulty of establishing regional institutions for cultural and political reasons, and low legitimacy or efficacy once established.

This in particular highlights the potential dangers of ad-hoc decision-making: the solution to one problem, at one scale, is often the cause of another, at a similar or different scale. It is therefore of prime importance to recognise that while the city is the main focus of socio-economic activity, and the associated pressures and impacts on the environment, it cannot be managed in isolation from forces and decisions that originate well beyond the city borders.

Despite or perhaps because of this complexity of urban systems, a piecemeal approach to urban management prevails in many cities; sprawl is seldom tackled as an integrated issue. In turn, issue integration is rarely matched by procedural integration through policymaking, problem analysis and impact assessment, planning, financing and implementation, precisely because of the wide scope of the issues involved. This constraint on effective urban management, already identified in the 1980s (European Commission 1990), still remains high on the political agendas (European Commission 2006).

There is a continuing perception of cities as isolated from their wider regional context. In reality, however, the functional influences of cities are recognised as reaching far beyond their immediate boundaries, and there are also multidimensional links between urban and rural areas that are becoming more and more apparent. Typically, in Europe today, cities flow imperceptibly across municipal boundaries, a process at different stages of development in different countries, but which occurs everywhere.

Largely because of this reality, and the relative inflexibility of administrative systems in responding to the socio-economic dynamic of the city, the responsibility for land use management remains divided between different administrations. This fragmentation of management, frequently exacerbated by the political tensions of neighbouring administrations, may furthermore lead to incoherent and uncoordinated land use management.

City-region governance structures

It has been demonstrated that the prime drivers of many environmental problems affecting European urban land originate outside the urban territory where the changes are observed. The global market economy, trans-European transport networks, large-scale demographic and socio-economic changes, cross-boundary pollution, as well as differences in land-planning mechanisms at national, regional and local levels, are the main drivers of change and environmental pressure on, and from, urban areas. As a result, there is now increasing awareness of the benefits of considering the city-region as an integrated unit for measures to counter urban sprawl and stimulate better coordination of policies and analysis of their economic, social and environmental impacts.

A key dimension of such frameworks is the division of responsibilities between the different levels of city and regional governance. Urban and regional managers at the local level have prime responsibility for the management of the city and its region. But the strategies and instruments to control urban sprawl strongly depend on the interconnectedness between local, regional and national conditions that are increasingly reshaped by the realities of Europe's spatial development. New planning responses to combat urban sprawl should therefore consider principles that recognise what is locally driven and what should be EU driven.

At the local level city-region governance structures need to support new policy interventions to counter sprawl focused on the need to supplement the logic of the market and be based on demand rather than supply-driven management. But identifying the necessary spatial trade-offs between economic, social and environmental objectives and the key requirements for the sustainable development of Europe's cities also requires an improved regional contextualisation of the respective assets that should be maintained, restored or enhanced.

This is the role devolved to spatial development in policy-making where the EU can support the envisioning of spatial planning of Europe's cities and regions to effectively address the issue of urban sprawl. This articulated vision of sustainable urban and regional development can provide the context for a range of integrated mutually reinforcing policy responses, offering a new policy coherence to be implemented at all levels.

It is already clear in the linkages between territorial cohesion and economic and social cohesion, two fundamental aims of the European Union (Article 16 of the Treaty), that many benefits can be secured from a broader vision of cohesion that encompasses the many dimensions of the development of territories, urban areas in particular, and their interrelationships. In response to this agenda a territorial dimension has been proposed for the conceptual basis of structural policies after 2007. The Commission has also proposed European territorial cooperation as an objective for Structural Funds interventions for 2007–2013 in support of territorial cohesion within the EU.

Furthermore even though the Lisbon Strategy has no explicit territorial dimension, one of its three main priorities calls for Europe to be made an attractive area in which to invest and work. This priority includes considerations relating to access to markets and the provision of services, as well as to factors relating to the creation of a healthy environment for enterprise and the family. The implementation of the Lisbon Strategy and future structural policies will take place in cities, regions, national territories and at European level (European Commission 2005). Therefore, a key question for policy-makers at different levels is to explore, identify, understand and select potential areas for development within their own territory in order to contribute effectively to this overall European strategy.

Overall, it is clear that the EU has a responsibility and a specific capability to challenge the wide ranging and powerful pan-European forces generating urban sprawl with impacts beyond the control of urban managers at the local level. For these reasons, policies at all levels need to have an urban dimension that tackle urban sprawl and help to redress market failures that drive urban sprawl and undermine a sustainable vision for the spatial planning of urban Europe. These impacts that are fully evident, for example, in the various visions for the future development of the Dresden–Prague region (see Box 3.5).

BOX 3.5   DRESDEN–PRAGUE: ECONOMIC GROWTH AND NEW TRANSPORT LINKS

German reunification and the collapse of the communist bloc led to changes in the economic regime from planned to market economy in both the former east Germany and the Czech Republic. Adaptation to the market economy caused many dramatic changes in traditional economic structures, such as a decrease in GDP and a high rate of unemployment, up to 25 per cent in Saxony. Towards the end of the 1990s, gradual but sustainable recovery of the economy commenced and political and social reforms took hold. These changes have created completely new driving forces for urban development. EU membership has also led to the growing engagement with European markets and access to EU development schemes e.g. TEN-T, ERDF, Cohesion Fund etc. For the new EU Member States (EU10) gross domestic product is expected to triple and the number of households is projected to double between 2000 and 2030 (European Environment Agency (EEA) 2005). But in contrast to economic growth, the demographic trends for EU10 show significant decreases of population, up to 7 per cent by 2030 (EEA 2005). It is clear that all the above-mentioned changes will have a strong impact on land use patterns in the area.

Future development paths: scenarios
*   *Business-as-usual*: extrapolates moderate 1990s trends of land use change, indicating that the land use patterns of the area will not change considerably over the next two decades.
*   *Built-up expansion*: elaborates the socio-economic projections of the European Environment Agency.
*   *Motorway impact*: evaluates the impact of motorway development (A17/D8 part of TEN Corridor IV).

Around Dresden new residential districts are situated adjacent to existing ones and lead to the merging together of former clusters. Construction of the new motorway around the city from west to south creates a new development axis for commercial and industrial areas. The simulation results for Prague show a very different, more clustered type of future development. The radial network of motorways connecting the city to different destinations attracts the development of commercial zones and produces more clustered patterns of growth. The municipalities located in the vicinity of Prague experience intensive residential development and hence it can be assumed that demand for new housing will remain strong.

The motorway A17/D8 can reinforce regional development and lead to the establishment of commercial and service areas adjacent to larger settlements and towns. In most cases the future growth pressures of Dresden and Prague will focus on agricultural land and natural areas around both cities.

Source: European Environment Agency 2006b

CITY-REGION GOVERNANCE: THE CASE FOR EUROPE

The EU White Paper on European governance provides the following framework of principles underpinning good governance that assists in defining a framework for intervention to counter sprawl at all levels:

- *policy coherence*: ensuring that policies are coherent and not sector-specific and that decisions taken at regional and local levels are coherent with a broader set of principles
- *cooperation in policy development*: development of systematic dialogue and increased cooperation with European and national associations of regional and local government
- *responsiveness to local conditions*: flexibility in the means provided for implementing legislation and programmes with a strong territorial impact.

Policy coherence

Policy coherence provides the first principle of good governance through which the EU aims to support initiatives to counter urban sprawl. Policies to be effective should deliver what is needed on the basis of clear objectives, in terms of time and with an evaluation of future impacts. Effectiveness also depends on implementing policies in a proportionate manner, on taking decisions at the most appropriate level, and ensuring that decisions taken at regional and local levels are coherent with a broader set of principles for sustainable territorial development across the EU. The framework for trilateral agreements between the EU, national governments and regional/local authorities (European Commission 2002) provides a specific example, and some agreements have already been signed, for example Milan (Laconte 2006).

However, cities also need a long-term sustainable policy vision to help synchronise the many critical success factors, including mobility, access to the natural environment, social and cultural opportunity, and employment, all of which form the basis for sustainable urban development.

EU Cohesion Policy (2007–2013) proposes a framework to build a coordinated and integrated approach to the sustainable development of urban and rural areas, to ameliorate the impacts of urban sprawl, with specific actions including the following:

- Coordination of land use policies, as well as Structural and Cohesion Funds investments between urban areas, rural areas, the regions and the national levels to manage urban sprawl. Initiatives to make urban areas and city centres attractive places to live and support the containment of urban sprawl.
- Encouragement to Member States to explicitly delegate to cities funds addressing urban issues within Structural Funds operational programmes, with full responsibility throughout the process for the design and implementation of the delegated portion of the programme.
- Investments to achieve compliance with EU laws on air quality, waste-water treatment, waste management, water supply and environmental noise. Active management of congestion, transport demand and public transport networks, with a view to improving air quality, reducing noise and encouraging physical activity all of which can assist in addressing the sprawl of cities.
- Co-financing of activities under the Structural Funds based on plans that address the key challenges posed by sprawl and the improvement of the overall environmental quality of urban areas.

Cooperation in policy development

Cooperation in policy development provides the second principle of good governance through which the EU aims to support initiatives to counter urban sprawl. The aim is to develop systematic dialogue and increased cooperation with European and national associations of regional and local government and other local partners including regional and city networks and other NGOs, to ensure that regional and local knowledge and conditions are fully taken into account when developing policy proposals.

The essentials of this approach are based on the development of a reinforced culture of consultation and dialogue, such as that attempted in the mobilisation of a broad range of partners with different skills by the Bristol Accord in which local partnerships including public, private, voluntary and community interests are viewed as essential to deliver sustainable communities. The aim is to develop and maintain partnerships over the long term based on flexible cooperation between the different territorial levels, so that regional and city networks and NGOs can make more effective contributions to EU policy development.

Responsiveness to local conditions

Responsiveness to local conditions provides the third principle of good governance through which the EU aims to support initiatives to counter urban sprawl. The principle emphasises the need for flexibility in the means provided for implementing EU legislation and programmes with a strong territorial impact. Thereby the EU aims to set the tone and direction for sectoral policy integration in cities while recognising that planning responses to the problem of sprawl must also be sensitive to the local and regional mix of priorities.

CITY-REGION GOVERNANCE: LOCAL MANAGEMENT

At the local level the key aim concerns the revision of the thrust of policy to counter sprawl, and the replacement of the dominant trends of urbanisation ('laissez-faire') with a new urbanism ('creative control') (Laconte 2006). At present, planning policy solutions at all levels of governance more typically reflect the logic of economic development rather than a sustainable vision of urban Europe.

The EU Urban Thematic Strategy offers an umbrella framework to support actions and solutions developed at the local level to support this new urbanism. The strategy offers a coordinated and integrated approach to assist Member States and local and regional authorities to meet existing environmental obligations, to develop environmental management plans and sustainable urban transport plans, and so to reinforce the environmental contribution to sustainable development of urban areas.

The Thematic Strategy provides a context in which good practice experiences of cities in combating urban sprawl (see Box 3.6 on Munich) can be applied and developed including:

- the development of long-term, consistent plans promoting sustainable development and the limitation of urban sprawl supported by monitoring and evaluation systems to verify results on the ground
- management of the urban–rural interface via cooperation and coordination between urban authorities and rural and regional authorities in promoting sustainable development
- policies for the rehabilitation of derelict brownfield sites and renovation of public spaces to assist in the creation of more compact urban forms
- policies for the avoidance of the use of greenfield sites and complementary urban containment policies
- identification of the key partners including the private sector and community, as well as local, regional and national government and their mobilisation in the planning, implementation and evaluation of urban development.

BOX 3.6   MUNICH: DEVELOPMENT OF THE COMPACT CITY

Munich is the capital of the Bavarian state and the third largest city in Germany. The MOLAND study area comprises the city of Munich (*Landhauptkapital*) and 44 surrounding municipalities (completely or partially). The total area is 791 sq. km and the resident population in 1990 was 1.69 million inhabitants. From 1955 to 1990 the population has grown by 49 per cent.

Munich – compact city

The Munich area has remained exceptionally compact when compared to many other European cities. It is the only urban area among the 24 urban areas studied where the built-up areas have grown at a clearly slower pace than the population. Another indicator of compactness is the share of continuous residential areas compared with all residential areas built after 1955. In all other western European cities studied almost all residential areas, built after the 1950s, are discontinuous in character, but in Munich only one-third is of this character and two-thirds is densely built.

Bavarian planning solutions

Munich was heavily bombed and mostly destroyed in the Second World War and immediately after the war the city's planners faced a decision whether to completely rebuild or to reconstruct what was destroyed. The outcome, in what later proved to be an excellent decision, was a mix of both approaches. The historical centre was rebuilt largely following the pre-war pattern and style. To ease traffic problems and to increase green urban areas, a combined park and traffic ring was constructed around the historical city.

By the early 1960s pressures to find new housing and transport solutions began to mount in Munich. The drivers for change were primarily the increased use of the private car, and strong inward migration from rural areas. At the same time at the Federal level in Germany, the new building law (*Bundesbaugesetz*) took effect. All these factors together influenced the far-sighted decision adopted by the Munich planners to move from traditional town planning to integrated urban development planning, providing guidelines for all municipal activities including economy, social issues, education, culture as well as town planning. The first integrated city-development plan of 1963 paved the way for Munich's modernisation.

In the late 1960s another innovative tool was also adopted as a response to citizens' opposition to the new development plans. The mayor organised an open discussion forum for urban development issues that became a permanent platform where the stakeholders and the city planners could exchange views and opinions. At the same time an independent department was created with the responsibility to coordinate all municipal planning activities, strengthen links with research and stakeholders involvement.

Regional cooperation was seen as the only way of safeguarding the balanced regional development of Munich and the mainly rural neighbouring municipalities. As early as 1950 the majority of the municipalities in the Munich region discussed common urban development issues in the form of a 'Planning Association of Munich's Economic Region' which became the Munich Regional Planning Association. However, this cooperation has remained on a voluntary and consultative basis and no planning authority has been transferred to the regional level, in contrast to other German city-regions.

The 1970s and 1980s were characterised by more incremental develop-ments and the planning vision became less clear. Nonetheless, the steps taken in the earlier period maintained the high planning standards and resulted in a compact and high-quality urban environment. The main objectives of this era were as follows:

- city in equilibrium where various economic, social and environmental interests are in balance
- development of areas inside the urban structure instead of urban expan-sion in the periphery supported by economic incentives, and made possi-ble by large brownfields vacated by industry, the military, the Federal Railroads (DBB) and the old airport in Riem
- strong emphasis on public transport and new road development limited to a minimum
- preservation of large green recreational areas around the city.

In the 1990s the comprehensive planning concept gained ground and a new version of the integrated urban development plan, called 'Munich Perspective', was adopted in 1998. The slogan of the plan is to keep Munich region compact, urban and green. The plan covers economy, social issues, transport, environ-ment and town planning. The main urban structure objectives include continued reuse of brownfields and avoidance of expansion. Mixed land use (residential, commercial, services) is seen as an important way of keeping the city compact. Improvement of public transport as well as pedestrian and cycling facilities and reinforcing regional cooperation are also seen as fundamental for the attainment of the plan objectives.

Key objectives and actions for the compact city
- integrated city development plan
- regional cooperation
- stakeholders' involvement in city planning
- emphasis on reuse of vacant brownfields
- continuously improving public transport with as few new roads as possible
- compact-urban-green – keep the city compact and urban and green areas green
- guarantee the necessary resources for implementing the strategies of all relevant policy areas (transport, housing etc.) for both 'business as usual' situations and through major renovation projects.

Source: MOLAND 2002

TOWARDS A NEW CITY-REGION GOVERNANCE

Land use patterns across Europe show that tensions are arising almost everywhere between our need for resources and space and the capacity of the land to support and absorb this need. Urban development is the main driver.

Throughout Europe in the 1990s, changes in land cover were mainly characterised by increases in urban and other artificial land development and forest area, at the expense of agricultural and natural areas. Anticipated growth of the urban population by 5 per cent in the coming decade, will further fuel these trends. Globalisation, transport networks, socio-demographic changes, societal aspirations for the 'urban culture' and uncoordinated land-planning mechanisms at various levels are the main sources of the environmental unsustainability of our cities.

The principles of multilevel governance stress the view that adequate decisions on urban development cannot be made solely at the local level. This is especially important in a European context where urban areas are becoming increasingly connected in order to realise common objectives, such as the Lisbon agenda for growth and competitiveness.

The potential exists for local policy to be isolated in overcoming the serious impacts of urban sprawl throughout Europe, a fact which highlights the requirement for urgent action by all responsible agencies and stakeholders. The EU Governance White Paper defines the preconditions for 'good governance' emphasising the need to assess whether action is needed at the EU level and the principles for action when required.

According to the good governance criteria the EU has specific obligations and a mandate to act and take a lead role in developing the right frameworks for intervention at all levels, and to pave the way for local action. Policies at all levels including local, national and European should therefore have an urban dimension to tackle urban sprawl and help to redress the market failures that drive urban sprawl. The provision of new visions for the spatial development of Europe's cities and regions is vital for the creation of a range of integrated mutually reinforcing policy responses.

The policy debate on sustainable visions for the spatial planning of urban Europe is already actively underway in the context of EU Cohesion Policy (2007–2013), and the Urban Thematic Strategy and provide the entrée for wider EU contributions to this debate on the visions. The aim is to set the tone and direction for sectoral policy implementation at all levels, and become the basis for the new urban planning model of city-regional development.

In developing integrated spatial planning for the key EU policy frameworks which make major contributions to policies to combat urban sprawl, transport and cohesion policies are crucially important dimensions for the delivery of positive outcomes. EU Cohesion Policy offers a new framework to articulate better coordination of land use policies and Structural and Cohesion Funds investments between urban areas, rural areas, and the regions that can effectively manage urban sprawl.

Good governance, in the context of the EU Urban Thematic Strategy, can be translated into the provision of support for actions and solutions developed at the local level to address urban management problems including urban sprawl. In this way the EU can directly assist in the transfer of good practice experience of the management of urban sprawl from one city to another and the dissemination of policy solutions that have proven effective.

There is no lack of best practices in the field of urban sustainability, and many regions and municipalities have made significant progress toward an integrated and sustainable urban development. Deeper understanding of city-region governance, awareness of interrelated systems, as well as optimal governance structures that are essential to address the gaps between sustainable development and the current reality, is clearly vital. Policies and especially investments can then be selected, prioritised and coordinated effectively based on new city-region governance strategies.

New city-region governance strategies

- Develop a region-wide, whole-systems view, so that policy-making is grounded in a shared understanding of the drivers of problems, as well as consequences of solutions.
- Adopt and follow a sustainable vision based on science-based sustainability principles and reflecting a whole-systems view. A participatory approach to visioning will ensure that the vision is a mutually agreed upon goal to strive towards among all stakeholders.
- Shape regional governance structures strategically: as transport patterns transcend municipal boundaries, the problem cannot be solved without regional coordination, which can take many shapes and evolve over time. National governments can play a key role by facilitating or even requiring coordination between regions. A common vision can serve as a springboard for change.
- Encourage national governments and the EU to support local and regional efforts towards the sustainable city; although the EU has no formal mandate for local or regional planning, it impacts in many ways, not least being its investment in transport through the structural funds.

REFERENCES

Ambiente Italia (2003) *European Common Indicators towards a Local Sustainability Profile.* Milan: Ambiente Italia.

Audriac, I. (2005) Information technology and urban form: Challenges to smart growth. *International Regional Science Review* 28(2): 119–145.

Bannon, M.J., Thomas, S.R. and Cassidy, A. (2000) *The Role of Dublin in Europe.* Research Paper prepared for the National Spatial Strategy Team. Dublin: Department of the Environment and Local Government (DoELG).

Blue Plan (2005) *A Sustainable Future for the Mediterranean: The Blue Plan's Environment and Development Outlook.* Edited by G. Benoit and A. Comeau. London: Earthscan.

Burton, E. (2000) The compact city: Just or just compact? A preliminary analysis. *Urban Studies* 37(11): 1969–2001.

Cameron, I., Lyons, T.J. and Kenworthy, J.R. (2004) Trends in vehicle kilometers of travel in world cities 1960–1990: Underlying drivers and policy responses. *Transport Policy* 11(3): 287–298.

Conference of Peripheral Maritime Regions (CPMR) (2005) Europe of the sea: Towards a maritime policy for the Union. Contribution to the preparation of the Green Paper. Technical Paper from the CPMR General Secretariat, France.

Couch, C. and Karecha, J. (2006) Controlling urban sprawl: Some experiences from Liverpool. *Cities* 23(5): 242–363.

Couch, C., Karecha, J., Nuissl, H. and Rink, D. (2005) Decline and sprawl: An evolving type of urban development – observed in Liverpool and Leipzig. *European Planning Studies* 13(1): 117–136.

Dura-Guimera, A. (2003) Population deconcentration and social restructuring in Barcelona: A European city. Cities 18(5): 355–364.

European Commission (1990) *Green Paper on the Urban Environment*. Communication from the Commission to the Council and the European Parliament. COM(1990) 218 final. Brussels: European Commission.

European Commission (2002) *A Framework for Target-based Tripartite Contracts and Agreements between the Community, the States and Regional and Local Authorities*. Communication from the Commission. COM(2002) 709. Brussels: European Commission.

European Commission (2005) *Cohesion Policy and Cities: The Urban Contribution to Growth and Jobs in the Regions*. Commission Staff Working Paper. Brussels: European Commission.

European Commission (2006) *Thematic Strategy on the Urban Environment*. Communication from the Commission to the Council and the European Parliament. COM(2005) 718 final. Brussels: European Commission.

European Environment Agency (EEA) (2005) *The European Environment: State and Outlook 2005*. Luxembourg: Office for Official Publications of the European Communities.

European Environment Agency (EEA) (2006a) *The Changing Faces of Europe's Coastal Areas*. Luxembourg: Office for Official Publications of the European Communities.

European Environment Agency (EEA) (2006b) *Urban Sprawl in Europe: The Ignored Challenge*. EEA Report 10/2006, European Topic Centre on Terrestrial Environment project team including David Ludlow (lead author), University of the West of England, Bristol; Jaume Fonts (task manager), Nuria Blanes, Oscar Gomez and Heimo Savolainen, assisted by EEA project officer Agnieszka Romanowicz, and JRC project team Marjo Kasanko (task leader), Jose I. Barredo, Carlo Lavalle, Laura Petrov, and Valentina Sagris.

Gkartzios, M. and Scott, M. (2005) *Countryside, Here I Come: Urban Rural Migration in the Dublin City-Region, Planning and Environmental Policy, UCD*: available www.ucd.i e/gpep (accessed 28/04/08).

Hall, P. (2002) *Cities of Tomorrow*. Oxford: Blackwell.

Handy, S. (2005) Smart growth and the transportation land use connection: What does the research tell us? *International Regional Science Review* 28(2): 146–167.

Laconte, P. (2006). Urban and transport management: International trends and practices. Paper presented at the Ecopolis Forum Eco-planning and Management for Adaptive Appropriate Human Settlement, Chongqing, 22–24 September.

Lyons, T.J., Kenworthy, J.R., Moy, C. and Dos Santos, F. (2003) An international urban air pollution model for the transport sector. *Transportation Research D* 8: 159–167.

Mitchell, C.J.A. (2004) Making sense of counterurbanization. *Journal of Rural Studies* 20: 15–34.

MOLAND (2002) MOLAND (Monitoring Land Use/Cover Dynamics) research project, reported in *Towards an Urban Atlas: Assessment of Spatial Data on 25 European Cities and Urban Areas*. European Environment Centre and DG Joint Research Centre of the European Commission. Environmental Issue Report 30/2002: available http://moland.jrc.it (accessed 28/04/08).

Muñoz, F. (2003) Lock-living: Urban sprawl in Mediterranean cities. *Cities* 20(6): 381–385.

Newman, P. and Kenworthy, J. (1999) *Sustainability and Cities: Overcoming Automobile Dependence*. Washington, DC: Island Press.

Ott, T. (2001) From concentration to deconcentration: Migration patterns in the post-socialist city. *Cities* 18(6): 403–412.

SCATTER (2002) EU Fifth Framework Programme project on sustainable land use and transport research forming part of Land Use Transport Research (LUTR) cluster grouped projects that studied and developed integrated planning tools to link urban transport to its impacts.

TRANSplus (2003) *Achieving Sustainable Transport and Land Use with Integrated Policies*. (Final Report) EU Fifth Framework Programme City of Tomorrow and Cultural Heritage Key Action (Energy, Environment, and Sustainable Development Research Programme).

Williams, K., Burton, E. and Jenks, M. (2000) *Achieving Sustainable Urban Forms*. London: E.&F.N. Spon.

Working Group (2004) Working Group on Sustainable Urban Transport, *Final Report*, January 2004. Brussels: European Commission.

Wu, J. (2006) Environmental amenities, urban sprawl, and community characteristics. *Journal of Environmental Economics and Management* 52(2): 527–547.

4

Decision-making Processes in Urban Design

Christopher Boyko and Rachel Cooper

The UK national government, through its Department of Communities and Local Government (DCLG), is wholeheartedly endorsing the creation and maintenance of prosperous and cohesive communities (Kelly 2006). They believe that, through effective and widespread policy, extensive cultural and economic programmes and citizen involvement, communities can be safe, healthy and sustainable. These ideas are being promoted heavily through the government's planning system, whereby more and more decision-makers and stakeholders in the private and public sectors are expected to address community and sustainability in building and urban design and development projects (Boyko et al. 2005).

To support the planning system and to help outline the relationship between communities, sustainability, planning and design, governmental and non-governmental organisations have published a number of reports and policy documents (e.g. Commission for Architecture and the Built Environment and Department for Environment, Transport and the Regions 2000, 2001; Communities and Local Government 2006; Office of the Deputy Prime Minister (ODPM) 2002, 2003, 2004, 2005a, 2005b, 2006; Urban Task Force 1999, 2005). These publications provide principles, guidance and information about the value of good design and planning and the need for the delivery of sustainable communities. While useful, greater effort needs to be expended to explain the implementation *process* through which well-designed and planned sustainable communities are created, developed and maintained. Knowing the stages and actions involved in the process can equip decision-makers with more information about when and how to make decisions and what to consider when making decisions.

The purpose of this chapter is to outline a normative process for urban design decision-making that allows a wide range of decision-makers to work together more easily in urban development projects (cf. Cooper et al. 2004, on the design and construction process). Researchers sought to establish this by first proposing a conceptual urban design decision-making process, originating from the relevant design and process literature. The conceptual process then was compared to practical processes, which were mapped from real-time urban development projects in the United Kingdom. The comparison allowed researchers to uncover gaps in the conceptual process (e.g. consideration of sustainability, and by whom), to highlight emerging issues and tensions and to suggest improvements for an updated (and normative) urban design decision-making process. This research is part of the larger *VivaCity2020* project, which aims to analyse urban planning, design and consultation processes to identify how and when key decisions relating to urban sustainability are made.[1]

To this end, the chapter begins with a description of urban design and the proposal of a conceptual urban design decision-making process. A brief description of three case studies in London, Sheffield and Greater Manchester follows, offering examples of urban design decision-making processes in practice. The chapter ends with key findings from the case studies and how these findings inform an updated urban design decision-making process that includes consideration of sustainability throughout.

URBAN DESIGN AND THE URBAN DESIGN DECISION-MAKING PROCESS

As a precursor to the research, it was important to first understand the definition of urban design. Doing so would set the context for developing the conceptual urban design decision-making process as well as for the case study work. Regarding the latter, researchers were able to use the definition of urban design to select appropriate urban development sites within the three case study cities (see below).

Urban design may be viewed as a multidimensional concept, emphasising transformation within the urban environment (Barnett 1982; Gosling 2000; Rowley 1994). Although such transformation is perceived mostly in physical terms (e.g. creating a park where previously there had been only a brownfield), people also play an important role in urban design. Through their changing social, psychological, aesthetic, functional and emotional needs, people act as drivers for urban design, shaping how urban spaces look, feel and are used. Thus, urban design is as much about transformation as it is about reaction to, and ongoing interaction with, the urban environment.

Taking the above ideas about multidimensionality, transformation and ongoing interaction into account, a definition of urban design may be offered: urban design refers to the dynamic art and process of designing, creating, making and managing spaces and places for people (adapted from Commission for Architecture and the Built Environment and Department of the Environment, Transport and the Regions 2000; Rowley 1994). From this definition, the idea of urban design as both a dynamic art and a process become evident.

Dynamic art emphasises creativity and specificity in context. While urban design may be part of a wider national policy, local authorities must be able to re-interpret the policy to suit their context (see Rogers and Power 2000, for a description of context). The private sector and other local stakeholders (e.g. community residents) also must be free to bring their particular insights to each situation and help to shape the urban design of an area (Commission for Architecture and the Built Environment and Department for Environment, Transport and the Regions 2000). Consulting and involving the community in urban design projects is part of the national government's remit for creating more sustainable communities (Communities and Local Government 2006; Office of the Deputy Prime Minister 2002, 2003, 2004, 2005a, 2005b, 2006).

Process emphasises following a method, procedure or series of actions, leading to the accomplishment of a result (Atkin et al. 2003; Oxford English Dictionary 2005). In general, the means to an end is often complex, non-linear and iterative (Rowley 1994), involving a host of people, issues and trade-offs over time. Illustrating a broad, conceptual guide to achieving an end attempts to highlight the complexity and gives decision-makers more knowledge about their roles, and who to work with, in the process.

A conceptual process for urban design decision-making may provide an appropriate balance between creativity and procedure. Such a process has the capacity to emphasise the dynamic and interrelated qualities and contexts of urban development projects. Information used to map urban design decision-making processes may come from the complementary collection of hard, quantitative data with soft, qualitative information (rather than a reliance on more rational processes in which only hard data is acceptable, for example, rational-comprehensive planning: Faludi 1973). The 'soft' information adds an extra layer of richness that may otherwise be lost to checklists, closed-end surveys and other quantifiable methods of obtaining information (Boyko et al. 2005).

A review of the literature on design processes revealed that an explicit process for urban design decision-making did not exist. Thus, a conceptual process was created as part of the *VivaCity2020* project, to be used as a starting point for understanding the complexity of urban design decision-making (e.g. how and when urban design decisions are made in urban development projects, what decision-makers use to make decisions, whether or not sustainability is considered in decision-making). This conceptual urban design decision-making process acted as a baseline process from which to compare real-world processes. In an effort to ensure that the conceptual process and the three processes mapped for the case studies were well founded, a panel of design, planning and regeneration experts examined the processes, provided feedback and validated them (see section on validation, pp. 93–94).

Design processes from various disciplines were consulted to understand what stages and actions within those stages were considered important. The disciplines included:

- architecture (Royal Institute of British Architects 1999)
- business (Smith and Jackson 2000)
- manufacturing, construction and engineering (Austin et al. 2001; Cooper et al. 2004; Woodhead 2000)
- non-governmental organisations (English Partnerships 2000; Heritage Lottery Fund 2000)
- planning (Bressi 1995; Nelessen 1994; Okubo 2000; Roberts 2003; Wates 1996, 1998)
- urban design (Biddulph 1997; Canadian Institute of Planners 2000; Rowland 1995; see also Macmillan et al. 2002).

Substantial overlap between urban design and the other disciplines meant that the urban design decision-making process could be streamlined into four stages, with four transition stages (see Figure 4.1).

Stage 1 – 'Creating teams, appraising the situation and forming goals' – is a preparation stage for an urban design project. Teams are formed, the site and its surrounding context are appraised, objectives for the project are developed, stakeholders are identified, funding is sought and timetables are created.

In Stage 2 – 'Designing and developing' – the main action is to create design options for an urban design project. This action will be based on a project design brief that is formulated by the team, an assessment and testing of ideas in the project brief and feedback from stakeholders.

In Stage 3 – 'Evaluating, selecting and creating a plan' – the design options will be evaluated with respect to the Stage 1 objectives and an option will be chosen. The selected option will be assessed again, stakeholders will be consulted on the decision and a plan will be prepared, ready to be executed.

Stage 4 – 'Implementing, monitoring and following up' – sees the implementation of the selected option via the construction process. Once built, the urban design project will be monitored for problems and a group will be established to manage the project in the future.

In between each stage are transition stages: 'Continuing to understand the context', 'Continuing to think about alternatives', 'Re-creating a plan' and 'Continuing the process'. The transition stages act as 'soft gates' for decision-makers to review their actions and plan their next steps (Kagioglou et al. 1998). They also reinforce the iterative nature of processes, as decision-makers may need to revise actions from a previous stage before moving on to a subsequent stage.

The information from the literature review, used to create this urban design decision-making process, is more conceptual than practical (i.e. abstracted from real-world examples). Having a conceptual process allows decision-makers to incorporate

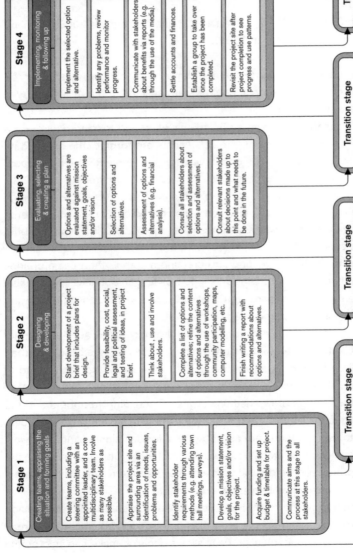

4.1

The urban design
decision-making
process taken
from the literature

Source: Boyko et
al. 2005

Stage 1

Creating teams, appraising the situation and forming goals

Create teams, including a steering committee with an appointed leader, and a core multidisciplinary team. Involve as many stakeholders as possible.

Appraise the project site and surrounding area via an identification of needs, issues, problems and opportunities.

Identify stakeholder requirements through various methods (e.g. attending town hall meetings, surveys).

Develop a mission statement, goals, objectives and/or vision for the project.

Acquire funding and set up budget & timetable for project.

Communicate aims and the process at this stage to all stakeholders.

Transition stage

Continuing to understand the context

Might require revision of goals & communicating further with stakeholders

Stage 2

Designing & developing

Start development of a project brief that includes plans for design.

Provide feasibility, cost, social, legal and political assessment, and testing of ideas, in project brief.

Think about, use and involve stakeholders.

Complete a list of options and alternatives; refine the content of options and alternatives through the use of workshops, community participation, maps, computer modelling, etc.

Finish writing a report with recommendations about options and alternatives.

Transition stage

Continuing to think about alternatives

Might require revision of report from Stage 2 to think more about alternatives.

Stage 3

Evaluating, selecting & creating a plan

Options and alternatives are evaluated against mission statement, goals, objectives and/or vision.

Selection of options and alternatives.

Assessment of options and alternatives (e.g. financial analysis).

Consult all stakeholders about selection and assessment of options and alternatives.

Consult relevant stakeholders about decisions made up to this point and what needs to be done in the future.

Transition stage

Re-creating a plan

Might require selection of new options and alternatives based on new information from the context, assessment of stakeholders, assessment of project brief, etc.

Stage 4

Implementing, monitoring & following up

Implement the selected option and alternative.

Identify any problems, review performance and monitor progress.

Communicate with stakeholders about benefits via reports (e.g. through the use of the media).

Settle accounts and finances.

Establish a group to take over once the project has been completed.

Revisit the project site after project completion to see progress and use patterns.

Transition stage

Continuing the process

Should require going back to Stage 1 with re-evaluation of context, re-assigning and re-assessment of goals, etc, upon considering use and users of project.

context-specific information into the process, thus creating a more flexible, less prescriptive guide to urban design decision-making for urban development sites. Real-world examples of urban design decision-making processes also may be compared to this conceptual process, providing details that may not have been highlighted in the review of design processes in the literature.

Nonetheless, the conceptual urban design decision-making process raises three issues. First, the process, taken from the literature, does not provide information about the decision-makers (Boyko et al. 2005). That is, one does not know who the decision-makers are in the process, what their specific roles are and whether or not they change throughout the stages of the process. To help understand decision-makers' roles, researchers on the *VivaCity2020* project employed a typology, adapted from Woodhead (2000), who purports that four decision-making roles exist:

- *Decision-approvers*: people who sanction decisions. These people often allocate funds for major capital investments.
- *Decision-takers*: people who meet regularly with teams developing proposals. These people ensure that quality proposals are given to the decision-approvers.
- *Decision-shapers*: people who develop the proposals and have their work approved, rejected and delayed by decision-takers and decision-approvers. These people use their expertise to create high-quality proposals to be given to decision-takers.
- *Decision-influencers*: people who are internal and external to the main decision-making organisation(s). These people influence the development of proposals in formal (e.g. at board meetings) and informal (e.g. telephone conversations) ways.

The second issue raised as a result of developing the conceptual urban design decision-making process is that there is no mention or consideration of sustainability at any stage in the process. Because sustainability is an important part of well-designed places (Commission for Architecture and the Built Environment and Department for Environment, Transport and the Regions 2000, 2001; Communities and Local Government 2006; Office of the Deputy Prime Minister 2002, 2003, 2004, 2005a, 2005b, 2006), more effort is needed to demonstrate who needs to consider it and how and where in the process it needs to be considered (Boyko et al. 2005).

Third, the urban design decision-making process needs to be considered in context within a larger urban design life cycle. For most urban development projects, there exist four stages: pre-design; design and development; use, management and maintenance; decline, demolition and/or regeneration (Boyko et al. 2006). These stages correspond to the development of a project (e.g. site, urban block, neighbourhood, large-scale urban area), from the moment an idea for development occurs, to the creation of a design and its realisation in built (and natural) form, to the upkeep involved in maintaining the project and, finally, to the project's degeneration and potential renewal. The urban design decision-making process comprises the design and development stage (i.e. creation of a design and its realisation), and overlaps with the use, management and maintenance stage (i.e. upkeep).

In the next section, three case studies will be discussed. The case studies highlight practical urban design decision-making processes, taken from three urban development projects in three different cities in the United Kingdom.

URBAN DESIGN DECISION-MAKING PROCESS CASE STUDIES

The case study cities of London, Sheffield and Greater Manchester were chosen for the *VivaCity2020* project because they had large populations (i.e. over 500,000 inhabitants) and high densities (i.e. over 1,000 inhabitants per square kilometre), and they possessed a host of urban issues relating to sustainability (e.g. noise, crime, access to public conveniences, adequate housing). Examining cities with these qualities – versus smaller towns and villages with smaller populations and lower densities and without a plethora of urban sustainability issues – provided greater opportunities for researchers to explore the important relationship between urban design decision-making and sustainability.

Once cities were selected, urban development projects within each city were chosen based on their scale and type of development. Researchers wanted to examine several different kinds of project to obtain a more comprehensive understanding of urban design decision-making in practice. Thus, small- (i.e. urban block), medium- (i.e. city centre neighbourhood) and large-scale (i.e. area comprising seven neighbourhood boroughs) developments were highlighted, each achieving different objectives: infill, repair and recovery and regeneration, respectively. From here, urban design decision-making processes for each urban development site could be mapped, providing practical examples that could be compared with the conceptual process. The processes for the urban development sites covered different timescales because each site had a different beginning point and researchers wanted to cover as much of the sites' history as possible.

London

A mixed-use development, approximately one block in size, was selected as the case study site. Located in Clerkenwell, just outside the heart of the city, the site offered an opportunity to map a smaller scale process that contained both contemporary and listed buildings. The process covered approximately ten years of the site's history.

Sheffield

The case study site selected for this city was a large, mixed-use quarter within the city centre. The mix of uses encompasses retail, office, residential and leisure spaces. An effort was made to map the urban design decision-making process for the area as a whole, rather than individual buildings or sites within the quarter. The process was mapped over a 25-year time period.

Manchester

The large site chosen for this case study covered 2,100 hectares and included seven boroughs and approximately 72,000 people. A vision and regeneration framework currently is being developed for the area to improve upon the extant deprivation (based upon an international design competition held by a local authority). The area suffers from a declining population, economic instability and poor health, among other issues. The process mapped for this site spanned three years.

Urban design decision-making processes for each urban development site were created by gathering information, later content analysed, from a range of sources. These sources included archival materials, observations, questionnaires and interviews with a range of decision-makers and stakeholders (e.g. academics, architects, developers, government employees, members of voluntary organisations, property surveyors, regeneration specialists, registered social landlords, resident and community groups, retailers). With each process map, a story unfolded. In particular, the stories detailed specific urban design decisions and who made those decisions, methods, tools and resources used in decision-making, who the stakeholders were, and what were the major issues involved in the urban development site.

FINDINGS FROM THE URBAN DESIGN DECISION-MAKING CASE STUDIES

The case study processes were chronologically mapped, using timelines to better distinguish discrete stages and actions by the various decision-makers and stakeholders. In the London and Manchester case studies (see Figures 4.2 and 4.3), specific actions and stages were uncovered that corresponded to some of the actions and stages in the urban design decision-making process, taken from the literature (Boyko et al. 2005, 2006).

In the Sheffield case study (Figure 4.4), the process took the form of five key decisions, rather than discrete stages and actions. Because several major decision-makers independently contributed to the development of the area, it made sense to understand how each decision-maker and their specific contribution impacted the overall area. With more time, detailed process maps could have been created for each of the five key decisions.

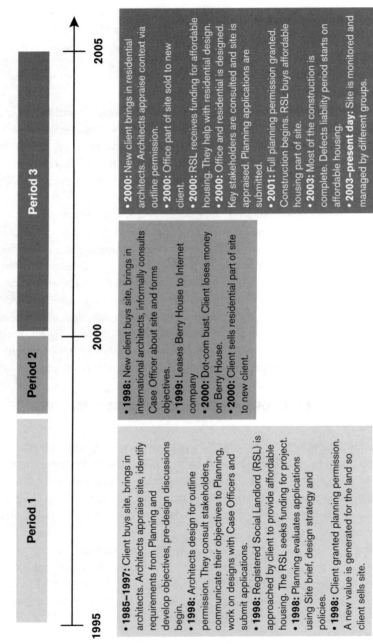

London & Clerkenwell: The Process (Brewhouse Yard)

1995   2000   2005

Period 1

Period 2

Period 3

Period 1

• **1985–1997:** Client buys site, brings in architects. Architects appraise site, identify requirements from Planning and develop objectives, pre-design discussions begin.
• **1998:** Architects design for outline permission. They consult stakeholders, communicate their objectives to Planning, work on designs with Case Officers and submit applications.
• **1998:** Registered Social Landlord (RSL) is approached by client to provide affordable housing. The RSL seeks funding for project.
• **1998:** Planning evaluates applications using Site brief, design strategy and policies.
• **1998:** Client granted planning permission. A new value is generated for the land so client sells site.

Period 2

• **1998:** New client buys site, brings in international architects, informally consults Case Officer about site and forms objectives.
• **1999:** Leases Berry House to Internet company
• **2000:** Dot-com bust. Client loses money on Berry House.
• **2000:** Client sells residential part of site to new client.

Period 3

• **2000:** New client brings in residential architects. Architects appraise context via outline permission.
• **2000:** Office part of site sold to new client.
• **2000:** RSL receives funding for affordable housing. They help with residential design.
• **2000:** Office and residential is designed. Key stakeholders are consulted and site is appraised. Planning applications are submitted.
• **2001:** Full planning permission granted. Construction begins. RSL buys affordable housing part of site.
• **2003:** Most of the construction is complete. Defects liability period starts on affordable housing.
• **2003–present day:** Site is monitored and managed by different groups.

4.2 London: the urban design decision-making process

Source: Engineering and Physical Sciences Research Council GR/S18380/01Vivacity 2020

Central Salford: The Process

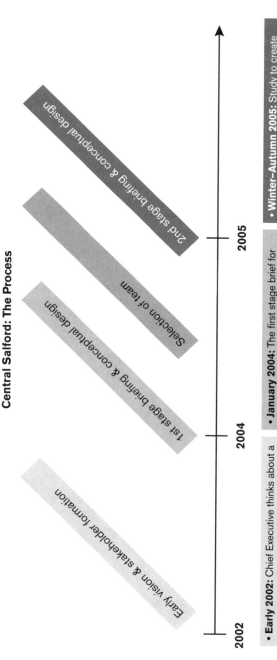

2002

- **Early 2002:** Chief Executive thinks about a unifying vision for Central Salford to improve quality of life.
- **Mid 2002:** Chief Executive asks a 'face' and others to join him.
- **August 2003:** A Steering Group is formed to help transform Central Salford. They believe a design competition is the best way to articulate a vision.

2004

- **January 2004:** The first stage brief for the design competition is written.
- **16 July 2004:** Expressions of interest returned by competition consortia.
- **27 July 2004:** Short-listing of consortia.
- **29 July 2004:** Tenders are issued.
- **12 November 2004:** Interview and presentation by competition consortia to the judging panel.
- **15 November 2004:** Appointment of winning competition consortium.

2005

- **Winter–Autumn 2005:** Study to create vision and regeneration framework is conducted. Various stakeholders are consulted.

Timeline phases: Early vision & stakeholder formation · 1st stage briefing & conceptual design · Selection of team · 2nd stage briefing & conceptual design

4.3 Greater Manchester: the urban design decision-making process

Source: Engineering and Physical Sciences Research Council GR/S18380/01Vivacity 2020

Sheffield & Devonshire Quarter: The Process

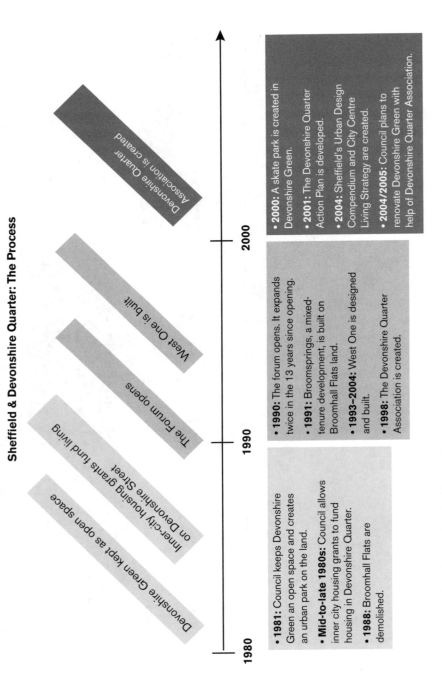

Devonshire Green kept as open space

Inner-city housing grants fund living on Devonshire Street

The Forum opens

West One is built

Devonshire Quarter Association is created

1980

- **1981:** Council keeps Devonshire Green an open space and creates an urban park on the land.
- **Mid-to-late 1980s:** Council allows inner city housing grants to fund housing in Devonshire Quarter.
- **1988:** Broomhall Flats are demolished.

1990

- **1990:** The forum opens. It expands twice in the 13 years since opening.
- **1991:** Broomsprings, a mixed-tenure development, is built on Broomhall Flats land.
- **1993–2004:** West One is designed and built.
- **1998:** The Devonshire Quarter Association is created.

2000

- **2000:** A skate park is created in Devonshire Green.
- **2001:** The Devonshire Quarter Action Plan is developed.
- **2004:** Sheffield's Urban Design Compendium and City Centre Living Strategy are created.
- **2004/2005:** Council plans to renovate Devonshire Green with help of Devonshire Quarter Association.

4.4 Sheffield: the urban design decision-making process

Source: Engineering and Physical Sciences Research Council GR/S18380/01 Vivacity 2020

The lack of knowledge brokers able effectively to link to European & national technical & policy networks is critical to the poor dissemination & translation of knowledge into formats appropriate to the various actors involved in promoting sustainable construction in different contexts. The development of checkdata codes & toolkits to prioritize sustainable construction has, in the UK for example, been less effectively devised & used than anticipated. This in part is due to the lack of individuals & agencies championing the transfer of knowledge within the domain & policy learning to the domain of organizational learning within firms, relevant agencies & local authorities

Sus can do INFORMING IDEAL

Examined across the three case studies, findings emerged about the urban design decision-making processes, decision-makers and sustainability. Each of these issues will be discussed in turn.

Urban design decision-making processes

In all three case studies, an explicit (e.g. written down, visual, tabular) urban design decision-making process was not followed, such as the one found in Figure 4.1. Rather, decision-makers had a tacit, or ad-hoc, process in mind that was shaped by their past experiences and knowledge and – particularly in the London and Sheffield case studies – by policy, private sector needs and public sector planning. These ad-hoc processes were shared within individual organisations (e.g. architecture firm), but required explanation when decision-makers from different organisations became involved (e.g. local planning authority and private sector developer).

In the Manchester case study, although an urban design decision-making process was not followed, a process for forming an urban regeneration company (URC) was being observed. The team involved with the URC – an agglomeration of public and private sector decision-makers – used guidance from the national regeneration agency, English Partnerships, to achieve this objective while concomitantly considering how best to approach urban regeneration (see www.urcs-online.co.uk for more information about forming a URC). The guidance provided suggestions about how to form a URC, and used guidance documents and past experiences from older URCs to help consider different strategies. Thus, the URC team in the Manchester case study was following a process for establishing a quasi-governmental body (which then would consider urban regeneration issues), not necessarily following a process for the sustainable design and development of urban areas.

Decision-makers

The decision-makers within the urban design decision-making process play specific roles, which have been created by the process itself. These roles may help to dictate a decision-maker's influence in the process and how that influence may lead to decision-making. Across the three case studies, the four different types of decision-makers, adapted from Woodhead (2000), could be discerned.

Decision-influencers were characterised consistently by local residents and businesses, community groups and other community-targeted organisations (e.g. voluntary group focusing on local employment). Representative democracy in the United Kingdom, in which citizens elect representatives to make decisions for them, means that the decision-influencers in the case studies will have less control over strategic decision-making on urban development projects. For the most part, local residents, businesses and so forth will elect someone else to take forward their concerns to decision-takers and decision-approvers. This stands in contrast to decision-influencers in other European countries, who live in more participative democracies and therefore have more involvement in how decisions are made.

Decision-shapers were more varied in the case studies. In London, the private sector architects and designers shaped the way in which the designs and plans were created. Furthermore, the registered social landlord involved in the urban development site specifically shaped the affordable housing component of the mixed-use scheme by referring to design guidance they created for affordable housing. In Sheffield, public and private landowners were the decision-shapers, as they helped to develop initial designs and plans and, in some cases, also acted as decision-takers and decision-approvers. Finally, in Manchester, the team who won the international design competition to take forward the vision for urban regeneration were the decision-shapers, as they had created an initial idea of what the urban development would look like in the short and long term.

Decision-takers and decision-approvers appeared to vary, depending on the sector – public or private – in which the decision-makers were involved. From a public sector perspective, the same decision-takers and decision-approvers were consistently present across the case studies. Decision-takers were officers found in local authority planning departments or who were leaders of an urban regeneration team. Once they made decisions about their respective urban development sites, they created reports for the decision-approvers. Elected representatives in the local authority, sitting on planning committees, represented the decision-approvers, who read the decision-takers' reports and made a decision to approve or deny a scheme. When considering the private-sector decision-makers in the case studies, decision-takers appeared to be the clients across the different urban development sites. Clients received information from their decision-shapers: the architects and additional consultants that they may have hired (e.g. landscape architects, interior designers). Before a decision was fully taken, however, the decision-approvers – in the form of financiers, insurance actors or, in some cases, the client – sanctioned the decision.

Examining the decision-takers and decision-approvers more closely, it is apparent that the private sector's 'bottom line' is financial more than anything else. The client, the financier and insurance actors have a monetary stake in ensuring a profit for the land and the urban development site that they are developing. Sustainability and high-quality urban design may be afforded secondary importance in many instances. In contrast, the public sector's 'bottom line' appears to be related more to design and planning principles.[2] Thus, a disconnect exists between the major decision-makers in the public and private sectors: even though both sides want the same outcome (i.e. an urban development), they both have different conditions placed on that outcome (i.e. profit versus good design), which may make discussions and negotiations about the urban development difficult.

Sustainability

Part of the objective for this research was to uncover gaps in the urban design decision-making process. One gap, which is significant for the larger *VivaCity2020* project, revolves around the consideration of sustainability: is sustainability considered at all and by whom? Through content analysis of the various source materials from the three case studies, it is apparent that sustainability, in its various guises, was explicitly considered in decision-making, albeit by different decision-makers, at different times and at different levels of detail.

Decision-makers

Most of the decision-makers who were identified as explicitly making decisions about the sustainability of the urban development projects in the case studies were located in the local authority planning departments. Local authority planners were responsible for examining the 'fit' of the urban development projects within the surrounding areas. Such examinations would have included decisions that ranged from fine-grain building details (e.g. the type and style of pointing used between bricks) to larger scale neighbourhood details (e.g. how the permeability of a site integrated with existing sidewalks and paths in a borough), all of which could contribute to the sustainability of the urban development projects.

Private sector property developers and architects also made explicit decisions involving sustainability. These decisions – made in consultation with clients, landowners, financiers and insurance actors – mainly concerned building-level details (e.g. use of recycled materials or combined heating and power) and rarely incorporated concerns about the sustainability of the wider neighbourhood. When explicit decisions involving the sustainability of an urban development project in its wider neighbourhood were made by these decision-makers, it was often at the behest of the local authority or because it was economically feasible to do so.

Timing of sustainable decisions

Explicit sustainable urban design decision-making by different decision-makers occurred throughout the process. In line with the stages of the conceptual urban design decision-making process (see Figure 4.1), decisions were made during brief preparation (by local authorities), while designing and developing the urban development sites (by local authorities and private sector developers, architects and registered social landlords) and when evaluating and selecting a design for planning approval (by local authorities). Thus, local authorities have more opportunities than other decision-makers to consider sustainability at many stages of the process.

Level of detail of sustainable decisions

When the topic of sustainability was broached in interviews, the economic dimension of sustainability was less acknowledged by decision-makers within the case studies than were the environmental and social dimensions. That is, decision-makers often discussed the environmental improvements that they could make in the design of their projects, the use of more sustainable materials in project construction, the need to reduce crime or the importance of public consultation. There was little discussion, for example, about the ecological limits placed on economic growth (Brown et al. 1987), or the idea that a local economy could flourish and be diverse as a result of creating urban development projects (Office of the Deputy Prime Minister 2003).[3] Thus, the concept of sustainability for interviewees seemed to embody the environment, and to some extent, societal concerns. Perhaps one reason why interviewees spoke more about the environmental dimension of sustainability was that climate change and global warming had been highlighted in various media at the time.

In London, sustainability was evidenced in local government policy, guidance and planning briefs. Planning and design officers also considered sustainability when writing reports to give to the planning committee, who were the ultimate decision-approvers for giving planning consent. Regarding the case study site, specifically, the planning and design officers said they thought about sustainability, but that it was not a concept that was fully enforced through the planning system at the time (i.e. the 1990s). The private sector architect working on the designs for the site echoed these claims. He stated that his designs emphasised sustainability by considering permeability, natural surveillance and creating car-free public spaces. However, due to restrictions on funding, he did not create a more environmentally sustainable design for the site (e.g. green roofs, greywater recycling). Moreover, the issue of not designing in environmental sustainability was muted at planning application meetings between the client and the local authority planners.

In Sheffield, it was shown that little local policy existed at the time that stressed sustainability. Perhaps due to other issues (e.g. building of Meadowhall and the debate about the importance of city centre retail: Mackay 2005), sustainability was not part of the agenda. Nonetheless, actions were taken by local authorities and the private sector throughout the development of the case study site that emphasised elements of sustainability. The decision by the local authority to keep a park as an open space, rather than develop on the land, has its roots in environmental (e.g. the park provides a green oasis in a dense, urban space) and social sustainability (e.g. the park is an amenity for neighbouring residents). Furthermore, the decision by an entrepreneur to create a mixed-use space for fledging retail businesses and for leisure activities (e.g. bar, café, restaurant) originated from his desire to help local businesses and to create 'a happening' in the city (i.e. promoting economic and social sustainability). Other decisions in the case study site – allowing inner city housing, forming a neighbourhood association, and creating a mixed-use site of office, retail and residential – showcase the importance of social, and to some extent, economic, sustainability.

In the Manchester case study, sustainability was rarely cited in the earliest briefing documents, which were used to guide design teams in creating a vision and regeneration framework for the international design competition. When it was mentioned, however, sustainability was found under a broader regeneration heading, which principally focused on economic growth (as opposed to the negative economic realities of the area) and social cohesion and consultation. Thus, design teams were not made fully aware of the sustainability challenges to the area. Furthermore, when it was time for the visions and regeneration frameworks to be judged by a panel – composed mainly of people from the public sector and several people from the private sector (Boyko et al. 2006) – sustainability was not prevalent among the criteria used for judging. Rather, the panel emphasised value for money, the visualisations of the visions and regeneration frameworks, creativity, market awareness, compatibility with government and aspiration (Felicity Goodey, personal communication, 3 December 2004; Councillor John Merry, personal communication, 9 February 2005).

VALIDATION OF THE URBAN DESIGN DECISION-MAKING PROCESSES

Once the case studies were completed, the researchers held an Expert Panel Day to discuss the processes (the conceptual urban design decision-making process also was discussed). A panel of experts in urban planning, design, development and regeneration was invited, chosen from industry and collaborating partners on the *VivaCity2020* project. It was believed they had valuable experience and knowledge about a range of issues relating to the urban design decision-making process and could provide critical feedback.

Each of the case studies and processes were presented – along with the conceptual process – to the expert panel. Researchers then asked the experts to discuss whether the case studies were fair representations of the process and whether anything had been omitted, including stages within all the processes. Through their discussions, the experts validated the processes and acknowledged the legitimacy of the urban design decision-making process, taken from the literature, in Figure 4.1. There were some concerns, however, that the panel felt were necessary to address if the process was to be improved (Boyko et al. 2006).

First, the experts believed that a timeframe needed to be incorporated into the process. A timeframe in days, weeks, months and years would show how long it took, on average, to complete a stage before moving onto the next stage. Providing a timeframe could help prevent the misunderstanding that all stages take similar amounts of time to complete or that the process, as a whole, could take a relatively short time to realise.

Second, members of the expert panel remarked that sustaining the interest and commitment of the community in long-term urban development projects may be difficult. They believed that local communities, particularly those who have lived through previous regeneration attempts, remain dubious about the successes of urban development when positive changes are not seen quickly enough, nor are sustained. Thus, developing some way to keep these decision-influencers engaged throughout the process – especially in the early stages with discussions about project goals and visions – and to actively communicate progress may be advantageous in the creation of more sustainable urban development projects.

Third, and perhaps most significant to the reality of making urban design decisions, the expert panel wanted the processes to reflect the non-linear nature of urban design and development projects. Actions within the different stages do not necessarily follow a prescribed order, nor are they ordered in importance. Instead, actions and stages may blur so that decision-makers may move from one action or stage to another, depending on the contextual issues involved with each urban development site. Therefore, visualising the non-linearity of urban design decision-making processes may help to better indicate the complexity of urban design decision-making.

NEXT STEPS

From the expert panel's comments and the researchers' comparisons across the case studies about the process, sustainability and decision-makers, the urban design decision-making process was updated. This updated process – a work-in-progress – is expanded from four stages to seven stages, and now overlaps with the pre-design stage, where the formation of ideas and an appraisal of opportunities before an urban development project are pondered (see Figure 4.5).

In response to the expert panel's concern about greater incorporation of sustainability into the urban design decision-making process, consideration of sustainability at varying levels of detail has been integrated into each stage of this updated process. For example, at Stage 0, 'Idea and opportunity formation', the person or people considering an urban development project should think about their own strengths and weaknesses, including reflection about their knowledge of sustainability.

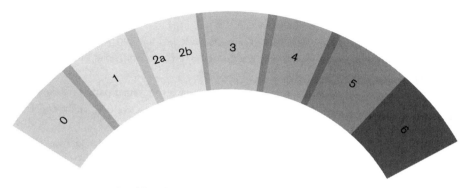

0   Idea/Opportunity formation
1   Creating teams, appraising the project,
    identifying stakeholders and forming goals
2a Writing the brief
2b Designing and developing a preliminary design
3   Evaluating and selecting a preliminary design
4   Detailing the design
5   Evaluating and selecting a detailed design
6   Implementation, monitoring and follow-up

4.5 The new urban design decision-making process
Source: Engineering and Physical Sciences Research Council GR/S18380/01 Vivacity 2020

At Stage 2a, 'Writing the brief', the person or people involved in brief writing should incorporate conceptual notions of social, economic and environmental sustainability, rather than being too specific and detailed, which may limit the creativity of architects, designers and planners.

The researchers are currently addressing the panel's other concerns. In addition, the researchers are planning to test the application of the updated process map with decision-makers (e.g. local authorities) and to create a matrix that will indicate who is making decisions throughout the process and what resources they are using in decision-making (cf. the City of Amsterdam's planning process, known as the *Plaberum*: City of Amsterdam Bestuurdienst 2005). From this work, researchers on the *VivaCity2020* project aim to create a truly normative process for urban design decision-making that will be utilised by decision-makers when creating sustainable urban development projects.

NOTES

1   *VivaCity2020* is a five-year research project, funded by the Engineering and Physical Sciences Research Council (GR/S18380/01). Any errors or omissions, however, remain the responsibility of the authors.

2   Financial considerations, however, are undoubtedly an important part of public sector decision-making, as local authority planning departments have to show that their services are delivering value for money.

3   Nonetheless, private sector developers, clients and landowners did acknowledge the potential return on investment on their properties. While it may be argued that return on investment helps to sustain these individuals or groups, financially, there is much less consideration for the economic sustainability of the neighbourhoods and cities in which their urban development projects are situated.

REFERENCES

Atkin, B., Borgbrant, J. and Josephson, P.-E. (eds) (2003) Conclusions. In *Construction Process Improvement*. Oxford, Blackwell Science.

Austin, S., Steele, J., Macmillan, S., Kirby, P. and Spence, R. (2001) Mapping the conceptual design activity of interdisciplinary teams. *Design Studies* 22(3): 211–232.

Barnett, J. (1982) *An Introduction to Urban Design*. New York: Harper & Row.

Biddulph, M. (1997) An urban design process for large development sites. *Town and Country Planning* 66: 202–204.

Boyko, C.T., Cooper, R. and Davey, C. (2005) Sustainability and the urban design process. *Engineering Sustainability* 158(ES3): 119–125.

Boyko, C.T., Cooper, R., Davey, C.L. and Wootton, A.B. (2006) Addressing sustainability early in the urban design process. *Management of Environmental Quality* 17(6): 689–706.

Bressi, T. (1995) The real thing? We're getting there. *Planning* 61(7): 16–21.

Brown, B.J., Hanson, M.E., Liverman, D.M. and Meredith, R.W. Jr. (1987) Global sustainability: Toward definition. *Environmental Management* 11(6): 713–719.

Canadian Institute of Planners (2000) *The Urban Design Process* available at www.cip-icu.ca/English/aboutplan/ud_proce.htm (accessed 24/06/04).

City of Amsterdam Bestuurdienst (2005) *The Planning and Decision-making Process for Spatial Measures 2006*. Amsterdam: City of Amsterdam Bestuurdienst.

Commission for Architecture and the Built Environment and Department of Environment, Transport and the Regions (2000) *By Design. Urban Design in the Planning System: Towards Better Practice*. London: Thomas Telford.

Commission for Architecture and the Built Environment and Department for Environment, Transport and the Regions (2001) *The Value of Urban Design*. London: Thomas Telford.

Communities and Local Government (2006) *Strong and Prosperous Communities: The Local Government White Paper*. London: The Stationery Office.

Cooper, R., Aouad, G., Lee, A., Wu, S., Fleming, A. and Kagioglou, M. (2004) *Process Management in Design and Construction*. Oxford: Blackwell.

Engineering and Physical Sciences Research Council (EPSRC) GR/S18380/01 *VivaCity 2020*. EPSRC, Swindon.

English Partnerships (2000) *Urban Design Compendium*. London: English Partnerships.

Faludi, A. (1973) *Planning Theory*. Oxford: Pergamon.

Gosling, D. (2002) *The Evolution of American Urban Design*. New York: Wiley.

Heritage Lottery Fund (2000) *Building Projects: Your Role in Achieving Quality and Value*. London: Heritage Lottery Fund.

Kagioglou, M., Cooper, R., Aouad, G., Hinks, J., Sexton, M. and Sheath, D.M. (1998) *A Generic Guide to the Design and Construction Process Protocol*. Salford: University of Salford.

Kelly, R. (2006) Speech by Ruth Kelly to the Local Government Association Conference (5 July) available at www.communities.gov.uk/index.asp?id=1501327 (accessed 27/02/07).

Mackay, L. (2005) *Shopping and Crime in Sheffield* (unpublished report). Salford: University of Salford.

Macmillan, S., Steele, J., Kirby, P., Spence, R. and Austin, S. (2002) Mapping the design process during the conceptual phase of building projects. *Engineering, Construction and Architectural Management* 9(3): 174–180.

Nelessen, A.C. (1994) *Visions for a New American Dream: Process, Principles, and an Ordinance to Plan and Design Small Communities*, 2nd edn. Chicago, IL: Planners Press.

Office of the Deputy Prime Minister (ODPM) (2002) *Sustainable Communities: Delivering through Planning*. London: ODPM.

Office of the Deputy Prime Minister (2003) *Sustainable Communities: Building for the Future*. London: ODPM.

Office of the Deputy Prime Minister (2004) *The Planning and Compulsory Purchase Act*. London: ODPM.

Office of the Deputy Prime Minister (2005a) *Planning Policy Statement 1: Delivering Sustainable Development*. London: ODPM.

Office of the Deputy Prime Minister (2005b) *Sustainable Communities: People, Places and Prosperity*. London: ODPM.

Office of the Deputy Prime Minister (2006) *The Office of the Deputy Prime Minister's Sustainable Development Action Plan. Securing the Future: Delivering UK Sustainable Development Strategy*. London: The Stationery Office.

Okubo, D. (2000) *The Community Visioning and Strategic Planning Handbook* available at www.ncl.org/publications/online/VSPHandbook.pdf (accessed 20/07/05).

Oxford English Dictionary (2005) *Definition of the Word 'Process'* available at http://dictionary.oed.com/cgi/entry/50189148?query_type=word&queryword=process&first=1&max_to_

show=10&sort_type=alpha&result_place=4&search_id=mN9p-XRa38f-2385& hilite=50189148 (accessed 08/03/05).

Roberts, M.B. (2003) Making the vision concrete: Implementation of downtown redevelopment plans created through a visioning process. Unpublished doctoral dissertation proposal, University of California, Irvine.

Rogers, R. and Power, A. (2000) *Cities for a Small Country*. London: Faber & Faber.

Rowland, J. (1995) The urban design process, *Urban Design Quarterly* 56 (October) available at www.rudi.net/bookshelf/ej/udq/56/udp.cfm (accessed 14/07/04).

Rowley, A. (1994) Definitions of urban design: The nature and concerns of urban design. *Planning Practice and Research* 9(3): 179–198.

Royal Institute of British Architects (RIBA) (1999) *RIBA Plan of Work*. London: RIBA.

Smith, J. and Jackson, N. (2000) Strategic needs analysis: Its role in brief development. *Facilities* 18(13–14): 502–512.

Urban Task Force (1999) *Toward an Urban Renaissance*. London: E&FN Spon.

Urban Task Force (2005) *Towards a Strong Urban Renaissance*. London: Urban Task Force.

Wates, N. (1996) A community process. *Urban Design Quarterly* 58 (April) *Supplement* available at www.rudi.net/bookshelf/ej/udq/58conf/cp.cfm (accessed 14/07/04).

Wates, N. (1998) Process planning session. *Urban Design Quarterly* 67 (July) *Special report: Involving Local Communities in Urban Design* available at www.rudi.net/bookshelf/ ej/udq/67_report/method_10.cfm (accessed 14/07/04).

Woodhead, R.M. (2000) Investigation of the early stages of project formulation. *Facilities* 18(13–14): 524–534.

5

Sustainable Urban Development and the Professions in the UK

Moving from a 'Zero Sum Game' Towards More Deliberative Practice?
Ian Cooper

The very notion of sustainable development – let alone its practical implementation – confronts the professions with serious challenges. For sustainable development is said to require integrated, whole-systems thinking whereas the professions arose out of the Enlightenment and subsequent moves to institutionalise divisions of labour. Sustainable development is also argued to need not only collaborative teamworking but also a degree of self-determination – in the form of people actively participating in making decisions that affect their lives. Conversely professionalism seeks to authorise and legitimate expert (as opposed to lay) judgement. This chapter is used to explore how these contending forces are being played out in the UK in the context of recent changes in the regulation and regeneration of the built environment. It is focused on a specific question. Can built environment professionals move beyond the tyranny of a 'zero sum game' approach, where one group has to lose in order for another to win, towards win-win outcomes, where both sides may benefit, achieved through using more deliberative forms of practice?

This chapter draws on recent work in the UK to try to examine how professional groups are currently responding to the need to regulate and implement two specific aspects of sustainable urban development – *sustainable construction* and *neighbourhood renewal*.[1] In particular, it is focused on whether, in practice, sustainable urban development is a terrain on which built environment professionals (planners, architects, engineers and constructors) are choosing to compete or to collaborate.

There are opposing social theories dealing with conflict and consensus (Joseph 2004) to draw on to think about how professions interact when responding to changing circumstances such as those presented by sustainable development. Conflict theory places emphasis on competition between social groups. The outcome of such competition may be likened to a zero sum game: one profession's gain has to be balanced by the losses experienced by another profession. From this perspective, if and when professions compete, the competition may result in winners and losers. For instance, in the UK, central government policy since the early 1990s has been predicated on the need to change the adversarial culture of construction industry (Latham 1994) – seen as pernicious not just within the industry between its component parts but externally too in its relations with clients and regulators.

Consensus theory, conversely, focuses instead on constructing agreement and on collaboration.[2] Through such collaboration, win-win outcomes may be available. So, for example, all the professions engaged in a particular collaboration may be able to profit from it in one way or the other. In game theory this is called a 'non-zero sum game' (see, for instance, Parrachino et al. 2006). Much of the effort expended in the major change management programme applied to the UK construction industry – variously called, since the early 1990s, the Movement for Innovation, Rethinking Construction, Accelerating Change and Constructing Excellence – has centred on trying to move both the demand and supply sides of the sector towards more collaborative forms of working (see, for instance, Adamson and Pollington 2006). More recently, this same kind of change management effort has been focused, following the Egan Skills Review, on the delivery of sustainable communities (Office of the Deputy Prime Minister (ODPM) 2006).

This chapter examines three types of challenge which built environment professionals may experience when confronted by sustainable development:

*   inter-professional competition
*   inter-professional collaboration
*   extended (including lay) participation in decision-making.

It examines these challenges in the context of two UK case study examples:

*   regulation of sustainable construction
*   engagement in neighbourhood renewal.

The chapter is used to ask, drawing on these case studies, whether built environment professionals are treating sustainable development as a zero sum game or as an opportunity for moving towards more deliberative forms of practice. As Forester (1999) attested:

> Because planning is the guidance of future action, planning with others calls for astute deliberative practice: learning about others as well as about issues, learning about what we should do as well as about what we can do . . . Because so few political or economic actors can act unilaterally, all by themselves, planners [like other built environment professionals] . . . typically work in between interdependent and conflicting parties.
>
> (Forester 1999: 1–2)

THE COMPETITIVE CHALLENGE OF SUSTAINABLE DEVELOPMENT FOR THE BUILT ENVIRONMENT PROFESSIONS

The first of these challenges is that of competition between built environment professions. Will the rise of sustainable development advance the interest of specific professions while undermining others? Definition of the problem here draws on the conflict theory of professions. Historically, professions arose, in part, to form and maintain boundaries in order to protect the interests of specific occupational groups. One of the ways in which professions do this is by mapping divisions of knowledge on to protected divisions of labour. Professions maintain these divisions, and the privileges that accompany them, by controlling admission to their work territory and behaviour within it. This is achieved by introducing regulated professional training routes, devising rules of conduct, setting standards, raising a shared set of ideals about behaviour and performance, and by constructing and defining a shared knowledge domain. Professions grew out of the divisions in knowledge set in train by the Enlightenment and industrialisation. As Burrage (1990: 19) noted, there was also an intimate and therefore causal relationship between the rise of professions and the rise of industrial capitalism.

From a conflict theory perspective, occupational groups are in a constant state of competition. Here, as Collins (1990) argued:

> Instead of merely responding to market dynamics . . . occupations attempt to control market conditions. Some occupations are relatively successful at this, others less so. Those that are especially successful are the ones which we have come to call 'the professions'.
>
> (Collins 1990: 25)

But occupational structures, like capitalism itself and markets in general, are not static; instead:

> They are constantly changing, as some occupations gain new resources in the struggle to gain closure over their markets, and other occupations lose some of the privileges they have gained.
>
> (Collins 1990: 25)

As a result, Collins argued:

> Groups are constantly manoeuvring over control. But their victory creates a new line-up of resources, which themselves become items for exchange and targets for further struggles.
>
> (Collins 1990: 27)

From the vantage point of conflict theory, sustainable development can be seen as both a threat and opportunity by individual professions. It is a threat to their existing order but also an opportunity for change, realignment and perhaps even expansion. On the positive side, it opens up access to new resources (new forms of knowledge) and new configurations (potentially new sources and areas of work, new clients, and new patterns of working). On the negative side, through redefining both the nature of what has to be done (production of a more sustainable built environment) and how this should be achieved (through more collaborative and participatory methods of delivery), sustainable development may also be a threat. Unless a professional organisation can capture and successfully exploit such new resources and configurations before its competitors do, then its existing market position, and the competitive advantages and privileges that go with this, may be eroded.

Similarly, drawing on Hayek (1982), Webster (2007) argued competition for advantage between professions can occur without being centrally directed, for example, by professional or educational institutions. There can be spontaneous shifts in professional values, practices, knowledge and skills which alter the pattern of relative advantage groups have in relation to each other, because

> professional cultures compete with each other over time. They compete consciously and unconsciously with the result that professions gain and lose dominance in particular roles and functions.
>
> (Webster 2007: 1)

Webster suggested that such changes can happen at the margin, because they work, rather than being driven centrally because of any formal knowledge about cause and effect,

> without us being aware of particular ways in which particular practices give advantage over others in achieving desirable outcomes. The competitive selection effect is cumulative ... Over time, practices that enhance the value added by members of a profession will accrue to the professional culture.
>
> (Webster 2007: 2–3)

From this, he concludes that, in the absence of professional bodies, the boundaries between distinct specialisms would shift fluidly over time (as they do in other labour markets). But profession institutions slow down such shifting by drawing boundaries around a corpus of knowledge on the assumption that successful professional action follows from conscious application of that knowledge:

> This view is no longer tenable. We know now that knowledge is as much generated in the world of practice as it is in universities [the sites of initial professional training] and that much, if not most, successful action happens as individuals apply experience and judgement in a way that is hard to codify.
>
> (Webster 2007: 4)

In these circumstances, he suggested, the role of a profession institution is now necessarily reactive, reduced to playing catch-up as it seeks to respond to the rapid expansion of knowledge, the rise of interdisciplinarity and the acceptance of complexity (Webster 2007: 5) – all of which are key features of trying to implement and operationalise sustainable urban development.

THE COLLABORATIVE CHALLENGE OF SUSTAINABLE DEVELOPMENT FOR THE BUILT ENVIRONMENT PROFESSIONS

There has been a practice-based alternative to the conflict theory of professions in the UK that has been promoted, with central government backing, since the early 1990s. This has been the drive towards what has variously been called interdisciplinary design or integrated teamworking (Adamson et al. 2007; Spence et al. 2001). This new imperative, which arose from the Latham (1994) report, *Constructing the Team*, was first strongly promoted within the UK construction industry itself. It has since been reapplied a decade later by the Egan Skills Review (ODPM 2004) to delivery of sustainable communities. This review identified the challenge with which built environment professions are confronted by sustainable development as being, not competition, but collaboration. Can specialists reach across the boundaries of their professional domains to collaborate effectively with each other in order to deliver sustainable communities?

Just as historically boundary formation and maintenance was necessary for the creation and rise of the professions, so now boundary crossing and penetration are often seen as central to the production, organisation and implementation of knowledge in advanced capitalist societies (Gibbons et al. 1994; Nowotny et al. 2001; Thompson Klein 1996). This has been identified as especially so in knowledge production for sustainable urban development (Cooper et al. 2005). Likewise, in discussing the skills and expertise required to deliver, for instance, sustainable communities, it has become an accepted wisdom in the UK to point, not to specific discipline-based skills but to generic, cross-discipline ones – such as visioning, leadership, stakeholder management and conflict resolution – as the missing ingredients necessary for effective implementation of sustainable development (Academy for Sustainable Communities

(ASC) 2006; ODPM 2004). This position is clearly articulated in Chapter 6 in this volume by Roberts (see pp. 127–128).

> While not wishing to deny or diminish the particular skills and understandings possessed by individual professionals, there are wider, more generic qualities that are essential elements in the making and maintenance of places [for sustainable communities]; these wider generic qualities reflect the requirement that places should be considered as entire complex systems in which a failure to deal with all aspects through an integrated programme of action can result in suboptimal outcomes.

In part, this focus of attention on more generic, interpersonal skills for professionals can also be traced back to beliefs that sustainable development requires not only integrated, whole systems thinking (Brandon and Lombardi 2005; Devuyst et al. 2001; Raliwal 2005) in order to deal with complexity (Jones 2003; Pusztai 2006) but, as we will see below, integrated, whole community, decision-making too (Okechukwu and Maser 2004; Warburton 1998).

These calls to collaborative working and integrated decision-making pose two related problems for built environment professions. Can their members acquire these apparently missing generic, cross-disciplinary skills that are seen as necessary for them to be capable of working together collaboratively to make integrated decisions? Even if they can acquire them and are able to work collaboratively, will they then be able to help make the required integrated decisions without losing their own competitive professional edge or undermining the privileges associated with it? Useful discussion of such questions is hampered, in the UK at least, by a lack of evidence. For, as Bartlett (2005) identified, there continues to be confusion about the application of sustainable development to the built environment in the UK precisely because there is a dearth of documented evidence about what is actually being done in practice.

THE PARTICIPATIVE CHALLENGE OF SUSTAINABLE DEVELOPMENT FOR THE BUILT ENVIRONMENT PROFESSIONS

A third challenge that sustainable development throws down for professions is how to respond to the involvement of lay participation in decision-making. For sustainable development is also argued to require a degree of self-determination – in the form of people actively participating in making decisions that affect their lives – whereas professionalism seeks to authorise and legitimate expert (as opposed to lay) judgement. This challenge focuses attention on what is currently seen as a major crisis facing the professions in general – their loss of legitimacy and public trust (Pfadenhauer 2006).[3]

In Britain, public participation is taken to be an essential element of planning and urban development, seen as necessary both to maintain trust and to deliver 'equity' (Benfield 1997):

> Planning is political [in liberal democracies and] . . . politics is only legitimate if it takes place in public. It has to be transparent. Anything latent, hidden, or not readily apparent is dismissed by liberal theory as non-existent, or as a matter to be relegated to the private, non-political realm of social life. The political game must be open and accessible, its processes defined by strict rules, procedures and public scrutiny to lessen distrust of political power.
>
> Benfield 1997: 4–5)

This is deemed necessary because a major justification of planning systems is that they resolve competing claims over the use of resources, especially land, and attempt to balance an uneven distribution of power while protecting the interests of weaker groups (Kivell 1993: 8).

Discussion of sustainable development has placed a heavy emphasis on the need to develop more democratic mechanisms for making decisions and for policy implementation (Evans et al. 2005: 13). This has focused attention on the need for joint governance by government and non-government (lay) actors. Indeed Christie and Warburton (2001) argued that 'good' (i.e. transparent and accountable) governance is central to sustainability:

> The fundamental driver of sustainable development must be democratic debate – decisions reached through open discussion, consensus based on shared goals and trust. Sustainable development needs representative democracy that is trusted and vibrant, and new forms of participatory democracy to complement it that can inspire greater engagement by citizens in creating a better world.
>
> (Christie and Warburton 2001: 154)

However, this focus on participation and equity is problematic for built environment professionals. As the experience of members of the BEQUEST 'concerted action' revealed (Cooper 2002), and as more recent work with both demand and supply-side members of the UK construction industry has repeated (Eclipse Research Consultants 2006), participation and equity are two of the principles underpinning sustainable development to which built environment professionals identify themselves as least committed.

These calls for participation and equity pose two more related problems for built environment professionals. Can their members embrace the new governance structures being proposed for sustainable urban development, based on increased lay involvement in decision-making, without forfeiting the legitimacy of their own expertise as a basis for contributing to such decisions? Can they achieve this without both losing their own competitive professional edge and the privileges associated with it? One response to engaging with this dilemma is Forester's (1999) notion of the 'deliberative practitioner' – someone who chooses to treat participation as presenting real opportunities for deliberative (even transformative) learning and action research since 'we learn in action not only about what works but what matters as well' (Forester 1999: 6–7). In this way, just as 'reflective practitioners' learn from experience (Schön 1983), Forester argued that 'deliberative practitioners' work and learn with others. Indeed, an important and defining characteristic of their professional skill is precisely their capability to operate effectively in this more inclusive way.

CASE 1: REGULATING SUSTAINABLE CONSTRUCTION IN THE UK

The first example examined in this chapter is focused on who has the professional responsibility for regulating sustainable construction in the UK and who has the technical capability to do so. It draws on the London School of Economics' Sustainable Construction Project (Rydin et al. 2006). This charted the emergence and potential impact of a new form of planning guidance in the UK – Supplementary Planning Documents on 'sustainable construction'. In the UK, responsibility for regulating permission to develop has been assumed by one profession (planners) while the technical capability for sustainable construction has been seen as residing with service providers in the construction sector (architects, engineers and constructors) as controlled by the *Building Regulations* (Department for Communities and Local Government (DCLG) undated a).[4] This has raised the problem of how one professional group (planners) can acquire the knowledge needed to regulate the behaviour of other professions (construction industry service providers). This problem of professional demarcation and competence has been compounded because the phrase *sustainable construction* lacks a consistent and concise definition in the UK. It has been used (alongside *sustainable communities* and *urban regeneration*) to cover a range of issues stretching from the design and construction of individual buildings right up to urban planning. But this inconsistency has not constrained policy initiatives on sustainable construction either at the level of the construction industry or at the urban scale.

This lack of consistent definition is aggravated (Rydin et al. 2006) by an unresolved split in sustainable construction in the UK between the planning system and the construction industry with broad policy guidance being aimed at urban planners and detailed technical issues addressed to construction service providers. This split arises, in part, from the division of responsibilities between central government departments. The Department of Trade and Industry (DTI) is responsible for promoting sustainable construction as part of its sponsorship role for improving the performance of the UK economy. Other government departments are also involved. The Department of Communities and Local Government has responsibilities relating to the production of the built environment – for planning policy guidance and for the Building Regulations. The Department for Environment, Food and Rural Affairs (Defra) presides, for instance, over waste management because of its responsibility for environmental sustainability.

Both the DTI and DCLG have seen sustainable construction as largely a matter for the construction industry itself to implement through innovation and self-improvement (productivity and efficiency gains) with enforcement, if necessary, through the Building Regulations. This laissez-faire approach was, until December 2006, reinforced by central government's continued emphasis on voluntary action, on demonstration projects and on best practice – in other words, on exhortation rather than regulation – to spread sustainable construction throughout both the demand and supply sides of the construction industry. Since December 2006, however, the UK government has shown a new willingness to embrace a regulatory approach as laid out in three documents, its so-called *Green Pack* (DCLG 2006a, 2006b, 2006c) covering both sustainable construction and climate change. These seek to set a regulatory framework and timeframe, consistent across both the planning system and building regulations, for achieving zero carbon in new housing at least by 2016.

However, before the appearance of the Green Pack, there was a vacuum – a lack of central government guidance on how to implement sustainable construction – caused by delays to the *Code for Sustainable Homes* (DCLG 2006b) and by the scaling down of the Code so that it deals only with new housing rather than all building types. Because of this vacuum at the national scale, individual English regional agencies and local planning authorities have been engaging directly with the sustainable construction agenda (Cooper 2006a). There has been a small industry producing development control checklists and codes for use by individual regional agencies and local planning agencies – to provide simple 'to do' formats for planners when dealing with the regulation of development proposals in England and Wales. (Scotland and Northern Ireland have their own arrangements.) This has resulted in a 'postcode lottery' in development control in the UK, with adjoining authorities choosing (or not) to adopt checklists and planning guidance documents with differing content and coverage.

These local Supplementary Planning Documents (SPDs) are typically focused predominantly on environmental sustainability by directly seeking to improve the environmental performance of buildings: they treat social and economic sustainability (if at all) only indirectly as second order issues. This is evident, for instance, from the contents list of the highest profile example – the so-called *Mayor's Code for London* (Greater London Authority (GLA) 2006) in Box 5.1.

Attempts to impose uniformity have been made through the emerging regional *sustainability checklists*, pioneered by the South East England Development Agency (SEEDA, undated). It has also been proposed through the 'model' local *supplementary planning guidance* produced jointly by the Local Government Association and Planning Officers' Society (LGA and POS 2006). In calling for national model guidance on sustainable construction, the LGA and POS made explicit the information sources on which they thought this guidance should be based, at least in the first instance (see Box 5.2).

Even a casual inspection of the sources included in Box 5.2 reveals that much of the knowledge the LGA and POS recommended for transfer is explicitly focused on environmental issues. For the most part, this has been generated by, within or on behalf of the construction industry and from very narrow evidence bases. (It is unlikely, for instance, that many (if any) of these sources of information would meet the stringent criteria outlined by Ehrlich (2003) for deciding whether evidence on climate change should be accepted or rejected.)

BOX 5.1   CONTENTS OF THE MAYOR'S CODE FOR LONDON

This Supplementary Planning Guidance covers:

- reuse of land and buildings
- maximising use of natural systems
- conserving energy, water and other resources
- reducing noise, pollution, flooding and microclimatic effects
- ensuring developments are comfortable and secure for users
- conserving and enhancing the natural environment and biodiversity
- promoting sustainable waste behaviour.

Appendix A contains Sustainability Appraisal methodologies and checklists and Appendix B lists Supplementary Planning Guidance and Best Practice guidance.

Source: Greater London Authority 2006

BOX 5.2   SOURCES OF KNOWLEDGE SPECIFIED BY THE LGA
AND POS FOR COMPILING THEIR MODEL GUIDANCE
ON SUSTAINABLE CONSTRUCTION

Building Research Establishment:
Ecohomes

Office of the Deputy Prime Minister:
Code for sustainable homes

Improving sustainability through
Sustainable and Secure Buildings
Act

Energy Savings Trust: best practice
standards

Constructing Excellence work

London and South East and East
of England toolkit

Welsh Local Government
Association: Delivering
Sustainable Development
through the planning system

Town and Country Planning
Association work, including
Sustainable Energy by Design

CABEspace (Commission for
Architecture and the Built
Environment) and UK Public
Health consortium study

English Heritage work: Consultation
on Sustainable Management of
the Historic Environment

Historic Environment Local
Management

Countryside Agency work on rural
design and sustainability: New
Vernacular principles

Concept Statements and Village
and Town Design Statements

Sustainable Procurement Taskforce
study

Department of Trade and Industry:
Consultation on Strategy for
Sustainable Construction

DTI led Better Buildings Summit and
Sustainable Buildings Task
Group

Office of Government Commerce:
Achieving Excellence

Defra Sustainable Procurement Task
Force

Defra Water Saving Group work

Defra Soils Team Built Environment
Work programme: Code of
practice for sustainable use and
management of soil on
construction sites

Soil guidance for Local Planning
Authorities and Regional
Assemblies

Regional Development Agencies:
development of regional
Sustainable Construction Charter

Recent local authority and regional
assembly studies, e.g. Tandridge
District Council: Sustainability
Appraisal for Woldingham VDS

East Midlands Regional Assembly
SDC study

WRAP work on recycled content
and recycling in construction

Demolition Protocol

DTI guidance on Site Waste
  Management Plans
Legal and sustainable timber
Incorporating biodiversity into Local
  Development Frameworks

WWF/ODPM Regional sustainability
  checklists
Any other work on SDC on home or
  non-home construction

Source: Local Government Association and Planning Officers' Society 2006

This focus on environmental issues should not be seen as surprising. As the Director of Sustainability for Constructing Excellence – the major performance improvement initiative within the UK construction industry – observed (Innes 2006), the industry's grasp of how to grapple with social and economic sustainability issues remains in its infancy. To generate robust knowledge about how to derive these types of benefits from property development and construction activities would, as a result, require planners to widen the base of expertise on which the construction industry currently draws.

Rydin et al. (2006: 9) suggested that the question of how technical knowledge, used for regulatory purposes, becomes embedded in the planning profession is an underexamined issue. The single instance examined above is illuminating. In the case of sustainable construction, at least, the planning profession has, on multiple occasions – and at a range of local, regional and national spatial scales – commissioned construction professionals to capture their industry's technical competence in guidance documents intended for use by planners. Planners now use this guidance in regulating the activities of property developers and construction industry service providers. Thus one group of construction professionals has sold its technical expertise, for the price of consultancy commissions, to another professional group, which then uses it to control construction service providers' behaviour and performance.

It remains to be seen whether planning professionals who work in development control in the UK's planning authorities will be able to acquire sufficient technical understanding, on the basis of this limited knowledge transfer, of the issues involved to do this effectively. Rydin et al.'s (2006: 14–15) study of London planning authorities suggested that capturing *technical* knowledge about sustainable construction produced by experts and then embedding and codifying this as *usable* knowledge within the bureaucratic procedures of the planning system is inherently problematic. They concluded that the hierarchical nature of development control sections, and the time-constrained performance metrics imposed on planning departments, will make the organisational learning necessary doubly difficult to achieve. In their judgement,

> the promotion of sustainable construction by planning practice faces planners with the need to develop new modes of practice based on an understanding of which construction practices are more or less sustainable. Otherwise, if this knowledge is confined to the development industry, the planning system will be able to do little beyond accepting the industry's assurances that they are promoting sustainability.
>
> (Rydin et al. 2006: 9)

The UK planning profession has also had to acquire such technical knowledge about sustainable construction at what, from the outside, may appear as relatively high a cost. In accepting the knowledge transferred by construction-based consultants as both sufficient and legitimate, planners have had to accept the property development and construction industries' self-definition of what sustainable construction is about – mainly the environmental performance of building and resource efficiency (Eclipse Research Consultants 2006). In this narrow framing of sustainable construction only residual attention is being given to using the planning system to deliver social and economic benefits that could be achieved by insisting that property developers and service providers in the construction industry adopt a more balanced, triple bottom line approach to delivering a sustainable built environment (Cooper 2006b).

However, both sides can point to gains here. Planners now possess a framework for regulating construction service providers' implementation of sustainable construction at the development control stage, and construction industry professionals get to be regulated on terms of their sector's own choosing and within a framework with which they presumably feel comfortable. So this outcome does not have the appearance of the 'zero sum game' postulated by conflict theorists as the likely result of competition between professional groups. Instead this apparently mutually beneficial outcome looks more like a win-win result. However, it remains unclear quite who is being manipulated by whom here – the gamekeeper or the poacher? Seen from the outside, from the vantage point of an independent, third party observer, the result also looks suboptimal. Planners are left in a position where they are being asked to regulate development on the basis of a superficially acquired technical understanding. Property developers and construction service providers are left to continue to frame their own contributions to a more sustainable built environment narrowly, with only a residual or vestigial regard for broader social and economic benefits. This suggests that even a consensual, collaborative approach to developing a framework for regulating sustainable construction can deliver an outcome that is, for the present at least, far from optimal.[5]

CASE 2: ENGAGING IN NEIGHBOURHOOD RENEWAL IN THE UK

In the UK there is a major programme to renew impoverished neighbourhoods. This is funded by central government under the title of Housing Market Renewal (HMR) (DCLG, undated b):

> These neighbourhoods have typically experienced long periods of economic decline, as job patterns have shifted and people have moved away to take up new opportunities. Though often situated close to or even within cities where the economy is growing, these neighbourhoods remain disconnected from the new jobs, with residents experiencing low skills levels, worklessness, high levels of crime or fear of crime, and poor facilities.

In 2002, nine English areas were identified by central government as in need of specific housing market renewal support though an HMR Pathfinder Programme. This is not just meant to be about housing: it is conceived of as part of a much wider concerted effort to revitalise communities and economies across the North and West Midlands in England. It has been put at the heart of efforts to make English cities more competitive: 'because we cannot reverse decline and attract skilled workers back to cities unless they offer the quality and choice of housing that people are looking for.'

Three years after the programme was announced, the Commission for Architecture and Built Environment (CABE) and the Royal Institute of British Architects (RIBA) undertook a study, looking 10 to 20 years ahead, to try to envision how neighbourhood renewal might be achieved (CABE and RIBA 2005). Part of the East Lancashire HMR area – Burnley, in the North West of England, an old industrial town with a declining population and struggling economy – was chosen to provide one of the neighbourhoods – Burnley Wood – used as case studies for the envisioning exercises (Platt and Cooper 2005).

An Urban Futures Game (CABE and RIBA 2005; RIBA 2008) was developed as a means of engaging, at the neighbourhood level, three interest groups: local government policy-makers, providers (including built environment professionals), and community representatives (local residents and community groups). The game was used in a workshop to air each group's aspirations and concerns, collated from previous interviews, about how the neighbourhood should be regenerated. The game gave the groups an opportunity to work together, face-to-face, to envision the regeneration opportunities open to them and to set criteria for assessing their success. The game was produced by CABE and RIBA 'to provide a template to re-establish playfulness, creativity and continuous learning back into the process of regenerating run down neighbourhoods' (Worthington 2005: 2).

Prior to the development of the Urban Future Games, Burnley Wood had experienced extensive consultation exercises, conducted by Burnley Borough Council, culminating in a masterplan that required extensive demolition of existing housing to provide opportunities for private investment in development (Platt and Cooper 2006: 25). This extensive consultation, commissioned by the Borough Council, had caused consultation fatigue. Residents and community groups' involvement in the master-planning exercise, undertaken by built environment professionals, had resulted in deep alienation. Even when done well, participation can have unwanted consequences, particularly if it is not adequately resourced and supported (Kagan 2006: 15): 'Participation can overburden some people, causing stress and burn-out, and the very skills, knowledge and energies essential for meaningful regeneration might be lost.' Unfortunately this is not an uncommon, if unintended, outcome of such exercises. Having examined the impact of participation on participants' well-being, Kagan concluded:

> regeneration professionals need to practise what they preach. Only when they themselves undergo the procedures they 'inflict on others' will they understand how it feels to be a participant.
>
> (Kagan 2006: 15)

As the draft masterplan for Burnley Wood emerged, residents and community groups became concerned by the destructive effects of the renewal programme and were keen to prevent further demolition: 'We don't want any more demolition. Instead we want to build on the fabric, build on what we have got' (Platt and Cooper 2005: 26). So they were desperate to retain the remaining families still in the neighbourhood and to preserve the vestiges of their community, stressing: 'We need to give the first chance for a new home to existing residents' (Platt and Cooper 2005: 26).

The council officers responsible for consulting the residents had not been able to give this assurance and found themselves in a difficult situation. As one remarked:

> I wouldn't like to see people in old communities driven out, but the town needs gentrification to become more prosperous. We are hopeful that developers will come in and build new homes, but people want, as far as possible, to stay in their community and have their homes redesigned or remodelled.
>
> (Platt and Cooper 2005: 26)

For policy-makers: 'Success will be measured in terms of house prices. Pushing them up would be a good thing, especially since we have the luxury of large amounts of social housing.'

To challenge what the Borough Council and its built environment professionals were proposing, one of the community groups and local residents commissioned their own architects to produce an alternative scheme for renewing the neighbourhood in accordance with their own aspirations. But policy-makers had not accepted this as a legitimate contribution to debate about the future of Burnley Wood (Platt and Cooper 2005).

It was in this charged and confrontational atmosphere that the Urban Futures Game was deployed (Platt and Cooper 2006: 250–259). The game brought policy-makers, providers and community representatives together and confronted them, using sets of playing cards, with each other's aspirations for and concerns about regeneration as previously captured through interviewing. At the workshop, all the participants were asked to use the cards to identify their own priorities. These were then transferred to wall charts. Figure 5.1, for instance, shows the gaps that the workshop identified between the two groups' priorities in terms of their aspirations for regeneration.

At the workshop, a set of options, again based on material captured in the interviews, were used to promote a dialogue between stakeholders about what might be done (see Figure 5.2).

As Figure 5.2 reveals, both sets of stakeholders expressed a preference for attempting to regenerate the neighbourhood using a small business incubator. Participants were also asked to identify which success criteria – again identified from the interviews – they thought should be used to judge whether regeneration should be successful. In this way, the game was used to structure and represent the wealth of material, collected from interviews with all three sets of stakeholders, via a common framework and process for shared dialogue.

Playing the game made evident differences between policy-makers and providers, on the one side, and community representatives, on the other (Platt and Cooper 2006: 254). These revolved around the balance between the future of the town as a whole and the needs of existing residents, respectively. But both sides preferred a regeneration option based on the small business incubator, and both wanted to use similar success factors for judging whether regeneration was a success. Despite the fraught circumstances in which it was played, Platt and Cooper concluded that:

> The game identified real opportunities here for consensus building. From this it would be possible to build an agreed platform about the way forward and also to identify areas of conflict that needed to be harnessed positively to being about successful regeneration.
>
> (Platt and Cooper 2006: 257)

Exercise 1 Aspirations

People	Housing	Community	Infrastructure	Economy	Education	Process	Leadership
1.1 Attract and retain dynamic young people	2.1 Have fewer but broader range of houses	3.1 Don't demolish, refurbish	4.1 Restore old mills and streets sympathetically and encourage conversion of mills into modern apartments	5.1 Establish the town as a major service centre for the area	6.1 Manage the transition from manufacturing to higher skilled service economy	7.1 Use an inclusive 'whole borough' approach to regeneration work	8.1 Get good news stories on regional TV
1.2 Create a more balanced community with a larger middle class	2.2 Push up house prices	3.2 Get rid of absentee private landlords	4.2 Make gateways into town attractive	5.2 Create more vibrant town centre capable of attracting department stores	6.2 Develop skilled service industry activities and small-scale creative industries	7.2 Use existing local capabilities and resources to deliver regeneration	8.2 Provide and market a new identity for the town that people can take pride in
1.3 Give existing residents first choice of new homes	2.3 Insist on adaptable high quality housing using renewable energy	3.3 Upgrade communities by reducing crime, improving facilities and providing better transport	4.3 Maintain and preserve Victorian heritage and built environment	5.3 Increase renewable energy and other green technologies, permaculture centre	6.3 Deliver greater levels of educational choice	7.3 Ensure people have faith in what Borough Council is doing by treating them well	8.3 Promote town as having affordable housing and fantastic scenery
1.4 Provide houses and facilities to attract young families	2.4 Demolish areas of decline and return them to woodland	3.4 Regain the urban village feel where local shops and where people care about each other	4.4 Regenerate neighbourhoods to benefit whole town not just existing residents	5.4 Provide jobs to attract families into the area	6.4 Develop workforce skills through training programme with local colleges	7.4 Develop a collective responsibility for delivering change	8.4 Provide evidence of early wins to show how regeneration can work
1.5 Encourage gentrification of the housing stock	2.5 There will be a market for sandblasted oversized lofts for people who can't afford to live in Manchester	3.5 Deliver mixed communities with greater breakdown in inter-area tensions	4.5 People need to be able to live in BW and walk down to the rapid transit station and be in Manchester in half an hour	5.5 Tackle poverty to reduce racism	6.5 Improve educational attainment to equivalent in rest of country	7.5 Respond to how the majority feel regeneration should go	8.5 Burnley could be a fantastic environment. A great place to get out of the city with a range of housing types
1.6 We will attract people by providing the sort of housing people want to live in and good schools	2.6 I know all the current thinking is about city living but people with kids want more space	2.6 I know all the current thinking is about city living but people with kids want more space	2.6 I know all the current thinking is about city living but people with kids want more space	5.6 Burnley's role in the regional economy has to be the major driving force	5.6 Greater university provision to attract and retain university students	7.5 Build a regeneration vehicle based on long-term relationships with lead developers	8.6 Make the town attractive to those commuting to Manchester and Leeds

5.1 Policy-makers/providers' and community representatives' aspirations for neighbourhood renewal in Burnley

Source: Platt and Cooper 2005

Burnley		Policy makers Providers	Community
1	Burnley's role in the regional economy has to be the major driving force	◯	⬤
2	Regenerate neighbourhoods to benefit whole town not just existing residents	◯	
3	Provide and market a new identity for the town that people can take pride in	◯	
4	Greater university provision to attract and retain university students		⬤
5	Insist on adaptable high quality housing using renewable energy		⬤

5.1 Continued

Burnley Borough Council chose not to pursue these opportunities further. In this, it is not alone. Such futures methods are largely absent from the toolbox currently being used for urban regeneration and neighbourhood renewal in the UK (Ratcliffe and Krawczyk 2007). Yet they could be used to mitigate many of the problems identified in the Urban Futures study. For instance, the use of cards to represent stakeholders' aspirations and concerns makes sorting and prioritising them fun. But the cards are also democratic. They mean that everybody's voice is brought to the table, anonymously, for joint consideration. Using wall charts makes stakeholders' opinions transparent. Aggregating these helps identify shared and unshared preferences. Options are a powerful way of engaging policy-makers and providers and the community in thinking about the longer term future of neighbourhoods and towns. Using a range of options can prevent participants from rushing to the 'lowest common denominator' shared vision – a common problem in futures exercises. But, perhaps most importantly, what this envisioning approach offers is opportunities for openly managing competing interests in a way that is more likely to build towards win-win results. Through using a more deliberative approach, each party not only may gain some benefit but also can understand the process used to reach any level of agreement they do manage to achieve.

Exercise 3 Options

5.2 Policy-makers/providers' and community representatives' aspirations for regenerating Burnley Wood

Source: Platt and Cooper 2005

Burnley	Policy makers Providers	Community
Option 1 Commuter Village	3rd	3rd
Option 2 Urban Wood	-	-
Option 3 Small business incubator	1st	1st
Option 4 Design-led regeneration	2nd	2nd

5.2 Continued

CONCLUSIONS

So can built environment professionals move beyond the tyranny of a zero sum game approach, where one group has to lose in order for another to win, towards win-win outcomes, where both sides benefit, achieved through using more deliberative forms of practice? It has become received wisdom, drawing on Gibbons et al.'s (1994) notion of *Mode 2* knowledge production, to argue that the *production* of knowledge in contemporary societies frequently requires boundary crossing to enable inter-disciplinary working. However, this attention to boundary crossing needs a much wider focus than just the production of knowledge. It also has to encompass the *transfer*, *integration* and *implementation* of knowledge too.

As the first example in this chapter indicates, regulation of how the built environment is made more sustainable is also going to require boundary crossing. This will be necessary to support the *transfer* of technical knowledge between, for instance, 'poacher' and 'gamekeeper' professional groups. As the second example illustrates, delivering sustainable urban development will also require boundary crossing, particularly across the interface for professional or public decision-making. This will be needed to support effective *integration* and *implementation* of both explicit/professional and tacit/lay forms of knowledge through more deliberative forms of practice.

Rydin et al. (2006: 30) outlined a set of requirements for effective knowledge transfer about sustainable construction to occur between construction professionals and planners working in development control in the UK. They argued that sustainable construction cannot be embedded and deployed effectively in decision-making for development control without:

- political champions to promote this new knowledge and mode of practice in planning departments
- knowledge brokers capable of translating expert, *technical* knowledge into *usable*, bureaucratic procedures
- boundary objects – such as codes and checklists – for transmitting and legitimating knowledge across the interfaces between expert and practitioner communities
- learning opportunities within planning departments to allow planners to share emergent modes of (best) practice
- planners with sufficient technical understanding of the sustainable construction technologies and practices, and their relationship to the standards enshrined in codes and checklists, to defend their decision-making on development control against objections from property developers and construction professionals.

Rydin et al.'s study (2006) of planning authorities in London suggested that not all of these requirements are currently being met.

These conditions may be necessary but they are not sufficient. The knowledge transfer currently enshrined in codes and checklists has been bought at the high cost of accepting as legitimate construction professionals' own narrow definition of their contribution to making the built environment more sustainable. At present, this is mainly limited to improving the environmental performance of buildings and resources efficiency with only residual or vestigial attention to delivering the broader social or economic benefits necessary for sustainable development. As a consequence, while the reported example of knowledge transfer across professional boundaries does have the appearance of a win-win outcome for both sides, the result looks suboptimal from an outside, independent third party perspective. Hence, even a consensual, collaborative, cross-professional, approach to developing a framework for regulating sustainable construction can deliver an outcome that is currently far from optimal from a non-professional standpoint.

Crossing professional boundaries to include non-professional, lay and especially tacit community-based knowledge is a clear requirement for sustainable development – as laid down in 1992 at the Rio Earth Summit (see, for example, United Nations Conference on Environment and Development (UNCED) 1992: paras 8.3 and 23.2). Implementing effective tools and techniques for achieving this, democratically, within the context of the UK planning system has proved difficult. The example of the Urban Futures Game illustrates that it is possible to use envisioning, for instance, to begin to build shared platforms that cross the competing interests of policy-makers, built environment professionals, and community stakeholders. But, as in the case of the

Urban Futures Game, such examples often operate outside, or as additional to, the formal planning system rather than within it. Such inclusive tools and techniques remain difficult to reconcile with the UK's representative, rather than participatory, mode of democracy.[6] However, the game does illustrate (Platt and Cooper 2006: 259–260) a number of the steps that have been used in recent attempts to move towards more deliberative forms of decision-making in the UK:

- establish a *forum* that brings stakeholders from different interest groups together
- devise a *framework* that clarifies and provides structure for effective discussion and testing of the issues raised by these stakeholders
- devise *options* that map out solutions and promote dialogue and negotiation pointing to a shared platform for moving forward
- report *preferences* and *priorities* that help create a positive and proactive climate of opinion about the future.

Operating in this way will require built environment professionals to do more than just acquire generic, cross-discipline skills. It will also require them to approach their engagement with both fellow professionals and community stakeholders as a 'non-zero sum game'. In this game, their most useful skill may turn out to be simply listening (Forester 1999: 128) in order to create the trust and the space in which each participant's stories (hopes, aspirations, fears and concerns) can be both voiced and heard.

One of the paradoxes of sustainable urban development would thus appear to be that, if built environment professionals want to maintain their influence, they will have to share their decision-making, not only with fellow professionals but also with lay members of the public. Both sets of stakeholders involved could benefit from such sharing. Professionals would gain access to alternative perspectives on how development should occur and members of the public could be empowered by being granted access to decision-making processes. However, for this to be a win-win experience, all parties involved are likely to have to practise the art of compromise.

NOTES

1   The perceived salience of issues confronting the professions can change rapidly. When Symes et al. (1995) examined the social and economic challenges facing architectural practices in the mid-1990s, they did not highlight in their index sustainable development, climate change, or public participation (although they did energy efficiency and quality of design). Yet, just five years later, the professional institutions for the built environment

jointly worked, under the aegis of the WWF and others, to develop a common curriculum framework for sustainable development covering both initial entry and continuing professional development (WWF-UK 2000).

2   In introductions to sociology, conflict and consensus theory are sometimes presented as 'ideal type' mirror opposites (e.g. Keel 2007). In practice, attempts to explain a situation are quite likely to resort to drawing on both perspectives, even if only implicitly. Following Hayek and others, it is possible to argue that constructive discovery can be delivered through competition. From this perspective (Webster and Lai 2003) constructive destruction occurs as entrepreneurs developed ideas that out-compete old ones. There is a constant jostling and shifting of collaborations, transactions and combination of knowledge and skills in search of more productive outcomes. Viewed in this way, competition is creative and positive and about collaboration in exchange. Competition tests the actions and products of entrepreneurs in a way that non-competitive production cannot.

3   Symes et al. (1995) argued that there are three conditions that have to be met for occupational groups to be seen as legitimate professions: specialised knowledge, legal sanction (such as registration or a licence to operate) and protection of the public interest. However, Greed (1999: 1–2) noted that, while built environment professionals stress the importance of 'public service', there is considerable public dissatisfaction with end product of their labours, particularly in relation to community and minority needs and to environmental considerations. Part of this dissatisfaction arises, she suggested, because of the demographics of these professions:

> If the majority of professionals come from a relatively narrow band of 'types' of people and are predominantly white, middle class, middle aged, male, and able bodied, their construction culture will lack richness and diversity, and there will be a lack of alternative, valid perspectives upon which to draw in the course of professional decision-making which ultimately will be reflected in the nature of the built environment itself.

> (Greed 1999: 1–2)

4   In England and Wales, control of the production of the built environment is split between planning and Building Regulation. The two systems are meant to be complementary, with the relationship seen in terms of a division of labour. The planning system is supposed to deal with design, siting and location of buildings, while the Building Regulations deal with their performance. Central government's Green Pack (DCLG 2006a, 2006b, 2006c) state that these two remits should not overlap:

> and effectively discourage planners from meddling in building control matters. However, this is not such a clear-cut distinction as the Government would like to believe. And trying to move planners away from considering details of building

design and construction methods that will deliver better performance is likely to hinder rather than promote the move to zero-carbon building.

(Rydin 2007: 91)

5   It is possible that, having agreed targets and timescales for improvement of environmental aspects of sustainable construction, the UK government may turn its – and the UK construction industry's – attention to further development of the social and economic dimensions of sustainability (Christopher Boyko, private communication, 2007). Evidence against which to test this proposition should be available in June 2008 when central government was due to publish its revision of the UK's Sustainable Construction Strategy.

6   Such engagement tools are limited in their outreach – in the number of people that they can be used to engage effectively in more deliberative decision-making. Employed on their own, they will not solve Europe's democratic deficit (Wikipedia 2007). They are more usefully in conjunction with broader techniques, like citizen juries (Jefferson Centre 2004), that can be employed to capture input from a group that is both informed about an issue and a better microcosm of the public.

REFERENCES

Academy for Sustainable Communities (ASC) (2006) *Making Places*. Leeds: ASC.

Adamson, D. and Pollington, T. (2006) *Change in the Construction Industry: An Account of the UK Construction Industry Reform Movement 1993–2003*. Abingdon: Routledge.

Adamson, D., Pollington, T., Thomas, K. and Macmillan, S. (2007) *The Business Case for Integrated Collaborative Working*. London: BRE Trust and Constructing Excellence in the Built Environment.

Bartlett, H. (2005) Understanding the implementation of sustainability principles in UK educational building projects. PhD, University of Cambridge.

Benfield, M. (1997) Injustice in planning in Europe. PhD, Newcastle University.

Brandon, P. and Lombardi, P. (2005) *Evaluation of Sustainable Development of the Built Environment*. Oxford: Blackwell.

Burrage, M. (1990) The professions in sociology and history. In M. Burrage and R. Torstendahl (eds) *Professions in Theory and History: Rethinking the Study of the Professions*. London: Sage.

CABE and RIBA (2005) *The Urban Futures Game: Visualising Neighbourhood Change*. London: CABE and RIBA. www.cabe.org.uk/default.aspx?contentitemid=604&field= browse_date&term= per cent202005&type=2 or www.buildingfutures.org.uk/research_ project.php?myid=12 (accessed 15/05/07).

Christie, I. and Warburton, D. (2001) *From Here to Sustainability: The Politics of the Real World*. London: Earthscan.

Collins, R. (1990) Market closure and the conflict theory of the professions. In M. Burrage and R. Torstendahl (eds) *Professions in Theory and History: Rethinking the Study of the Professions*. London: Sage.

Cooper, I. (2002) Transgressing discipline boundaries: Is BEQUEST an example of 'the new production of knowledge'? *Building Research and Information*. 30(2): 116–129.

Cooper, I. (2006a) *Sustainable Construction and Planning: The Policy Agenda*. London: LSE SusCon Project, Centre for Environmental Policy and Governance, London School of Economics. www.lse.ac.uk/collections/geographyAndEnvironment/CEPG/sustainable construction/reportsinPDF/PolicyAgenda.pdf (accessed 14/05/07).

Cooper, I. (2006b) Towards sustainable construction: What are the potential policy measures and actions in Europe? Input paper to Infrastructure and Built Environment Workshop, Forescene: Development of a Forecasting Framework and Scenarios to support the EU Sustainable Development Strategy, Wuppertal Institute, www.forescene.net/schedule. htm (accessed 14/05/07).

Cooper, I., Hamilton, A. and Bentivegna, V. (2005) Networked communities, virtual organisations and the production of knowledge. In S. Curwell, M. Deakin and M. Symes (eds) *Sustainable Urban Development, Volume 1: The Framework and Protocols for Environmental Assessment*. London: Routledge.

Department for Communities and Local Government (DCLG) (2006a) *Planning Policy Statement: Planning and Climate Change*. Consultation document. London: DCLG. www.communities.gov.uk/index.asp?id=1505140 (accessed 14/05/07).

Department for Communities and Local Government (2006b) *The Code for Sustainable Homes: A Step Change in Sustainable Homes Building Practice*. London: DCLG. www.communities.gov.uk/index.asp?id=1162094, (accessed 14/05/07).

Department for Communities and Local Government (2006c) *Building a Greener Future: Towards Zero Carbon Development*. Consultation document. London: DCLG. www.communities.gov.uk/index.asp?id=1505157 (accessed 14/05/07).

Department for Communities and Local Government (undated a) *The Building Regulations*. London: DCLG. www.communities.gov.uk/index.asp?id=1130474 (accessed 14/05/07).

Department for Communities and Local Government (undated b) *An Overview of Housing Market Renewal*. London: DCLG. www.communities.gov.uk/index.asp?id=1140278 (accessed 15/05/07).

Devuyst, D., Hens, L. and de Lannoy, W. (2001) *How Green is the City? Sustainability Assessment and Management of Urban Environments*. New York: Columbia Press.

Eclipse Research Consultants (2006) *Where Next for Sustainable Construction?* Workshop report to the UK Sustainability Forum, London. www.cief.org.uk/pdf/where_next_ construct_Dec05.pdf (accessed 10/05/07).

Ehrlich, R. (2003) *Eight Preposterous Propositions: From the Genetics of Homosexuality to the Benefits of Global Warming*. Princeton, NJ: Princeton University Press.

Evans, B., Joas, M., Sundback, S. and Theobald, K. (2005) *Governing Sustainable Cities*. London: Earthscan.

Forester, J. (1999) *The Deliberative Practitioner: Encouraging Participatory Planning Processes*. Cambridge, MA: MIT Press.

Gibbons, M., Limoges, C., Nowotny, H., Schwartzman, S., Scott, P. and Trow, M. (1994) *The New Production of Knowledge: The Dynamics of Science and Research in Contemporary Societies*. London: Sage.

Greater London Authority (GLA) (2006) *Sustainable Design and Construction: The London Plan Supplementary Planning Guidance*. London: GLA.

Greed, C. (1999) *The Changing Composition of the Construction Professions*. Occasional Paper 5. Bristol: Faculty of the Built Environment, University of the West of England.

Hayek, F.A. (1982) *Law, Legislation and Liberty*. London: Routledge.

Innes, S. (2006) The view from Constructing Excellence. Sustainable Construction: Policy, Planning and Implementation Conference, Centre for Environmental Policy and Governance, LSE, London, 15 June.

Jefferson Centre (2004) *The Citizen Jury Process*. www.jefferson-center.org/index.asp?Type=B_BASIC&SEC=percent7B2BD10C3C-90AF-438C-B04F-88682B6393BE per cent7D (accessed 29/06/07).

Jones, M. (2003) *Liberating the Leaders: Applying Complexity Science to Sustainable Development*. Authentic Business. www.authenticbusiness.co.uk/archive/complexity/ (accessed 10/05/07).

Joseph, J. (2004) *Social Theory: Conflict, Cohesion and Consent*. Edinburgh: Edinburgh University Press.

Kagan, C. (2006) *Making a Difference: Participation and Well-being*. RENEW Intelligence Report. Liverpool: RENEW North West.

Keel, R. (2007) *Conflict Theories of Deviance*. www.umsl.edu/~rkeel/200/conflict.html (accessed 28/06/07).

Kivell, P. (1993) *Land and the City: Patterns and Processes of Urban Change*. London: Routledge.

Latham, M. (1994) *Constructing the Team*. Final Report of the Joint Government/Industry Review of Procurement and Contractual Arrangements in the United Kingdom Construction Industry. London: HMSO.

Local Government Association (LGA) and Planning Officers' Society (2006) *Planning Policies for Sustainable Building. Guidance for Local Development Frameworks*. London: LGA. www.lga.gov.uk/Publication.asp?lsection=0&ccat=28&id=SX9E04-A783D652 (accessed 14/05/07).

Nowotny, H., Scott, P. and Gibbons, M. (2001) *Re-thinking Science: Knowledge and the Public in an Age of Uncertainty*. Cambridge: Polity.

Office of the Deputy Prime Minister (ODPM) (2004) *The Egan Review: Skills for Sustainable Communities*. London: ODPM.

Okechukwu, U. and Maser, C. (2004) *Evaluating Sustainable Development: Giving People a Voice in their Destiny*. Sterling, VA: Stylus.

Parrachino, I., Stefano Zara, S. and Fioravante Patrone, F. (2006) *Cooperative Game Theory and its Application to Natural, Environmental and Water Resource Issues*. Washington, DC: The World Bank, Development Research Group, Sustainable Rural and Urban Development Team.

Pfadenhauer, M. (2006) Crisis or decline? Problems of legitimation and loss of trust in modern professionalism. *Current Sociology* 54(4): 565–578.

Platt, S. and Cooper, I. (2005) *Urban Futures: Embracing Change*. London: CABE and RIBA. www.carltd.com/downloads/UrbanFutures.pdf (accessed 15/05/07).

Platt, S. and Cooper, I. (2006) Democracy and development. In P. Malpass and L. Cairncross (eds) *Building on the Past: Visions of Housing Futures*. Bristol: Policy.

Pusztai, C. (2006) The emergence of sustainable communities: The potential of a complex systems approach in planning for local sustainability. In K. Richardson, W. Gregory and G. Midgley (eds) *Systems Thinking and Complexity Science: Insights for Action*. Mahwah, NJ: ISCE Publishing.

Raliwal, P. (2005) Sustainable development and systems thinking: A case study of a heritage city. *International Journal of Sustainable Development and World Ecology* 12(2): 213–220.

Ratcliffe, J. and Krawczyk, E. (2007) Imagineering sustainable urban development: The use of prospective in city planning. In L. Kosela and P. Roberts (eds) *Towards the Foundation of Theory for the Built Environment*. International Symposium, Salford Centre for Research and Innovation, University of Salford.

Royal Institute of British Architects (2008) *Building Futures Game: Developing Shared Visions for Neighbourhoods*. London: Building Futures, RIBA. www.buildingfutures.org.uk/projects/building-futures/the-building-futures-game (accessed 22/04/08).

Rydin, Y. (2007) Making zero-carbon housing a reality. *Town and Country Planning* 96(3): 90–91.

Rydin, Y., Amjad, U., Moore, S., Nye, M. and Whitaker, M. (2006) *Sustainable Construction and Planning: The Academic Report*. London: LSE SusCon Project, Centre for Environmental Policy and Governance, London School of Economics. www.lse.ac.uk/collections/geographyAndEnvironment/CEPG/sustainableconstruction/reportsinPDF/TheAcademicReport.pdf (accessed 14/05/07).

Schön, D. (1983) *The Reflective Practitioner: How Professionals Think in Action*. London: Temple Smith.

South East England Development Agency (SEEDA) (undated) *SEEDA Sustainability Checklist*. Guildford: SEEDA. http://southeast.sustainability-checklist.co.uk/ (accessed 14/05/07).

Spence, R., Macmillan, S. and Kirby, P. (eds) (2001) *Interdisciplinary Design in Practice*. London: Thomas Telford.

Symes, M., Eley, J. and Seidel, A. (1995) *Architects and their Practices: A Changing Profession*. Oxford: Butterworth Architecture.

Thompson Klein, J. (1996) *Crossing Boundaries: Knowledge, Disciplinarities and Interdisciplinarities*. Charlottesville, VA: University Press of Virginia.

United Nations Conference on Environment and Development (1992) *Agenda 21*. New York: UNCED. www.un.org/esa/sustdev/agenda21text.htm (accessed 15/07/07).

Warburton, D. (1998) *Community and Sustainable Development: Participation in the Future*. London: Earthscan.

Webster, C. and Lai, L.W.C. (2003) *Property Rights, Planning and Markets: Managing Spontaneous Cities*. Cheltenham: Edward Elgar.

Webster, C. (2007) Successful professional action and the rules of learning. Editorial. *Centre for Education in the Built Environment Transactions* 4(1): 1–7.

Wikipedia (2007) Democratic deficit in the European Union. http://en.wikipedia.org/wiki/ Democratic_deficit (accessed 29/06/07).

Worthington, J. (2005) Introduction. In Building Futures (2005) *The Urban Futures Game: Visualising Neighbourhood Change*. London: Commission for Architecture and the Built Environment and RIBA.

WWF-UK (2000) *Professional Practice for Sustainable Development, Project Management Group*. Godalming UK: WWF.

6

Sustainable Communities
Policy, Practice and Professional Development:
A Model for Europe
Peter Roberts

This chapter argues in support of the requirement to go beyond token interdisciplinary and inter-professional collaboration and to move towards new forms and methods of education, training, research and practice. At the heart of this new skills and knowledge agenda is the realisation that sectoral, single profession thinking and action is, on its own, unlikely to be able to resolve the deep-seated problems which confront many towns, cities and regions. This realisation is hardly revolutionary; some thinkers and practitioners, such as Ebenezer Howard, advocated the adoption of an integrated comprehensive approach to placemaking during the closing years of the nineteenth century. So why has it taken so long for the wisdom of the integrated approach to placemaking to become accepted practice and what does this imply for the education, training and deployment of sustainable communities professionals? In attempting to answer this question this chapter makes reference to the origins and evolution of the sustainable communities approach in the United Kingdom and elsewhere in the European Union. Specific attention is also paid to the skills and knowledge element of the sustainable communities agenda, and what this implies for the future development of professional activities in this field.

At the outset it is essential to provide some definitions which can help to set the boundaries, or zones of interaction, for the wider debate. The term 'zone of interaction' is used deliberately here in order to emphasise that one of the key objectives of the sustainable communities skills and knowledge agenda is to transform closed disciplinary and professional territories and boundaries into an open institutional landscape. In this new open institutional landscape, belonging to the sustainable communities team of professionals and other actors can be regarded as a more important consideration than maintaining the traditional isolation of the individual professional. While not wishing to deny or diminish the particular skills and understandings possessed by individual professionals, there are wider, more generic qualities that are essential elements in the making and maintenance of places; these wider generic qualities reflect the requirement that places should be considered as entire complex systems in which a failure to deal with all aspects through an integrated programme of action can result in suboptimal outcomes. This requirement for the adoption of teamworking in order to transcend the traditional territoriality associated with some professional groups has been recognised for many years, both by the professional bodies themselves and through independent assessments of the skills and knowledge requirements associated with placemaking (Office of the Deputy Prime Minister 2004). Equally, in reviews of the scope and content of diverse areas of policy and practice, such as urban and rural regeneration, it is evident that the full range of professional skills encompasses community health and social work, at one end of the spectrum, and construction, surveying and civil engineering, at the other end (Roberts and Sykes 2000).

This takes the discussion to the next point of definition: what is the sustainable communities agenda and why has it emerged in recent years as a discrete area of thinking and action? As noted earlier, while some of the major component parts of the sustainable communties approach have their origins in the ideas espoused by an earlier generation of thinkers and practitioners, the modern formulation emerged in response to the weakness associated with partial, sectoral or individual professional attempts to resolve the problems associated with various types of placemaking. Although these individual efforts may have been representative of the leading edge of practice in a single field of activity, they were, nevertheless, not in themselves sufficient to bring about the desired outcomes. For example, and as is now evident, it proved impossible to create new communities by simply building houses; rather, it is now firmly established that it is necessary to bring together a range of professions and other actors in order to design and deliver better places. In the context of this discussion, sustainable communities can be defined as the spatial manifestation of the principles of sustainable development – they are places where people want to live, work and enjoy a good quality of life, now and in the future. As a consequence, it is possible to trace a direct link between the work of the World Commission on Environment and Development (WCED 1987), the agreement of the Agenda 21 work programme which resulted from the WCED report (the Brundtland Report), the development and implementation of the work programme at local level through Local Agenda 21, and the emergence of the sustainable communities approach. In essence, the sustainable communities model is built upon eight components which are brought together and delivered through the ninth master component of placemaking (Office of the Deputy Prime Minister 2005a). The sustainable communities model is illustrated in Figure 6.1.

A second question follows from the definition of a sustainable community which has been given above: how does such a model and means of approach help to deliver sustainable development? The model embodies the principles of sustainable development:

- sustainable communities aim to balance and integrate the environmental, social and economic components of the community (the balanced development principle)
- sustainable communities attempt to satisfy the requirements of the present generation and of future generations (the futurity principle)
- sustainable communities respect the needs and desires of other communities locally, regionally, nationally and internationally (the equity principle).

Although no two communities will adopt an identical programme or follow an identical development pathway, it is evident that the sustainable communities model and

6.1 The Sustainable Communities Model
Source: Office of the Deputy Prime Minister 2005a

approach provides a common set of guidance; this observation can be illustrated by reference to cross-national reviews of sustainable community and associated practice (see, for example, Academy for Sustainable Communities (ASC) with ECOTEC 2006; Drewe 2000). In addition, it is evident from European Union and other policy statements that it is now acknowledged that there are many links between the various components of sustainable development and sustainable communities. For example, the Commission of the European Communities (2005: 3), in discussing the sustainable use of environmental resources, notes the extent to which such resources are 'crucial to the functioning of the economy and to our quality of life' and, therefore, advocates integrating 'environmental concerns into other policies that affect environmental impacts of natural resource use'.

Having identified and defined sustainable communities, and having positioned sustainable communities as the spatial manifestation of sustainable development, the final consideration at this stage of the chapter relates to the spatial application of the model and approach. All of the major policy statements at UK and European levels (Office of the Deputy Prime Minister 2003, 2005a, 2005b) emphasise the applicability of the model to all communities: urban and rural, new and old, large and small. A more helpful framework for distinguishing the different spheres of application of the model would consider three types of place:

- *New places*: here active intervention by public, private and voluntary sector actors is aimed at the establishment of a sustainable community – examples include public sector new towns and cities, private sector large scale new developments and voluntary sector urban villages.
- *Regenerating places*: here active intervention by public, private and voluntary sector actors is aimed at the regeneration of a place that has been the subject of environmental, social or economic failure – examples include regeneration schemes of all types and scales which engage all three sectors.
- *Evolving places*: the majority of places in the UK are not the subject of significant or exceptional active intervention, rather they are transformed through a gradual process of evolution – such places are guided through this process by public, private and voluntary sector policies, efforts and encouragement; all professionals working in the sustainable communities field can contribute to this process of evolution.

In all three types of place the desired end state is the creation of a sustainable community. One implication of the adoption of such an approach is the eventual diminution of regeneration as a major activity; this can be seen to be a consequence of the introduction of the sustainable communities principles into the planning and management of potentially failing places and the creation of new places. In the context of this discussion regeneration can therefore be defined as the retrospective application of the sustainable communities approach to a place which has failed. Success in this context would see the need to regenerate or diminish as the sustainable communities principles are applied; while such a state is unlikely to emerge rapidly, it should be regarded as a central objective of policy. What is implied here is a shift from an 'accident and emergency' approach to placemaking to a 'preventative medicine' model. Figure 6.2 illustrates this desired progression from the current situation to a future state in which the sustainable communities principles have been applied in all aspects of practice.

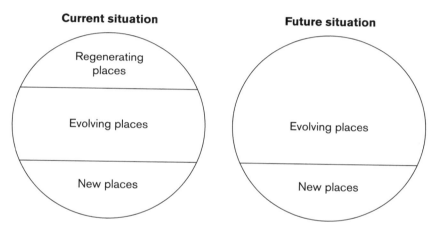

6.2 Types of sustainable community
Source: Roberts 2005

The implications of these various transformations in perception, policy and practice associated with the creation and management of places are highly significant. In particular, there are profound implications for the education, training and continuing development of all sustainable community professionals. Equally, the adoption of the sustainable communities model implies that the provision of skills and knowledge needs to extend beyond the traditional professional audience in order to equip communities themselves with the competences they require so that they can play an active role in making the gradual evolution of places the norm. This requirement to provide skills and knowledge to community actors reflects both the inherent logic of the sustainable communities model and the emerging policy priorities of UK central government. One example of these new policy priorities is provided by the current proposal to provide 'an enhanced focus on place' accompanied by the objective of 'improving the citizen voice, giving local residents more say over what happens where they live' (Department for Communities and Local Government 2007: 10) Such an enhancement of capability and competence suggests the need both for new professional skills, and for new ways of working, especially between professionals and members of local communities.

The following section of this chapter considers the implications of the issues and points of discussion which have been outlined in this extended introduction; this section also identifies some of the possible challenges which will confront the sustainable communities professions. A third section of the chapter offers conclusions and points for future research.

POLICY, PRACTICE AND THE PROFESSIONS

In the first section of this chapter it was argued that the sustainable communities policy system both reflects many of the traditional concerns evident in the best practice of placemaking and management, and represents the spatial manifestation of the sustainable development principles set down in the Brundtland Report. This section of the chapter expands upon this argument, and it then proceeds to consider the implications of the emergence of the sustainable communities policy agenda in relation to the skills and knowledge requirements of professionals and others who are involved in the implementation of the agenda.

As has also been argued above, it is, perhaps, unhelpful to divide the discussion between the various spatial 'problem sets' represented by the three types of place in which professionals and other actors operate (see Figure 6.2). Rather, it is evident that there are many common challenges, ways of working and lessons from best practice. These common learning, organisational and knowledge resources can be deployed in regenerating, evolving and new places. Irrespective of the particular form of practice application, it is evident that there are also certain generic skills and capabilities that are likely to produce positive results; these generic skills and capabilities are at the heart of the sustainable communities skills and knowledge agenda and they are required by all professional and other actors. The evidence base to support this statement is extensive: the Egan Review of Skills for Sustainable Communities (Office of the Deputy Prime Minister 2004), Diamond and Liddle (2005), English Heritage (2007) and the Bristol Accord (Office of the Deputy Prime Minister 2005b) all advocate the provision of a generally similar programme of generic skills and knowledge.

Although the transition towards the provision of generic skills and knowledge is now an established trend across a considerable number of the sustainable communities disciplines and professions, it is also acknowledged that there is a proven need for the continual upgrading of specialist capabilities. However, even with regard to the balanced promotion of generic and specialist skills, it is also wise to sound a note of caution against assuming that the application of skills and knowledge follows a similar pattern in all places. Space and place continue to matter, and there is a considerable danger in assuming that a single template (or a limited palette of templates) for spatial development can be established. Indeed, it is possible to regard the making and management of place as the weaving of a spatial 'cloth': the 'warp' of common generic and specialist skills and knowledge is interwoven with the 'weft' of the natural and built features, socio-economic characteristics and cultural history of a particular place. Although similar 'yarns' may be employed in the making and management of a place, the resulting pattern will differ both spatially and over time; rather like the clan tartans of Scotland, different applications of common 'yarns' will produce distinct and distinctive spatial arrays.

These messages about the need for a common approach to the making and implementation of sustainable communities policy reflect the need to develop generic and specialist skills, on the one hand, and an appreciation of the implications of place and space, on the other hand. The messages are also deeply rooted in many of the sustainable communities disciplines and professions. One example of these antecedents may be sufficient to illustrate this point. As was noted in the first paragraph of this chapter, a number of influential thinkers and practitioners who were working around the end of the nineteenth century began to develop models for the integrated and comprehensive development of place; these were to be places which offered a better quality of life for all and which were to be developed and managed by both professionals and citizens. Among the most prominent of these thinkers and practitioners was Ebenezer Howard. *Tomorrow: A Peaceful Path to Real Reform* (Howard, 1898) argued the case for the creation of what Howard called a 'social city', a place which would conform to certain guiding principles and which would rely equally upon professional and community 'pro-municipal work' for its establishment and maintenance; this point will be discussed at greater length later. The comparison between a 'social city' and a sustainable community is interesting because of the broad similarities which exist in terms both of content and the means of expression (Roberts 2005). Box 6.1 illustrates the two models and, despite the differences of language, the relationship is readily apparent. Although the application of 'social city' was principally intended to occur through the development of new garden cities, it was argued by Howard that the model could also be applied to existing settlements in the same way as the sustainable communities principles can be used to guide the transformation of a place that has failed, that is a place which is the subject of active intervention through regeneration.

Returning to the point made in the preceding paragraph, 'social city' relied for its establishment upon two sources of influence and effort; 'pro-municipal work' comprised both the activities of professionals and the input of contributions from

---

BOX 6.1   SOCIAL CITY AND SUSTAINABLE COMMUNITY

Social city	Sustainable community
Happy people, social opportunity	Active, inclusive and safe
Concert and cooperation	Well run
Beauties of nature	Environmentally sensitive
Beautiful homes and gardens	Well designed and built
Easy access, admirable sanitary conditions	Well connected
Higher wages, abundant employment	Thriving
Low rents, advancement for all	Well served
Bounds of freedom widened	Fair for everyone

Source: Roberts 2005

---

members of the community. Howard (1898: 139) considered that such contribution could best be achieved through harnessing 'the greatest, the most valuable and the most permanent of all vested interests – the vested interests of skill, labour, energy, talent, industry'. The sustainable communities approach incorporates a similar ethos and places considerable emphasis upon widening access to the skills and knowledge required to create and maintain quality places. By stating that it is necessary to widen access to skills and knowledge, two points are of importance: first, the need to increase the number of people entering the various sustainable communities disciplines and professions, second, the need to ensure that ordinary members of communities can gain access to the necessary skills and knowledge. In the United Kingdom, responsibility for the strategic management and guidance of enhanced access to sustainable communities skills and knowledge is vested in specialist government agencies, one of which is the Academy for Sustainable Communities (ASC). The ASC is responsible for ensuring the provision of skills and knowledge to professionals and others contributing to the creation and maintenance of sustainable communities in England. Although the ASC has a primary concern with ensuring that there are sufficient skilled and experienced professionals working in the sustainable communities field, it also seeks to ensure that local community leaders and actors have access to skills and knowledge, and that young people are made aware of the sustainable communities model and of the careers available should they wish to engage in such activities (Academy for Sustainable Communities, 2006). In developing and delivering the necessary skills and knowledge the ASC works with a wide range of professional

---

BOX 6.2 THE BRISTOL ACCORD

The Bristol Accord was agreed in December 2005 at a meeting held under the UK Presidency of the European Union. The Accord included a number of matters related to sustainable communities:

- an endorsement of the characteristics of a sustainable community and an agreement to compile good practice case studies that demonstrate sustainable communities' characteristics to an agreed template;
- an acknowledgement that the European Investment Bank (EIB) can contribute to a sustainable communities agenda and an agreement that an expert group should be established to consider how to enhance the impact of EIB loans;
- an agreement on the importance of fostering skills for successful placemaking and the value of cooperative activity on this theme across Member States, this would include support for a skills symposium as the first step in a longer term programme of European cooperation for skills development.

Source: Office of the Deputy Prime Minister 2005b

---

organisations, regional delivery bodies (known as Regional Centres of Excellence or RCEs), universities and colleges, local authorities, private and voluntary sector organisations, and a range of community-based groups.

Whilst the ASC has a direct mandate for the delivery of sustainable communities skills and knowledge development in England, it also has a wider role as part of a Europe-wide community of interest. Alongside other similar institutions, the ASC is the UK focal point in a European network of national sustainable communities skills and knowledge organisations. Returning to the earlier discussion of the Bristol Accord (Office of the Deputy Prime Minister, 2005b), the ASC and the partner national organisations representing the other 26 EU Member States work together to share expertise and experience related to the development of sustainable communities skills and knowledge. Although the focus of this work is on improving the skills and knowledge of new and existing professionals, there is also a common awareness that it is essential to delivery local and community competence and capability.

Returning to the central theme of this section, the elaboration and application of sustainable communities policy in the UK and elsewhere in the EU, together with evidence from practice across Europe, indicates the presence of a common set of conclusions regarding the need for professional generic skills. First, such generic skills have often been neglected in the past, with emphasis placed instead on developing specific or specialist skills, often to the full or partial exclusion of the inculcation of wider generic competences. This exclusion or neglect of generic skills has had two consequences: it has made it more difficult to bring professionals together as a team – teambuilding takes time and is often not undertaken for single projects – and it has led to difficulties in terms of the adaptability of the professional workforce. These consequences have contributed to suboptimal professional performance and have exacerbated the absolute shortage of suitable qualified and experienced professionals. Second, the broad content of the generic skills portfolio is generally similar across EU Member States. Research (ASC with ECOTEC 2006) has indicated that key skills gaps identified across European countries include leadership, negotiation and influencing, financial and project management, multidisciplinary working and better project coordination. This pattern of skills shortages also reflects the findings of the Egan Review. Third, the priority for skills development across the EU Member States is the provision of integrated teaching and learning about the sustainable communities principles, as agreed at Bristol (ODPM 2005b) and summarised in Box 6.2, and about the generic skills necessary for their implementation. The generic skills needed are outlined below in Box 6.3, which indicates the generic skills required by all sustainable communities professionals, including a wide range of core and associated occupations from community health and social workers, through the built environment professions, to implementers and decision-makers. This listing is based on the Egan Review (Office of the Deputy Prime Minister 2004) and the ASC with ECOTEC (2006) report.

In November 2006, at a European Skills Symposium organised by the ASC and equivalent bodies based in other EU Member States, the observations made in the previous paragraph were endorsed. Among the most important findings and conclusions from the Symposium were the following points:

- A clear agreement exists between Member States on the importance of the sustainable communities agenda and on the vital role played by skills in delivering this agenda.
- A shared understanding is evident regarding the need to develop a common terminology or vocabulary that crosses professional, disciplinary and other boundaries.
- A recognition exists that the challenge facing Member States varies, with certain states facing less severe challenges in some sectors than others.
- An acknowledgement is evident that the ability of some Member States to enhance their provision of skills and knowledge is less developed than is the case elsewhere.

BOX 6.3 KEY GENERIC SKILLS FOR SUSTAINABLE COMMUNITIES' PROFESSIONALS

Key generic skills include:

- *Visioning and strategy development*: innovative thinking and approaches to engaging and including the community, including the ability to develop and articulate a vision and strategy and gain support.
- *Project management*: defining project objectives and providing the means of delivery, including team building, project plan preparation, coordinating actions.
- *Leadership*: inspiring others to contribute to the development and implementation of strategy and projects.
- *Team and partnership working*: developing and implementing multidisciplinary teams and partnerships, including the provision of skills, the establishment of positive attitudes and the use of common terminology.
- *Creative thinking*: making links between policy areas and people, negotiation and influencing others, thinking laterally and innovating.
- *Effective delivery*: identifying and overcoming constraints, challenging unrealistic targets, identifying practical solutions, reconciling conflicting interests.
- *Process and change management*: managing and improving processes, identifying and managing change, introducing improvement.
- *Resource management*: ensuring that environmental, social and economic costs are understood, understanding risk and reward, identifying and securing resources, presenting a business case.
- *Managing stakeholders*: establishing and maintaining relationships between stakeholders, reviewing partnerships and refreshing them, identifying roles and responsibilities.
- *Conflict resolution*: negotiating and influencing the structure and content of programmes, identifying the sources of actual or potential conflict and resolving problems.
- *Analysis, decision-making and evaluation*: marshalling and using evidence, evaluation, preparing alternatives and taking decisions, monitoring, review and evaluation, exemplars and mentoring.
- *Communication and feedback*: being able to communicate to all stakeholders and actors, expressing vision and strategy, media management, engaging with customers and providing feedback.

Source: Academy for Sustainable Communities with ECOTEC 2006

- An acceptance is present of the importance of ensuring that all stakeholders in placemaking have good access to decision-making skills and information.
- A desire exists to develop further and more fully exploit existing knowledge and learning about skills for sustainable communities.

Given this new emphasis on the objectives of mobilising sustainable communities principles and providing the associated skills, it is important to identify and overcome any barriers which might prevent or hinder the full implementation of these objectives. Although in principle these barriers should not prove to be significant, in practice they are often considerable, due in part to institutional and organisational inertia and professional elitism. The presence of 'silo thinking' has also been identified as a major cause of inefficiency and reduced effectiveness. Typically the various professions involved in a major programme or project span the full range of sustainable communities occupations, of which there are over 30 broad categories. This wide team of professionals will have been educated and trained in a particular discipline and will possess a range of specialist skills. However, many members of the team are likely to possess a somewhat restricted or outdated portfolio of generic skills and will possibly have only a hazy awareness of the sustainable communities principles. In themselves these deficiencies are not insurmountable, and can be addressed through either active continuing professional development (CPD) or learning through experience.

While experiential learning and CPD provide a solution for professionals working in practice, it is also essential to introduce common learning units on sustainable communities principles and generic skills into the initial education and training of all relevant pre-degree, degree and postgraduate programmes, preferably on the basis of teaching students in mixed subject groups. Such an approach would reflect the realities of best practice, where groups of professionals with various skills and from different backgrounds have to work together, often despite the constraints imposed by their initial education, specialist training, separate codes of practice or the inherent restrictions of their professional experience. Providing more adaptable and corporate opportunities for education and training has also been identified as a priority issue by a number of professional organisations. Moving beyond the conventional boundaries of their existing educational guidelines, a number of major professional institutes have agreed partnership commitments with the ASC which are intended to encourage universities and colleges to introduce common sustainable communities learning outcomes and teaching materials into their taught programmes. Examples of such commitments include those agreed with the Chartered Institute of Housing, the Royal Institute of British Architects, the Landscape Institute, the Institution of Economic Development and the Royal Town Planning Institute. Similar inter-professional agreements are now emerging in other European countries and the concept of the sustainable communities 'team' is now moving towards realisation. In the UK, the first graduates of an innovative inter-professional development programme, called Raising Our Game, have already demonstrated in practice the merits of enhanced team working and learning.

Although the idea of transforming the existing sustainable communities skills and knowledge deficit through the provision of more appropriate education and training has now gained general acceptance, there is still a need to address both the requirement to retrofit new or enhanced skills and knowledge to the competence portfolios of existing professionals, and to address the longstanding problems associated with an absolute shortage of professionals due to an insufficient number of entrants into the sustainable communities professions. The first of these challenges is, in part, being addressed through the partnership commitments agreed between the ASC and the professional institutes and is also the subject of specific action to encourage the establishment of pan-professional CPD programmes (Carmichael 2006). A pan-professional CPD programme provides opportunities for professionals from different occupations to participate in learning programmes focused on generic skills and common topics of interest, such as how to develop and implement sustainable community strategies, how to bring about property consolidation in an area which is the subject of regeneration, or how to establish social infrastructure in a new settlement. Early results from such experimental programmes indicate the significant benefits which are associated with providing joint CPD opportunities and encouraging the implementation of teamworking approaches.

With regard to the second challenge, two general responses have been made: first, introducing learning materials into the secondary school curriculum at a point in time when young people are making their initial career and study choices, and second, providing opportunities for inter-professional transfer and skills enhancement. The skills shortage difficulties that these initiatives are seeking to address are substantial, and the evidence base upon which policy has been constructed points to the potential for even greater difficulties in the future (Ernst and Young 2004). Using UK evidence to illustrate the difficulties encountered in ensuring an adequate supply of qualified and experienced sustainable communities professionals, it is evident that:

- There is an absolute and serious shortfall of supply in certain key occupations, including civil and structural engineering, planning and social development.
- There are other absolute supply shortfalls in occupations such as project management and transport.
- There is, in general, an adequate supply in certain other professions.
- But there are major doubts regarding the effectiveness of many professionals due to the lack of generic skills and the absence of a common and shared

understanding of their respective roles in the wider sustainable communities team.

These findings (Ernst and Young 2004; Office of the Deputy Prime Minister 2004) reflect earlier studies in the UK and elsewhere in the EU. Summarising the situation, it has been argued that it is essential to make best use of the existing professional workforce by supporting the introduction and development of 'the skills needed to allow integrated working' (ASC with ECOTEC 2006: 13).

As a consequence of these and other assessments, the responsible national bodies in the various EU Member States have been taking action to ensure that sustainable communities careers are made more attractive and that skills enhancement possibilities are extended. In the UK the ASC has been charged with the development and delivery of learning at secondary school level regarding sustainable communities and with the provision of advice and support for those young people who wish to pursue a career in one of sustainable communities occupations. An innovative teaching programme, Making Places (ASC 2006), has been introduced into the secondary school curriculum and careers material and advice has been offered through careers conventions and other media. As noted above, the second strand of this challenge, careers transfer, has been assisted through the introduction of pan-professional CPD. Furthermore, the provision of common learning material at pre-degree, undergraduate and postgraduate levels will enhance the potential for career transfer and, as a consequence, will also offer professionals a clearer understanding of the wider objectives of sustainable communities activities, irrespective of the location and type of such professional activities.

A final issue to be discussed in this section relates to the provision of sustainable communities skills and knowledge to the wider community audience. One of the most serious aspects of the failure to deliver sustainable communities policy and best practice over the past decades can be attributed to the lack of attention given to working 'with' communities, rather than doing things 'to' communities. A number of studies of successful practice in regeneration and other aspects of placemaking have pointed to the need for the engagement of residents, landowners, employees and other people who have a stake in a neighbourhood. Research findings point to the desirability of engaging stakeholders, including ordinary citizens, at an early stage in the development of a sustainable community strategy (Burwood and Roberts 2002; Joseph Rowntree Foundation 2000), and this research evidence is reflected in recent UK central government statements of policy regarding the behaviour of a wide range of local government, professional and other actors responsible for the making and management of places (DCLG 2007). As noted in Box 6.3, many of the generic skills required by all sustainable communities professionals are aimed at helping to develop the ability to deliver this more responsible and responsive approach to the engagement of the ultimate customers for professional services: the people who live or work in an individual place. Above and beyond the merits of engaging citizens in the development of sustainable communities strategies, it is also evident that citizens are essential contributors to the delivery of strategies and to the long-term management of place. Local 'ownership' of a place (including the policies for its management) is one of the necessary preconditions for the successful evolution of a community, and gradual evolution, rather then radical action following catastrophic failure, would appear to be the preferred method of place management. For professionals, this implies a transformation of attitudes and behaviours: away from professional elitism and towards the establishment of a wider placemaking team which values and incorporates contributions made by the people who live and work in a community.

CONCLUSIONS AND FUTURE RESEARCH PRIORITIES

The most important messages from the review of evidence and practice which has been presented in this chapter relate to the nature, content and structure of the education and training of professionals. Three aspects are of particular importance: the nature of the relationship between individual professionals and between professionals and other stakeholders, the content of the professional portfolio of skill and knowledge, and the structure of organisations, institutions and operational teams. Each of these points is now reviewed.

A first cluster of conclusions reflects much of the earlier discussion, especially regarding the elements related to the skills deficit associated with the continuing presence of 'silo' working and the desirability of introducing a wider understanding of common issues and skills requirements into the initial and continuing education and training of all sustainable communities professionals. In order for this provision to be effective, it is necessary to introduce opportunities for cross-cutting learning into the curriculum and, furthermore, to encourage the adoption of a team approach to both learning and practice. Teamworking between professions is already accepted as the preferred mode of organisation and operation; applying this experience, it has also been demonstrated that extending the team to include local people produces further benefits (Jeffrey and Roberts 2005). The priorities for future research and practice which emerge from this conclusion include the need for further reviews and evaluations of the alternative methods of team building and management; of the desirability or otherwise of providing model professional team templates; of the contribution of role models, exemplars and mentors to the education of professionals; and of the most effective ways of extending the sustainable communities team in order to involve local stakeholders and citizens.

The second cluster of conclusions relates to the content of the professional portfolio of skills and knowledge which is necessary in order to develop and deliver sustainable communities. The generic skills portfolio required by all sustainable communities professionals and other stakeholders, including local citizens, was outlined in Box 6.3, and these skills provide the substance of the cross-cutting learning that was referred to in the previous paragraph. Developing and delivering such learning requires reforms to both the learning outcome guidelines that are issued by professional bodies and the content of the individual learning programmes provided by universities, colleges and other education and training institutions. A call for the introduction of a common sustainable communities module that can be studied by all professionals across Europe has been made by URBACT (an EU initiative which promotes networking between EU cities) and this call is echoed by the representations made by skills development organisations in individual EU Member States (ASC with ECOTEC 2006). One intention in introducing such a module would be to provide greater occupational mobility and flexibility, while another consequence would be to encourage and support greater geographic mobility. Introducing common modules (or common units of study which could be incorporated into existing modules or courses) would also allow for cross-disciplinary learning to be established – it is argued that if you educate and train professionals together, it is likely that they will find it easier to work together. Such learning provision could also be extended to others, including local authority officers and members, other public and private sector staff, community professionals working in the voluntary sector, and local community leaders and participants. By increasing the spread of the delivery of learning it should prove possible to achieve greater scale economies and thereby reduce the unit cost of learning. Research and practice evaluations should focus on identifying and developing the most effective ways of ensuring the continuing development of learning materials and methods for their delivery. A further issue is: who should pay for this extended education, training and provision of knowledge? At present, much of the financial burden is carried by the public sector, professional bodies and individuals. In future, a much greater contribution will have to be made by the private sector, especially the larger high income consultancy firms and by other companies who profit from the processes of creating and maintaining sustainable communities.

A third cluster of conclusions is associated with matters of structure. Even the best interdisciplinary and cross-profession learning and knowledge provision will not, in itself, deliver effective practice. Despite the best efforts of universities, colleges, professional institutions, responsible employers and individual learners, there is no guarantee that the acquisition of skills and knowledge alone will lead to better outcomes. What is also required is a package of reforms related to how sustainable communities programmes are developed and delivered. Such reforms might include the provision of central government or joint professional institution guidance on the structure of operational professional teams; the establishment of education and training partnerships between professional institutions and with universities and colleges; and the introduction of legal, financial and other incentives to support cross-sector working. Research and practice reviews to support such innovations should focus on identifying and evaluating alternative institutional and organisational structures, assessing how best to remove barriers to inter-professional working and how to stimulate more effective working between professionals and other sustainable communities stakeholders, and on identifying and evaluating examples of good and best practice in this field of activity.

Finally, and accepting that many of the examples used to illustrate this chapter reflect the situation in the UK, it is important to emphasise that the issues discussed herein are now acknowledged as matters of concern across the EU. The Bristol Accord and the agreement reached at the meeting of EU ministers held in Leipzig in May 2007 provide the foundations for a new agenda for professionals and others who are involved in the making and management of sustainable communities. However, the realisation of the objectives associated with this agenda is a task for the professional institutes, national strategic bodies (such as the ASC), universities and colleges and individual professionals who seek to practise in an effective manner. The expected outcome will be lasting sustainable communities and a higher quality of life for all.

REFERENCES

Academy for Sustainable Communities (ASC) (2006) *Making Places.* Leeds: ASC.

Academy for Sustainable Communities with ECOTEC Research and Consulting (2006) *Skills for the Future.* Leeds: ASC.

Burwood, S. and Roberts, P. (2002) *Learning from Experience.* London: British Urban Regeneration Association.

Carmichael, S. (2006) *Pan-Professional CPD.* Liverpool: RENEW.

Commission of the European Communities (2005) *Thematic Strategy on the Sustainable Use of Natural Resources.* Brussels: Commission of the European Communities.

Department for Communities and Local Government (DCLG) (2007) *Place Matters.* London: DCLG.

Diamond, J. and Liddle, J. (2005) *Management of Regeneration.* London: Routledge.

Drewe, P. (2000) *The Challenge of Social Innovation in Urban Revitalization.* Delft: Spatial Planning Group, Delft University of Technology.

English Heritage (2007) *Suburbs and the Historic Environment.* London: English Heritage.

Ernst and Young (2004) *Evidence Base Review of Skills for Sustainable Communities.* London: Office of the Deputy Prime Minister.

Howard, E. (1898) *Tomorrow: A Peaceful Path to Real Reform*. London: Swan Sonnenschein.

Jeffrey, P. and Roberts, P. (2005) *Intelligence Report 1: Lessons from the Exemplar Programme*. Liverpool: RENEW.

Joseph Rowntree Foundation (2000) *Key Steps to Sustainable Area Regeneration*. York: Joseph Rowntree Foundation.

Office of the Deputy Prime Minister (ODPM) (2003) *The Sustainable Communities Plan*. London: ODPM.

Office of the Deputy Prime Minister (2004) *The Egan Review: Skills for Sustainable Communities*. London: ODPM.

Office of the Deputy Prime Minister (2005a) *Sustainable Communities: People, Places and Prosperity*. London: ODPM.

Office of the Deputy Prime Minister (2005b) *The Bristol Accord*. London: ODPM.

Roberts, P. (2005) Establishing skills for tomorrow. *Town and Country Planning* 74: 296–297.

Roberts, P. and Sykes, H. (2000) *Urban Regeneration*. London: Sage.

World Commission on Environment and Development (WCED) (1987) *Our Common Future*. Oxford: Oxford University Press.

Part II

Changing Institutions

7

Sustainable Construction and Urbanism in the Netherlands and the Czech Republic

Challenges of Today's Political and Professional Context

Thomas Scheck, Ivan Dejmal and Ger de Vries

Human behaviour everywhere is based on very similar, if not identical mechanisms. But context, history, culture and traditions, as well as characteristics of geographical position, climate, nature and landscapes, or economical, political and social evolution make the idea or objectives of sustainable development or sustainable urbanism in different places rather different.

Is it realistic and honest to explain to people who are struggling and fighting to feed their family that they should act in a different and a more sustainable way for all? Such a context combined with a new strong economic development can provoke enormous new problems, for example, in Asia where big cities are growing by 1 million people a year each, consuming imported natural resources on a huge scale, and destroying other regions at distance. Locally, the 'natural' balance between human beings and their environment is unlikely to withstand severe stresses and strains.

European countries have experienced a certain number of periods of strong growth and specific large-scale urban development. The examples range from Hausmann's scheme for Paris (now perceived as 'classical Paris structure'); the Industrial Revolution in the UK (Manchester, Liverpool) and on the European continent; the economic and urban development after the First World War; the schemes for rebuilding European regions after the Second World War; the Communist totalitarian production of large-scale urban schemes and mono-functional and mono-spatial specialisation with no concern for environment; and, in the early 1990s, the new freedom in central and eastern Europe and a new emphasis on environmental concern in 'western' countries.

This chapter looks at two quite small but socially and economically well-developed European countries and compares their most significant characteristics of the past as well as recent and the current evolution concerning sustainable urban development: the Netherlands and the Czech Republic.

THE NETHERLANDS

For two hundred years before the golden age of Dutch expansion on the world seas in the seventeenth century, the Batavian people were struggling against natural elements and a daily threat by the sea. At the same time, the young 'Republic of provinces' was able to stay independent only on the condition that Catholics and Protestants would hold together. With a helping hand from Erasmus, the practice of mutual respect and dialogue is still a Dutch trademark. The geographical position of the Netherlands made this complex of land and water a strong European trade and transport centre. The Dutch progressively mastered the flood risks and developed techniques for building dykes and windmills, making it possible to create new land called polders. The new Dutch marine ruled over the seas and dominated the Far East trade. Dutch urban development has been rational, based on a pragmatic geometrical logic of land division and development, based on the right balance between land and water, respecting often till now the old *verkaveling* (quite narrow strips of land surrounded by canals allowing evacuation of water).

The present-day Dutch economy is prosperous, situated for a significant part in the western provinces in an almost uninterrupted urban belt starting in the south at the Belgian border and continuing to Amsterdam, including Rotterdam, The Hague, and also Utrecht, Leiden, Haarlem and other cities. One of the most densely populated zones in the world, it is a complex mixture of traffic infrastructure (motorways, railways, rivers and canals leading to major ports, urban transport), urban expansion, industry and intensive agriculture. In this context, the Dutch traditionally espoused dialogue and a reasonable degree of sustainability in their daily activities. Social and ethical motivations remain strong. Politically, there is no bipolar system and the parliament and government action is based more on dialogue and balance. In professional practice, architects and urban planners are being trained as 'engineer-architect' or 'engineer-urban planner', and a daily pluridisciplinary practice is the rule.

In the early 1990s, new inputs in environmental and sustainable policies were initiated. The specificity of the Dutch practice is the strong will to transform experiments into new design standards in order to contribute as rapidly as possible to a friendlier and richer environment, sustainable urban design and management and energy saving concepts. In the section on the Netherlands, Ger de Vries describes the evolution of environmental care, new experimental building and urban design from the early 1990s up to now.

THE CZECH REPUBLIC

After two hundred years of an extremely rich spiritual, cultural, scientific and economic period (Charles IV, Jan Hus, Comenius, Rudolph II), Prague and the Czechs were dominated for centuries from the early seventeenth century to the end of the First World War by the Habsburg dynasty. A prosperous period followed between the world wars, with the young Czechoslovakia becoming, in spite of its limited size, the seventh largest economy in the world (Bohemia and Moravia having formed the most productive part of the Austro-Hungarian Empire). At the end of the Second World War, even though the US Army was progressing through Bohemia, the world leaders decided Czechoslovakia should be freed by the Soviets, losing precious time and lives. Through application of this world logic, Czechoslovakia ended up 'behind the wall', separated from the free world when communists took over in February 1948. Czechoslovakia became one of the very few socialist countries where the private sector completely disappeared and state party power was the only rule.

After the 'velvet revolution' of November 1989, the new freedom offered a happy period of new brotherhood. At the same time, it was easy for certain persons to consider, following a 'state manages all' period, a 'the market should manage all' era. Any social argumentation or regulation was considered suspicious for many, basically because the people were (and some of them still are . . .) afraid to lose the new freedom. Fortunately, the post-communist president Vaclav Havel was a kind of moral and humanist guarantee and complementary to the liberal economic forces. The Czech nature and country are quite romantic, comprising mountains and hills covered with woods, lakes, rivers and not much agricultural land. Before 1989, the real life was the weekend life in the countryside, leaving the communist daily life behind. In the early 1990s, personal benefit and fortune logically reappeared. People discovered not only a new freedom, but also the strongly polluted industrial zones, soviet military bases and nature destroyed by superficial mining and acid rain in the north of the country. In the section on the Czech Republic, Ivan Dejmal describes briefly a historical overview of Czech urban development and points out principal features of the communist period as well as current situation and perspectives.

THE EVOLUTION OF SUSTAINABLE BUILDING IN THE NETHERLANDS

Sustainable building ceased being a novelty in the Netherlands some years ago. The way in which the term has changed since the mid-1970s is indicative of the developments. Sustainable building has evolved from focusing on a few aspects of a home or a building to involvement with an integrated concept – sustainable development, management and maintenance of the entire built environment. The development has moved in a nutshell from idealistic pioneers to a permanent item in building policy and regulations.

Prior to the energy crisis, the Netherlands experienced a period of growing prosperity and increasing energy consumption. The report *The Limits to Growth* from the Club of Rome in 1972 and the 1973 energy crisis shortly afterwards revealed the other side of prosperity only too clearly. Unless something was done, there would be shortages of food and raw materials in the foreseeable future. The earth was facing an unavoidable ecological disaster. Government regulations dating from the period around the energy crisis were concerned primarily with the interior environment and health. These included such subjects as reducing damp and noise problems and providing ventilation, heating and daylight. After the energy crisis, the focus shifted to saving energy.

The energy crisis provoked a new central government energy policy and in the period from 1973 to 1990 energy efficiency and diversification were the key subjects. The first solar energy projects were completed in Boxmeer in 1975 and Zoetermeer in 1977. Many new programmes were started in housing, offices and other commercial and industrial buildings. Around this time the Dutch Government Buildings Agency also had energy-saving programmes and it experimented with *energy efficient building* in pilot projects (see Box 7.1).

The government responded to the energy crisis by publishing its Energy Policy Document in 1974. This is the beginning of the history of energy saving in new and existing housing. The government set up a number of bodies for the purposes of information and demonstration in order to implement the energy policy effectively. Shortly thereafter, in 1978, the National Insulation Programme was initiated. The programme set out to subsidise the insulation of 2.5 million homes by 1990.

BOX 7.1   PIONEERS

For many years pioneers have been striving for a better world and a better environment. De Kleine Aarde in Boxtel is an example. De Kleine Aarde built some spherical recycle homes under the banner of *environmentally friendly and ecological building*. The design was aimed at making the occupants self sufficient with regard to raw materials and energy. The homes incorporated a number of environmental measures that are still seen as progressive today, such as a compost toilet and a methane gas installation.

Around this time energy savings also started being taken into account in renovation work. Subsidies for new buildings were scrapped and those for existing buildings were raised. Spijkenisse Town Council wanted to know how an energy efficient home could be built for an additional budget of only 10,000 guilders. The architect Kristinsson responded with a plan for homes without central heating, and Schiedam Town Council had the design built as a practical experiment. Ultimately this resulted in 1983 in the minimum energy homes, which were also eligible for the PREGO scheme introduced in the mean time (see Box 7.2).

Alongside these activities driven primarily by energy savings, conventional designs for the interior environment continued to be a focus of attention. The combination of additional insulation and moisture in homes resulted in a great deal of investigation. There were also other aspects that played a part in influencing the regulations. For instance, the policy was also directed at emissions of volatile compounds and the use of waste materials in construction. As far back as 1980 concern arose with regard to reducing waste, including construction and demolition

---

BOX 7.2   PREGO

The PREGO scheme (Proefprojecten Rationeel Energie-gebruik in de Gebouwde Omgeving – Pilot Projects for Rational Energy Utilization in the Built Environment) was introduced by the government in 1980. This scheme subsidised fifteen experimental energy friendly housing projects. The PREGO-plus scheme was aimed at demonstration projects that showed how different building methods could be employed in an energy friendly war. A number of different experimental projects were implemented, such as the large-scale underground storage of solar energy in Groningen, homes with heat pumps and wind energy in Huizen and the Experimental Energy Garden in Hoofddorp (1984). It was recognised at that time that parcelling out land so as to obtain maximum benefit from the sun did not take up any additional space. For example, Haarlemmermeer Town Council decided on the basis of the experience gained in this area that the new Overbosch residential district would be laid out so as to maximise the use of sunlight. The project was completed in 1987. The *E'novatie* programme, aimed at existing stock, was initiated in 1988 in order to demonstrate that home improvements and energy savings in post-war housing go together very well indeed and that this combination results in comfortable and sought-after rental housing.

waste, the asbestos problem, radon in homes and, later, reducing the exposure of painters to harmful substances. In 1986 the *Interior Environment Memorandum* was published, followed in 1988 by the *Living in a Healthy Interior Environment Memorandum*, with an overview of the knowledge in the field at that time. Energy was incorporated in the building regulations with the focus on energy savings and improving the interior environment and climate. Private organisations and research institutes supported this interest in a healthy interior environment. A focus on people and environmentally friendly and healthy building and living got off the ground through pioneering projects that were usually initiated by private parties. The homes in Goirle and 's-Hertogenbosch dating from 1986 are an example. This trend was also manifest in the NMB-Postbank building (now ING) in Amsterdam, which was built in 1987 in accordance with the principles of organic architecture.

The publication in 1987 of the Brundtland committee's report *Our Common Future* energised Dutch policy-makers. Greater priority was needed for sustainable global development in addition to a healthy interior environment and energy savings. This vision was expressed in the RIVM (National Institute of Public Health and the Environment) report *Zorgen voor Morgen* (*Looking after Tomorrow*) and the policy response in 1989 was the National Environmental Policy Plan (Nationaal Milieubeleidsplan or NMP). The 1989 National Environmental Policy Plan was based on three policy spearheads that served as guidelines for the development of sustainable building in the first few years. These were integrated chain management, energy conservation and promotion of quality. Shortly thereafter a new government came to power and a more focused plan, the National Environmental Policy Plan-Plus with a Sustainable Building appendix, was published in 1990.

In 1991 the municipality of Rotterdam introduced an Environmentally Friendly Building premium and provided an overview of the materials to be used together with alternatives. In 1992 Amsterdam incorporated a list of environmental materials to be used in its Requirements and Recommendations for New Buildings. Both city councils used the instruments that had been developed in the mean time to facilitate realisation of the environmental ambitions for homes – the DCBA scheme (see Box 7.3) and the Sustainable Renovation Manual. In 1992 Delft and the housing associations formulated environmental requirements for social housing development.

The *Sustainable Renovation Manual* gave lists of environmentally preferred measures and products with a score. Later this 1992 method was combined with the *Sustainable Housing Manual* published in 1993 in the National Sustainable Building Package; 1992 also saw the publication of the Environmental Classification of Building Materials based on the principles of people and environment friendly building. This was used primarily in practice in bio-ecological architecture. By then there was a cascade of initiatives in the form of policy notes, programmes and declarations relating

---

BOX 7.3   DCBA SCHEME

The DCBA scheme differentiates between four levels: D = normal building practice, C = correcting for the environmental harm caused by normal building practice, B = restricting environmental impact to a minimum and A = autonomous situation with minimal environmental impact. Measures and alternatives were defined for each level. In 1989 this method was developed in preparation of the Ecolonia project in Alphen aan den Rijn.

---

to sustainable building. They were at central government level as well as at local authority level.

- In the Government Buildings and the Environment policy document published in 1991 the government made an effort to introduce sustainable building in relation to new government premises.
- Themes like health and water were assigned greater priority in the 1991 Cleaner Living programme from the Stuurgroep Experimenten Volkshuisvesting (Public Housing Experiments Steering Group) and Building Healthy Offices in 1992. In 1994 the Buildings and Interior Environment Policy Memorandum indicated agents and their sources for homes, offices and schools.
- National construction industry organisations laid the basis for a systematic approach to environmental policy in the building sector in 1993 with the 1995 Construction Industry Environmental Terms of Reference Policy Declaration. One of the policy spearheads to arise out of the environmental terms of reference is the encouragement of the use of renewable raw materials, with regard to which the 20 per cent More Timber in Buildings campaign was initiated.
- Local authorities demonstrated that they were taking sustainable building seriously. Requirements were already being set in Amersfoort, Schiedam and Dordrecht for the development of new locations and housing projects. In the urban region of 's-Hertogenbosch a Sustainable Building Covenant and Basic Package for New Housing was agreed by the local authorities, the housing associations and local building firms. Many other local authorities were to follow suit.
- In 1994 the Quality on Location Programme placed sustainable building and landscaping in a broader context. The goal of the project was to integrate town

planning, environmental and public housing quality at the VINEX (Fourth Memorandum on Physical Planning Plus) locations.

- The long-term future of housing was addressed in the Sustainable Technological Development interdepartmental research programme (DTO-1993). The goal of this programme was to reduce the environmental impact by a factor of 20 by 2030. In 1994 four teams of architects were commissioned to design a sustainable office concept for 2040. Sustainable district development was also studied in Rotterdam. There were publications relating to the whole DTO programme after it ended in 1997.

The 1995 Sustainable Building Plan: Investing in the Future marked the beginning of a programmamatic approach by central government. It was clear that by then a substantial quantity of knowledge about sustainable building had been acquired. Projects like The Ecological Town as Mission in 1995 from the Dutch National Spatial Planning Agency and the strategies closely allied to it such as the Ecopolis Strategy in 1992 were evidence of this.

The National Sustainable Building Packages aimed at making knowledge about sustainable building available on a large scale. A series of five were produced:

- National Sustainable Building Package – housing (1996)
- National Sustainable Building Package – management (1997)
- National Sustainable Building Package – commercial and industrial building (1998)
- National Sustainable Building Package – urban development (1999)
- National Sustainable Building Package – road building and civil engineering (1999).

Based on the housing package, the Ministry of Housing Spatial Planning and the Environment developed a yardstick for sustainable housing development in order to promote investments in sustainable building – the Tommel yardstick.

Another vehicle for disseminating knowledge and information about sustainable building was set up in 1996 – the National Sustainable Building Centre. The centre focused primarily on professionals in the construction industry. By then a number of regional sustainable building information points had also been created. However, dissemination of knowledge is not enough. The financial possibilities also had to be expanded if sustainable building was really going to be given a chance. The scope of the Green Project Scheme therefore extended in 1996 to encompass sustainable building. The aim of this scheme is to make the financing of a range of environmentally friendly projects less expensive and through this to stimulate them. Interest and dividends received by private investors in 'green organisations' are exempt from income tax. Consumers may take out a green mortgage financed in this way. The interest is 1–2 per cent lower than market interest rate. Assets in the construction sector that generate an environmental profit come under the Free Depreciation of Environmental Investments (Vrije Afschrijving van Milieu-investeringen – VA-Mil) scheme.

In 1995 the Energy Performance Coefficient (EPC) was incorporated into the building regulations. The standard for this performance coefficient was made tougher, and this contributed to the rapid introduction of cost-effective energy measures. In 1995 the World Wide Fund for Nature joined in by promoting projects with a very good energy performance coefficient. In 1996 the Temporary Sustainable Building Encouragement Scheme for existing buildings came into effect. Under this scheme some 56,000 existing homes were renovated in a sustainable way. In 1997 SEV and Novem published a sustainable housing management manual for existing buildings under the name DUWON (Duurzaam Woningbeheer – Sustainable Housing Management). A start was also made on the integration of sustainable building into the Urban Regeneration Investment Budget scheme.

The Exemplary Sustainable and Energy Friendly Building Projects programme was launched at the beginning of 1996 by the Public Housing Experiment Steering Group (SEV) and Novem. This programme evolved from the Sustainable Building Plan and the Third Energy Policy Document published in 1995. The aim of the programme was to provide broad-based access to experience with sustainable building. Ultimately in 1997 this status was granted to 50 projects. A comprehensive report on the programme was published in April 2000 in book form by the Dubo Centrum (Sustainable Building Centre). Later this approach was continued through the Intensive Use of Space Stimulation Programme (StIR-1997) and the Industrial, Flexible and Easy Dismantled Building (IDF-bouwen – 1999) project (see Box 7.4).

The Dutch Government Buildings Agency developed instruments in order to determine the environmental costs of buildings (Environmental Cost of Government Buildings – 1996). An analysis was made of the environmental impact of building materials throughout their entire life cycle and the environmental impact of a building while it is in use. Calculations were made for several projects, for example the Dynamic Office in Haarlem. Later these types of calculations were used as grounds for selecting the most appropriate design. For example, the design selected for the Directorate-General for Public Works and Water Management's building (2000) in Terneuzen was the one with the least environmental impact. But there was also a change starting in the way that clients and project developers of office projects looked at sustainable and healthy building and management. The Arthur Andersen offices in Amstelveen (1996) are a good example.

BOX 7.4   SENTERNOVEM WEBSITE

Turning policy into reality

SenterNovem is an agency of the Dutch Ministry of Economic Affairs. We promote sustainable development and innovation, both with the Netherlands and abroad. We aim to achieve tangible results that have a positive effect on the economy and on society as a whole.

Our core competence is converting government policy into reality. On behalf of the Dutch government we implement policy regarding:

- innovation
- energy and climate change
- environment and spatial planning

SenterNovem also works on behalf of international organisations such as the European Union, the International Energy Agency (IEA) and foreign governments. Through us these organisations gain access to a broad Dutch network of knowledge institutes, research centres, trade associations, companies and government officials. We also participate in numerous international platforms and counselling groups.

With the knowledge and experience gained in the Netherlands and abroad, we can help you assess your specific project. We offer a wide spectrum of products and services that can be used by the government in public-private partnerships. From developing and disseminating knowledge, to monitoring and developing policy instruments and to managing subsidy schemes. We act as a full partner, e.g. as programme manager, participant or programme adviser. We can help you convert your policy into reality.

Our products and services

These web pages offer an overview of SenterNovem's wide array of domestic and international projects.

For general information on SenterNovem, contact our Front Office:

Tel: +31 30 239 35 33

Email: frontoffice@senternovem.nl

www.senternovem.nl

Source: V&L Consultants

The Second Sustainable Building Plan (1997) defined a new course. The plan encompassed local authority decision-making, existing stock and urban development, commercial and industrial building, road construction and civil engineering and consumers. Sustainable building was stimulated in the commercial and industrial sector through the government's own efforts and through the introduction of the Sustainable Commercial and Industrial Building Register.

The IBN-DLO complex (1998) in Wageningen and the Directorate General for Public Works and Water Management's building (2000) in Terneuzen were topical exemplary projects. A town planning instrument was developed for the local energy infrastructure, the Energy Performance on Location (EPL) and a programme for designing an optimal energy infrastructure (OEI). The EPL was used in 1998 to start pilot projects, which were successful. The Directorate General for Public Works and Water Management played an exemplary role in the civil engineering sector. Incidentally the principles of sustainable building had been applied widely in this sector without the activities necessarily being labelled as sustainable building.

A milestone for sustainable building was reached in 1998 when the environment was added to the Housing Act as a fifth cornerstone and the translation of sustainable building measures into building regulations started. The requirements relating to energy efficiency were made more stringent for residential, commercial and industrial building. There was also greater focus on change of use of buildings and redevelopment of areas. This coincided to some extent with the Intensive Use of Space Stimulation Scheme and the Urban Regeneration Investment Scheme. The regulations for a material-related environmental profile of a building (Materiaalgebonden Milieuprofiel van een Gebouw or MMG) was an important addition to the fifth cornerstone. The MMG is an extension of the approach using a Life Cycle Analysis (LCA) as applied in some instruments relating to sustainable building.

A number of instruments were developed in order to enable consumers to put sustainable building and living into practice. The Sustainable Odd Jobs project, for example, was concerned with consumer information and improvement of the ranges of sustainable products in the do-it-yourself sector. The development of the Woonwijzer-Wizzard (Home Tips Wizard), a manual for adapting individual homes for sustainable use, was another example.

Instruments were developed so that professionals in the building industry could use an LCA analysis to calculate the environmental impact of an entire building. EcoQuantum and GreenCalc are particularly useful. Suppliers to the construction industry also made efforts to provide unambiguous information about the environmental impact of products. To this end Environmentally Relevant Product Information was introduced in 1999 by the Dutch Construction Industry Suppliers Association.

The *Action Plan for Sustainable Building: Investing in the Future* was published in 1995. This was a goal-oriented and practical document that was aimed to give sustainability a stronger and, in the long term, fixed place in the decision-making process on the layout and use of buildings and their environment. This document marked the beginning of the government's programmed approach to sustainable building. The Second Action Plan of 1997 built upon the results of its predecessor. In consultation and close cooperation with the representative organs of all the parties involved in the building process, once again, a selected list of actions and projects was drawn up. The aim was to help the further development and application of sustainable building along various policy lines. By 1999 it can be ascertained that both plans had had much effect. In the mean time, sustainable building had become an issue and is now more and more often taken as a theme in building processes. However, it is still too early to drop the programmed approach. More time is necessary for the knowledge and experience with sustainable building to be broadly applied and firmly embedded in the daily practice of construction. In addition a number of extra stimuli in specific sectors are necessary. The Policy Program on Sustainable Building: 2000–2004 addresses these needs. With the creation of the essential preconditions and by undertaking concrete actions, it is intended to bring sustainable building definitively to a higher level. If, in the beginning, sustainable building was primarily aimed at improving the environmental efficiency of buildings, in the meantime, the objectives have widened. It is about the sustainable development, retrofitting and maintenance of buildings and their environment as a whole, including the demolition and removal of buildings.

This has led to a greater focus on the existing stock. The Investment Budget for Urban Regeneration (ISV, published in 1999) was brought to life for investment in towns. The ISV is a collection of mostly already existing subsidy measures in the field of accommodation, space, environment and the physical conditions for economic activities. The ISV is a powerful instrument for applying sustainable building and sustainable development to existing towns. The Policy Program represented an additional stimulus for sustainable urban development, consumers and energy, and it devoted additional attention to knowledge and innovation.

Until 2002 the Policy Program on Sustainable Building: 2000–2004 has been monitored and evaluated. At that time a decision has been made to adjust the programme in the direction of energy saving and carbon dioxide reduction in order to limit emissions by the built environment. Besides, the use of environmental friendly building materials received extra attention as well as the indoor environment.

But a tendency in practice has also been recognised: the 'greening' of the economy and good governance. Moreover, studies argue the central government has to stimulate and facilitate local and regional parties, and the central government has not only to bring sustainable building more to the attention of the citizens but also to reward good environmental behaviour. It has to show what sustainable building means in practice, not only by knowledge development and knowledge dissemination but also in realised projects and the possibilities of an integrated design process.

Some remarkable projects have already been started as a private initiative. In the municipality of Culemborg the EVA-Lanxmeer project has been developed. The plan originated in 1993 inspired by Marleen Kaptein, who founded the Educational, Informational and Advisory Centre for Ecology (EVA) to promote integral, sustainable urban design, and to show in an example, the EVA-Lanxmeer project (Figure 7.1). The first 100 of about 250 dwellings had been delivered in 2000 and the project is still in development at the time of writing. Another project that had been started as a private initiative was De Kersentuin, realised in 2003 in Leidsche Rijn, a new development of about 30,000 houses of the city of Utrecht. The project has 94 dwellings.

In 2003 an evaluation of the performance of the Green Fund Scheme appeared. The Green Fund Scheme is a governmental tax incentive instrument that has been used by the Dutch government since 1995 to encourage environmental initiatives. In 2004 Triodos Bank introduced its 'Triodos Vastgoed Fonds', a fund for financing sustainable real estate in the Netherlands. The fund is especially focused on commercial real estate such as offices, shops and commercial buildings in the Netherlands.

Since 2000 several updates have been realised of instruments and methods for developing sustainable building and sustainable development focused on the built environment in general, for instance, LCAs, GreenCalc, EcoQuantum and instruments for the development of sustainable sites and locations, and also methods for improvement of the quality of the built environment conform to the triple P model: ecological, social and economic aspects.

In 2005 the book *Sustainable Urban Design: Perspectives and Examples* (Adriaens et al. 2005) was published containing the results of a monitoring and evaluation project. The authors described in a clear and accessible manner sustainable urban design as it is practised at the present time. By means of a historical sketch and clear, richly illustrated examples of present-day projects, the authors showed that sustainable urban design is no utopia. The book reviewed five projects extensively and ten projects in short. The main projects are: the GWL site in the city of Amsterdam, influence of water on urban transformation (1996–1998, apartments, high density), EVA-Lanxmeer in Culemborg, the ecological district as a practical utopia (2000–2007, private initiative, mostly single family houses, average density), Schalkwijk in Haarlem (restructuring, rainwater discharge and reduction of roads), Business City Fortuna in Sittard (1999–2010, business park, water storage, park management and traffic control) and De Hutten in the municipality of Ulft (2005–2010, reconstruction of two old industrial sites).

In 2005 the State Secretary for Housing, Spatial Planning and the Environment presented the new plans of the Dutch government with sustainable building. Since then, the central government has no longer been an initiator of sustainable building. Instead it supports initiatives of the market for the integration of sustainable building as a part of quality improvement in the building industry. The new policy is oriented on carbon dioxide reduction in general as also in the built environment, including improvement of the energy performance of new and existing buildings.

Until 2007 there were few initiatives for big leaps forward in the field of sustainable building in the Netherlands. However, since the movie *An Inconvenient Truth* by Al Gore was shown in the Netherlands in 2007, a renewed awareness for sustainable development has been awakened in business and policy decision-making, leading perhaps to a new chance for sustainable building in the Netherlands.

7.1 EVA-Lanxmeer
Source: V and L Consultants Archief Rotterdam

THE EVOLUTION OF URBANISATION AND SUSTAINABILITY IN THE CZECH REPUBLIC

The problem of (un)sustainable urbanism is an international one. Up to the Industrial Revolution, the population density and the structure of residential settlements, with the exception of several tens of harbour and mining towns and towns situated on the traditional trade routes, was fully dependent on the fertility of the land. The terrain configuration strictly influenced land access and thus also the density of the first agrarian settlements and the agricultural methods within their surroundings. Usually the maximum effective distance of arable land from a settlement was less than half an hour walking. Bigger settlements, meaning bigger municipalities with specialised craft production and trade, and small towns serving as administrative and spiritual centres, were limited in size – and to a great extent also in their importance – by the fertility of the surrounding land and by the needs of its agrarian settlements. The most remote settlement was situated half a day's walking distance from the local centre, so that the people had time to return home to look after their livestock. The area of interaction, as well as the territorial distribution and density of the local centres with their surroundings, was strictly limited by these factors. A similar relationship was maintained also in links to their larger vicinity and this limited the growth of towns on regional or state levels. For similar reasons, the distance between them was measured in a half-day's horse ride. Between big administrative centres, for practical reasons, the distance was one or more day's horse riding.

The Industrial Revolution stands at the beginning of the development of present day urbanisation. It radically altered traditional settlement patterns, particularly because of the concentration and mass production of certain types of products and the need to trade these products at least in the wider regions. The fertility of the land and the effectiveness of its agrarian support thus ceased being the primary condition for the growth of the industrial settlements. This became dependent on the sale of products produced by the local industry and primarily supplied to big and distant towns and trade centres. The growth of the settlements became therefore dependent on the development of new transport routes which connected industrial centres with trade centres, and on the discoveries of raw material deposits and sources of energy.

From the end of the nineteenth century, the loss of consciousness of the duality between the public and the private added to this process and caused deepening of the territorial separation of functions and social groups. When the new Prague borough – Kralovske Vinohrady – was built at the end of the nineteenth and the beginning of the twentieth century, the block construction with a public front facing the street and a private one inside the yards was still asserted. Explicitly functional and social regulations were applied: shops only on the ground floor, offices only at one level, flats of all categories inside one house including a poor-quality caretaker's flat in the basement or ground floor and attic rooms for students or bohemian artists.

At the same time the individualisation of the style of building began for the newly emerging middle class. Their houses left the street line, neighbours and the city. In the newly established boroughs, such as Prague's Hanspaulka or Orechovka or in newly emerging satellite towns of Cernosice or Dobrichovice, they were situated in the middle of garden plots surrounded by green vegetation. Soon this type of housing was transferred to the poorer clientele – but with less comfort and in the less attractive locations (such as Chodov, Zahradni Mesto). However, the effect is the same: the street was no longer a social space with social control, instead new demands on space and the transport infrastructure were increasing. This separated residential development with its spread at the fringes of the existing settlements also disturbed the previously more or less sharp boundaries defining what is outside and inside a settlement.

As a reaction to these changes, several attempts were made to return to the compact town. With the exception of some distinguished operations such as Gocar's rehabilitation of Hradec Kralove and Le Corbusier's design of a linear town made of high-rise blocks in Zlin, most of the proposals remained on paper. After the Second World War, the new Ostrava borough of Poruba and the completely new town of Havirov were established as compact towns. This was followed up to a certain point also in Havlicek's and Bubenicek's tower blocks in Kladno-Rozdelov in the 1950s. These attempts are, however, connected to the ideology of collectivisation and similarly to 'Koldum' (Kolektivni dum = Collective house) in Litvinov embody the ideas of an important leftwing intellectual of the 1920s and 1930s: Karel Teige and his vision of the 'minimal flat'.

The majority of Czech small and medium settlements grew additively, by progressive expansion from the previously existing structure of the town through clusters of independently standing capacity blocks of flats and clusters of small family houses, preserving the idea of garden cities. These however were built on small plots.

Larger and very large settlements differed by having sets of complete housing estates with concentrated services – shopping centres, nurseries, schools, restaurants, sports facilities, sometimes even cinemas and larger cultural establishments. Specific to this building development were the mostly residual areas of car parks and garages for the residents and also the proximity of large areas of small gardens, where some of the inhabitants of the neighbourhood looked for compensation for the monofunctional life in prefabricated concrete blocks of flats.

Such types of building construction are generally closely connected to increasing stratification of functional segregation of the spaces into sectors for living, for work, for shopping, for administration and for leisure activities. As opposed to other European countries, the size of Czech socialist neighbourhoods was often also determined by political ideology. For example there was a large industrial zone built in the eastern part of Prague in the attempt to maintain a significant proportion of working class within the city population.

However, since the beginning of the 1960s, the spatial functional segregation started to develop on a very large scale over the whole country. At the state and regional levels, living areas and industrial agglomerations as well as agricultural and recreational zones were gradually being defined and separated factually and administratively. The natural need of the inhabitants to spend at least short periods of time in the countryside led to many open and naturally attractive places being overpopulated – becoming instead noisy townships of densely built weekend houses or huts at allotment gardens. Many of these colonies increased in size to such an extent that the human weekend concentration was similar to city streets on a Saturday afternoon. The mountainous and sub-mountainous parts of the country saw the development of special recreation centres built for trade union members from state companies. At present these are being replaced in the attractive parts of the country by clusters of 'apartment blocks' or huts in 'recreation villages' built most often by foreign and especially Dutch investors.

Conversely, the regions of the country with mineral raw materials with high potential energy value were seen specifically as 'industrial' and were sacrificed for this purpose. For example, in the mining region of North Bohemia, 89 settlements including the historical royal town of Most were destroyed due to mining activities. In conjunction with coal mining, important steel production based on the import of raw iron minerals, were developed in the regions of Ostrava and Kladno. Other settlements, without mineral and energy deposits, such as towns in the river Labe catchment area (Pardubice, Kolin, Neratovice, Lovosice, Usti nad Labem) were developed as the centres of chemical industry. Some small border towns, for example Rumburk, Varnsdorf or Nachod, were established as the centres of the textile industry. This regional separation of production functionality, originating in the totalitarian era, persists to the present, both in the original form and in the emergence of serious social problems in places where the industries ceased to exist. At present, new industrial agglomerations are being established as industrial parks and zones on the free land close to bigger towns. These occupy more often areas of 200–1000 hectares of high quality agricultural land.

All of this functional separation has shifted transport into the role of the main urbanisation tool and caused a problem. It is necessary to convey daily large quantities of raw material and products, and also people from their dwellings to work and back. It is also necessary to transport them or give them the opportunity to transport themselves to do their shopping, travel for entertainment and at weekends to travel there and back to areas of recreation. The trips for such daily needs are no longer an occasion for meeting and expectations, rather they become an everyday, tedious, time-consuming and expensive necessity for everyone. This leads not only to further concentration of people in conglomerations (reduction of expenses and distances) but also to increasing speed and capacity of communications, because the speed shortens time and perceived distance.

Territories through which speedy communications pass pay the price for this mental shortening of distance between points A and B. For a long time high speed thoroughfares directed on the traditional routes through the centres of naturally established municipalities and towns had a divisive effect. But shifting them outside settlements brought new problems. By taking completely new routes, they broke existing natural relationships, settlements, and transport in the area and become parasites on its space. For example, the problems with establishing the motorway Prague – Dresden through natural reserves of Ceske Stredohori or Saske Svycarsko is leaving both cities and the target metropoles Berlin and Vienna cold. The towns and regions through which the motorway is passing are 'foreign' and difficult areas, just obstacles to the highway which have to be overcome.

Alongside this, the continually increasing residential and industrial conglomerations become parasites on the space of surrounding countryside through their consumption of energy and materials. A network of innumerable power lines, heating and gas pipes covers the landscape. Extensive systems of water works – from the dams, through water mains to supply reservoirs are built for the requirements of conglomerations. Large trading and storage areas are being created consuming space around the speedy communications.

A significant example of new settlement parasitism is the growth of a new wave of living in family houses and villas close to large towns. It is a matter of either entirely new formations for rich clients, which are usually fenced and guarded and so completely separated from the public space of settlements, or there are big development areas without any community and social facilities which are built within existing municipalities. Soon their inhabitants will exceed the original population of small rural communities and ultimately completely break up their coherence and community, which could actively share in maintaining and shaping the urban structure of a settlement. Urban agglomerations during their territorial expansion have already swallowed hundreds of settlements and destroyed the identity and hierarchical structure of hundreds of others in their surroundings without consideration for the consequences of the expansion, be it for the life and structure of their own conglomeration.

Current situation and perspectives

In the 1990s there was also the very new phenomenon of 'restitutional urbanism'. After the 'velvet revolution' (November 1989), properties were privatised and restituted to the original owners or their families. After restitution, the new landowners wanted to convert their agricultural land as quickly as possible into building sites and the inexperienced or corrupt civil service was unable to prevent them in unsuitable cases.

The problem of not-sustainable urbanism is international. In Europe, the new EU Member States might have an advantage. Because of capital deficit, the consequences of the non-sustainable development and urbanism are for the time being limited and linked to important residential or industrial agglomerations. The Czech Republic has a network of reasonably coherent little towns and villages. Since the early 1990s, those entities are being developed on a rational base thanks to the Regeneration of Rural Municipalities Programme, in which corrective completion and redevelopment of rural municipalities is subject to state support and subsidies.

No such instrument is unfortunately available for towns on operational or theoretical levels. The new building law (183/2006 Sb.) includes under the paragraph concerning territorial planning, that any plan of territorial development as well as the local strategic planning have to include evaluation of influences on sustainable development of the territory. In practice however, these concerns are limited to economic development of the territory and preservation of existing employment and development of new opportunities.

Apart from the specific political and general social influences, the professional urbanistic circles have always had a prominent role in the new urban development in the Czech Republic. Before the 1990s, the system was a total state-run system ruled by the communist party, including architecture and urban planning units and offices. Until now, the specialist schools did not take complex urban problems into account. They did not change the paradigm of the education of new architects and urban planners and they continued to cultivate in them the idea that they are the creators of new realities, creators who are allowed not to take in account factual territorial connections and the real social needs of the users of their creations.

But to be fair – urbanism cannot in itself be permanently sustainable on its own. It must correspond to the principles of the administration and life of a permanently sustainable society. But Czech society has not so far seen sustainability of its behaviour through urban development. Up to now severing the links between settlement and the surrounding countryside is understood as freedom without any limit. Up to now it was not necessary to feel as a loss the great areas of often most fertile land on which garden cities of family houses, landfill or transport infrastructure from the metropolis encroached.

Acting as 'engaged observers' from a new EU Member State, we notice that it is possible to import wheat from Canada, beef from Argentine, soya for pigs from India and perhaps fresh strawberries by plane from Israel. The affected areas are far away, and that is why for the territorial expansion of Paris, Munich or Prague they cannot be and they are not an obstacle, even such serious problems as threatening degradation of Canadian and American arable land caused by monoculture grain production, felling trees for pastures in South America, or contamination of Indian water and land by pesticides caused by soya production.

In the world of territorial detachment of the beginning from the end, of the use from the origin, of the profit from the impact, there is not and cannot be the understanding of these events as being the natural territorial limits of the settlement development and the urbanisation of the territory.

If we know nowadays that the only known basic prerequisite for such existence is to place as much as possible of material energy flows in the smallest possible territory where people could directly see the beginning and the end of the processes and correct their behaviour accordingly, then it is clear that present urbanism is in detail and in its general direction miles away from permanently sustainable development. But it is certainly not its task to discover the principles of administration and life of the sustainable society. That is the task for social discussion from which the informed cultural model is derived. It remains to be seen whether this is at all possible without us reaching the end of the journey of our unsustainable development.

SOME FINAL THOUGHTS

Why are two (in some respects) comparable European countries with a similar economic and social potential sufficiently different to make a comparative study worthwhile? This is definitely not a case of 'good' and 'bad'. Instead it involves an attempt to talk briefly about evolution, development, growth and its consequences and side effects. Of course, the Czech consciousnesses about sustainability is not yet developed to the level of the Dutch. However, it will be interesting to see in the near future whether the Czechs will be able to do better, learning from sustainable practices in the Netherlands and other older EU countries. The 'new' Europe is the Europe of initiative, development, and both growth and limits to growth, it is the place to be, an experience to live. And pieces of this 'new' Europe and new European practice are present in both of the countries examined.

Landscape and urban context

Most of the Dutch landscape in the critical parts has been created by people, fighting against the sea and mastering rational land division and complex water systems. The extremely high density of population and the intensive industry and agriculture in those regions logically put forward a most complete range of problems of sustainability. It is for these reasons that the Dutch have progressively developed a high level of expertise.

The Czech landscape is a romantic and natural one, linked to the pleasure of spending some time every weekend in the countryside. On the other hand, as we have seen, the spatial specialisation under communism led to the destruction of some natural regions and industry and Soviet army bases did not care at all about pollution. New aggressions against nature and traditional urban units now take the form of large-scale infrastructure projects and construction. The preservation of certain valuable not yet exploited archaeological sites is not guaranteed under the pressure of capital. Yet these elements represent nowadays the Czech motivation for a more sustainable approach.

Social, economical and political aspects

Accustomed to wealth, political stability and traditionally caring for the 'dense but good living together', the Dutch are used to social and political involvement and debate. Every opinion should be respected and if possible integrated in any social or political evolution, as well as building or urban project. Conscious about the environmental problems on local but also on planetary levels, the population is motivated to invest itself personally and to contribute to the general interest.

Even though Czechs are conscious about an old democratic tradition between the First and Second World Wars, the majority of the population lived under communist dictatorship where not only personal freedom and initiative, but also perspective or debate were banned. In consequence, the practice of democracy after the 'velvet revolution' is recent and people are not used to being asked for their opinion before taking important decisions concerning large-scale transport infrastructure or urban development schemes. The possibility to take initiatives, work hard and make money is also recent. The country is oriented to get its place back among the wealthy nations. For these different reasons, both growth and consumption are blossoming and limits are not on the horizon for the time being.

Instruments and sustainability orientations

As described above, the Netherlands have developed a large and very complete variety of political, economical, financial and fiscal as well as methodological and evaluation instruments. From concerns about energy, the emphasis has moved on to building materials, waste and water management, and health. From the experience of sustainable building, guidelines for sustainable urban design have been developed. Successful experiments were rapidly used in building standards and implemented on a large scale. Nowadays, the accent is on a healthy environment, conditions for a good life, economy and more sustainable development.

The Czech Republic does not have many tools at the disposal of willing politicians, local authority managers or professionals involved in urban planning. The interest is however slowly but surely growing. The legal instrument arsenal is also becoming more complete and sophisticated. In the field of sustainability, the main orientations are energy efficiency for evident economic reasons, pollution treatment and strategic planning on a large scale.

Difficulties to be overcome
Recently, the Dutch have experienced rapidly rising wages and prices and these have produced rather non-traditional, more personal-interest behaviour. Economic and demographic growth as well as strong expansion of demand for individual space and demand for new decentralised construction on premium locations have provoked the two major 'black points': on one hand, an invasion of built environment reducing more and more 'natural' areas to 'urban natural reserve'; on the other hand an invasion of transport infrastructure and more or less blocked traffic flows (vehicle numbers have doubled since 1990).

In the Czech Republic, sustainability is not for the moment a major concern for political parties and leaders. In the current period of strong economic growth and social and political evolution, only the most visible damage to the environment is being treated. The first concern is with economy, followed by social and health care. On the other hand, the decentralisation of decisions poses, as in other European countries like France, the problem of competence at the local level. A significant part of the population still lives in the residential buildings of the communist era. In Prague, for example, half of the population lives in these large schemes around the city centre. In spite of the creation of private, exclusive complexes for the new wealthy, living in those prefabricated neighbourhoods is not considered as a punishment and a real social mixture remains for the time being. But for how long? The Czechs do not have a Dutch variety of sustainability instruments at their disposal. Fortunately, it is probable that in the near future, due to the continuous international exchanges, European projects and EU standards, specific methods and tools for sustainability will become available to Czech decision-makers and professionals.

CONCLUSION

The Netherlands is one of the leading actors in sustainable building and urbanism, but at the same time, daily life brings new difficulties and the weight of the two 'black points' described is growing. For us, the instruments, the practice and the technical solutions developed in the Netherlands are most relevant and useful to study and serve quite often as inspiration or example. The Czech Republic is developing with the objective of joining the most developed EU Member States in the shortest time. The match is on between the pulsation of economic growth and its pressures and the evolution of regulatory instruments and the social aspects of sustainable urban development. But, as we all know, in most cases, our species is only ready to invest itself and modify its behaviour when it is almost too late. It might look realistic that the Czechs, with help from the more experienced, will manage to achieve a more sustainable urban development before losing too much.

REFERENCES AND FURTHER READING

Note: This selection is oriented towards those publications likely to be accessible to an international readership.

Adriaens, F., Dubbeling, M. and Feddes, F. (2005) *Duurzame Stedenbouw: Perspectieven en Voorbeelden (Sustainable Urban Design)*. Wageningen: Blauwdruk.

Berends, J., Geelen, V. and Góedman, J. (1995) *De ecologische stad als missie – naar een duurzame ontwikkeling van stedelijke systemen*. The Hague: Rijksplanologische Dienst.

CROW (1999) *Nationaal pakket Duurzaam Bouwen Grond-, Weg en Waterbouw*. Ede.

Haas, M. (1992) *NIBE-Milieuclassificatie Bouwmaterialen*. Naarden: Nederlands Instituut voor Bouwbiologie en Ecologie.

van Hal, A. and de Vries, G. (2000) *Kiezen voor verandering: Duurzaam bouwen in Nederland. Opting for Change: Sustainable Building in the Netherlands*. Boxtel: Aeneas uitgeverij van vakinformatie.

Meadows, D. (1972) *Rapport van de club van Rome – Grenzen aan de groei*. Utrecht: Aula-boeken 500, Uitgeverij Het Spectrum.

Ministerie van Volkshuisvesting, Ruimtelijke Ordening en Milieu- beheer (1988) *Wonen in een gezond binnenmilieu*. The Hague.

Ministry of Housing, Spatial Planning and the Environment (1999) *Policy Programme Sustainable Building 2000 – 2004: Firmly embedding (Summary)*. (VROM 991176/h/01-00) The Hague.

Ministry of Housing, Spatial Planning and the Environment (not dated) *Green Financing, Environmental yields in the Netherlands*. Novem, Laser.

Nationaal Dubo Centrum (1999) *Nationaal Pakket Duurzame Stedebouw*. Rotterdam.

Novem bv (1992) *Ecolonia Demonstration project for energy-saving and environmentally aware building and living*. Sittard.

Novem bv/Bouwfonds Woningbouw bv (1995) *The road to Ecolonia Evaluation and residents' survey*. Sittard.

RIVM, Samson H.D.(1989) *Zorgen voor Morgen: Nationale Milieuverkenning 1985–2010*. Alphen aan den Rijn: Tjeenk Willink.

Silvester, S. and de Vries, G., (1999) *Woonsatisfactie, bewonersgedrag en bewonerswensen bij Voorbeeld projecten Duurzaam Bouwen*. Delft: Technische Universiteit Delft / V&L Consultants, Delft.

Stichting Bouwresearch (1998) *Nationaal pakket Duurzaam Bouwen Utiliteitsbouw*. Rotterdam.

Stichting Sureac (1997) *GreenCalc*. Bussum.

Thijssen, I. and Engelen, M. (1992) *Milieubewust wonen in Eclonia – Handleiding voor de bewoners van Ecolonia in Alphen aan den Rijn Woon/Energie*. Sittard.

Tjallingii, S.P. (1992) *Ecologisch Verantwoorde Stedelijke Ontwikkeling*. Wageningen: Instituut voor Bos- en Natuuronderzoek.

de Vries, G. (not dated) *Bouwen en Milieu deel 5 Voorbeeldprojecten*. Rotterdam: V&L Consultants.

World Commission on Environment and Development (1987) *Our Common Future*. Oxford: Oxford University Press.

8

Institutional Dynamics and Institutional Barriers to Sustainable Construction in France, the United Kingdom and the Netherlands
Eric Henry and Magali Paris

This chapter discusses institutional dynamics and institutional barriers, looking at the way policy towards sustainable construction has been developed, and at the introduction of environmental standards and guidelines to traditional methods and traditional contracts. The three countries have introduced measures to conserve energy, use more renewables, manage the use of water and reduce air pollution. In France and the Netherlands, the creation of a code of sustainability, supported by the huge evolution in heating regulations, involves new competencies and a different management of projects by involving professionals, users and local politicians differently. In France, policy has focused on specific building projects and on achieving measurable goals over a specific range of criteria and on environmental project management. In the Netherlands, a national tradition of creating consensus in planning policies has been harnessed to the control of natural resources in sustainable urban design and sustainable building design. In the United Kingdom, a broader agenda has been pursued, emphasising improvements in the quality of life. However, construction industry tendering methods and forms of contract have made this agenda harder to implement.

The dynamics are not sufficient to break down the numerous institutional barriers which contribute to professional identities, to decision-making and to the organisation of everyday life. However, much individual and collective learning have been set in train.

ISSUES COMMON TO ALL THREE COUNTRIES

All three countries and their inhabitants have been involved in the global climatic evolution that questions the future of our planet and especially the sustainability of its development. But everybody is not concerned the same way. Sustainable development is not fractal (Godard 1994). Its implementation cannot be reproduced from one country to another, from time to time, because it is dependent on a political, economic, cultural and institutional context and on the past events which model the historical development of that country. In Europe, the singularity of each country lies in the heterogeneity of these paths, even if the European Union leads its members on different levels.

The preservation of resources, energy efficiency, and environmental quality are recurrent themes in which the European Union is strongly involved, with votes for directives and the implementation of international standards. The European member states translate and reinterpret the directives and the international standards in their own regulations and standardisation.

Our desire to focus on a comparative analysis of the building sector in three countries, Netherlands, United Kingdom and France, involves research at the heart of histories and national developments.

In each country, sustainable development actions – led at different scales (state, regions, cities etc.) – do not necessarilly fit into each other but they produce new interaction systems.

Our decision to study the 1990–2005 period is because it is significant for understanding the stakes and the evolution of the main institutional dynamics of sustainability in each country.

New actors

First of all, the sustainable development question seems to provoke, in all the countries, the increase in the power of two actors at the local scales of neighbourhood and of cities: on the one hand the inhabitants and on the other hand the politicians (Gilli and Courdurier 2000). This important change may modify institutional and power games and some of the choices and decision criteria for briefing, design, use and consumption.

We may underline two factors. First, the pressures exercised by the users are outside the predetermined schemes of the professional logistics which simply take into account the environmental requirements that are linked to a common political logic. The environmental performance of a building is evaluated by the users only if it satisfies them at the same time as their demands for space organisation, use and costs. Second, the current interest (in France and the United Kingdom) or the previous interest (in the Netherlands) of politicians for sustainable urbanism and construction makes developers more careful about environmental and investment choices in the long term as well as more concerned about the loss of profitability for their operations which can come from innovation. However, strong sustainability requirements from authorities for big city planning and construction operations (Paris, Rotterdam, Lyon, Delft or Grenoble) will make the developers and builders progress and also constitute a marketing reference for them to gain a part of a new market area.

Sustainable development, as we could observe in its national evolution,[1] implies new ways of drawing up the objectives and the requirements for design. Sustainable development often brings conflicts between professionals, politicians and users. The arrival of new specialists in sustainable development brings changes to the habits of professionals of the building sector.

The construction sector in turbulence

The actors of the construction sector have cultural references and common techniques whatever the identity of each professional group. What gathers the actors together is a way of working structured by local projects and accompanied by a particular relationship with nature, with space modelling and materials. The construction sector is a world of transformation which taps strongly into natural resources and which produces a great deal of rubbish. The construction sector is a world which is still anchored locally and nationally but involved indirectly at the global scale with suppliers, the search for labour, the energy crises, the greenhouse effect, the waste of resources.

Professional institutions and rules in each country surround the local and national life of the construction sector, and these are bypassed by a new dynamic for more sustainable cities and construction. For builders and planners, the rules of setting up a project, the rules of cooperation between actors and the rules of contracting are changing.

Some of the national and local initiatives reinforce this dynamic for change, whereas other initiatives put a brake on this dynamic. The former initiatives refer to formative and stimulating actions resulting from new guidelines and new actors during all the setting-up stages, during all the design stages and during all the management stages of the project. The latter initiatives are the small number of convincing actions led by public authorities, polemical and conflicting positions taken by worried professionals (often destabilised) and types of traditional contracts which lead to a standstill.

Institutions and rules challenged

What should be understood by institutions and rules? In 2002, at the request of the Ministry of Dwelling, Planning and Environment, Van Bueren and Priemus (2002) (of the University of Delft) set out the position of institutions based on work by previous researchers on administration and organisation in Northern Europe and United States (Klijn and Koppenjam 2000; March and Olsen 1984).

This position takes two aspects into account when evaluating change, on the one hand the formal and institutional rules,[2] and on the other hand the informal rules and the interaction models which structure and regulate but do not predetermine the behaviour of professionals and their way of selecting problems and choice criteria.

The thesis of March and Olsen (1984), essentially interactionist, proposes that every organisation is problematic and can be understood through its ways of cooperation and interaction (between actors). The ways of cooperating and interacting allow the organisation to be reproduced and to exist despite its weakness, its contradictions and its conflicts. This thesis concentrates less on power games than on the canalisation of these power games by institutional criteria for choice and by organisational procedures. The change of reference framework, consisting of guidelines for design and of new rules, which is due to a greater consciousness of sustainability, alters the legitimacy of decision criteria, common methods of cooperation and models of interaction. The evolution of regulations and acts reinforces or inhibits such a change.

The beginnings of a new market

Sustainable building, sustainable construction and design are 'constructions durables' (sustainable buildings) or 'constructions HQE' (High Environmental Quality buildings) in the French version. In Europe, the terminology varies from one country to another but all countries show, after about ten years, a huge but recent change in the ways of exchanging, of cooperating, of taking decisions in the briefing, the design and the realisation of construction.

Since 1992, with programmes of encouragement, the creation of standards and regulations (more and more numerous), especially in France and in the Netherlands, a new market area has emerged. This is due to converging results of scientific studies on climatic change, on the reduction of biodiversity, on the effects of different types of chemical pollution etc. The increasing demand for sustainable dwellings could become permanent.

In the international and European context of the 2004–2006 period, our research focused on France, the Netherlands and United Kingdom. These three countries have different building cultures, different state and territorial organisations and very different contracting systems. Each country has a particular path (which seems more or less efficient) regarding the initial purposes for promoting sustainable development of the dwelling and the city.

We will develop a comparison of the dynamics of change and the difficulty of achieving the initial purposes, by presenting successively

- a short history of national regulations and standards and political change in the sustainable construction sector
- guidelines for sustainable construction which create a dynamic for institutional change and renew methods of cooperation
- the advance of sustainability, the constraints on its institutionalisation and the progressive learning of new ways to cooperate and to make decisions.

A SHORT HISTORY OF NATIONAL REGULATIONS AND STANDARDS AND POLITICAL CHANGE IN THE SUSTAINABLE CONSTRUCTION SECTOR

The environmental societal stakes (reduction of greenhouse gas emissions, protection and recycling of resources, urban densification and social mix, demographic evolution of cities) are global. However, the national paths of the building and urban design worlds are different from one country to another. They are closely linked to public opinion, to the organisation of professions (training, contracting systems, systems of practice) and to the territorial and political organisation, as well as to the national economy of the sector, to the new investment dedicated to sustainable development and to the sharing of innovation between states, cities, developers, designers and users.

France

A research and development programme was launched in 1992 by PUCA with researchers and professionals.[3] After the agitation of late 1970s and 1980s around solar energy and the creation of an agency for the management of energy (AFME), the research and development programme of 1992 constituted the first major initiative in the construction area. The socialist Ministry of Housing initiated this programme, the results of which are to be seen in the 1996 methods and tools of environmental quality evaluation and in a code for high environmental quality called 'HQE' which is centred on building (Olive 1999; Rialhe and Nibel 1999).

In 1993, 11 experimental 'green building sites' were launched with the help of PUCA and ADEME.[4] Later 100 REX (Research-Experimentations) called HQE were undertaken for social housing from 1994 to 1998. These operations were not really convincing because the principles of sustainable building were applied in the wrong way.

Then, environmental quality high schools were developed in the area of Paris supported by ARENE and in the northern area supported by the new regional council directed by an ecological elected representative and the CERDD.[5] The concept of 'Eco-lycée' (Eco-high school) was launched and was spread to other regional councils in which there were ecological elected representatives. These projects presented many requirements which were difficult to evaluate a posteriori. The ecological nature of materials and their toxicity were debated.

Some professionals and ecological elected representatives extolled the use of traditional materials such as soil, straw and hemp. A black list of industrial materials with energy costs, and/or known to be toxic, appeared. Then, the industrial firms – gathered in the AIMCC – joined with the High Environmental Quality Association to set up a standardisation of products through AFNOR.[6]

Thus, the commission NF-P-01E, created in 2000, was in charge of defining and codifying the environmental quality of building construction products. At the same time, legislation was very active. From 1992 to 1996, laws were voted on water, landscape, noise, air, the protection of the environment and on sustainable development in urbanism and planning. These laws prepared the ground for local urban sustainable development initiatives. The plan of decentralisation and of local public action was completed with several laws, one attributing urban design competences to urban collectivities (1999), another on solidarity and urban renewal (SRU 2000) and another for neighbourhood democracy (2002).

Finally, a plan for the climate was published in 2000 to satisfy the Kyoto agreements. The National Plan for Sustainable Development (PNDD) was not published until 2002, ten years after the Earth Summit in Rio de Janeiro. This plan concludes the set of institutional reforms and gives the initiatives a stronger local dimension, as the Netherlands has had since 1982. The HQE reasoning and its code – composed of 14 targets structured in 4 areas (see Chapter 9 by Debizet and Symes) – stimulates the world of construction but is often criticised for its lack of strong requirements, in particular regarding energy performance. Otherwise, the 'HQE' reasoning requires the actors to deliberate about the targets to be chosen and to involve the users in questions concerning major targets of environmental quality, comfort and health (Bornarel and Akiki 2003; Hetzel 2003).

Since 1998–2000, a dynamic of innovation has been carried forward by a group of professionals – we call them founders – who have created the HQE association and have registered the trademark 'HQE' in 1996. The HQE reasoning focuses on environment and building and thus is different from the reasoning about sustainable development which takes place in France, today, at the scale of urban design of the commune, the smallest administrative division. Since 2002–2003, the HQE reasoning has been reinforced by the certification of tertiary buildings implemented by two organisms: CERTIVEA (certification organ of the CSTB) and the AFNOR and overseen by the HQE association.[7] In the same period, CERQUAL (certificating organ of QUALITEL, an association for improving the quality of housing) and AFNOR created a certification of environmental quality of housing based on a simplified guideline composed of seven targets and on an audit of the management of the project at each important step of the project (in the same way CERTIVEA has done for certification). The Union for Single-family Housing and AFNOR have also created a certification of HQE for such projects (see Chapter 9 by Debizet and Symes). All these certifications underline the requirement for strong performance, especially performance in energy efficiency. The developers and the communes follow this dynamic of certification. Thus the HQE association, the National Union of Property Developers (SNAL) and ADEME in 2005 began an experimental programme to set up a guideline for sustainable urban design composed of 11 targets, whereas the Association of the Ecological Mayors (éco-maires) and ADEME have launched in the same period an experiment with sustainable development in communes. Simultaneously, ADEME set up an environmental and urban approach (AEU) based on 50 experimental projects (Schmitt and Debergue 2006). This experimentation on a territorial scale is quite new in France, but is a common practice in the building world. Urban design and building experimental programmes are now being developed in the same way as they have been developed in the Netherlands since the mid-1990s. Since the year 2000, a new market is emerging through legislative and normative measures and through a noticeable increase in experimental projects.

The Netherlands

Initiatives on energy efficiency for buildings, on the management of water and on the recycling of waste have been conducted since 1990 through experimental programmes at the scale of buildings and communities.

The social-democratic government has played the parts of instigator and regulator with several actions: since 1972 the concept of an 'ecological way of life' has been set up, in 1980 the urban planning department was created, then in 1993 environmental planning for grouped housing composed of more than 200 dwellings was initiated. In 1989, national plans, concerning energy efficiency, renewable energy, management of natural resources and waste, and the development of welfare, were promulgated. These plans have been followed by several experimental projects and always debated with the enterprises of the building sector, the housing associations and the counties. These plans have been evaluated since 1996. The purpose of the first experimental projects was to show what could be done in terms of sustainable building. Then, rapidly (after 1997), sustainable urban design became a main strategy (spatial proximity, transport, landscape, urban facilities), and the state began to devolve its responsibilities to the counties.

Since 2001, the assessment of national plans has taken an important place. This assessment is quite positive despite gaps having been revealed in the support by professionals, and in the residents not being sufficiently involved in the projects, and in the higher and higher standards of regulations being difficult to implement (Sunnika 2001). The state, the materials producers, and the professionals of the building area together created in 1996 the Dubo Centrum (Centre for Sustainable Building) which completes the institutional organisation system of the building sector: the other components are the SBR (Scientific and Technical Centre for Building), the NOVEM (Agency for Energy and Environment) and the NVOB (National Research and Development Centre for the Building Contractors). The Dubo Centrum was in charge of setting up, disseminating and providing training about the new requirements for sustainability, which are gathered in the guidelines called the NP (Nationaal Pakketen Durzame Bouwen) and accompanied by some recommendations for design. These guidelines are sorted by type of building and are based on the first experimental projects and on negotiation between the professionals of the building sector.

The debates about materials are quite similar in France and in the Netherlands. Due to the emergence of a black and white list of materials, the industrial producers chose to disseminate environmental and health information about materials. Then a standard on environmental and health information on products was created. This standard, called MRPI, is based on the EN 14021 and 14024 published in 1998. The MRPI standard is more concise than the French equivalent standard called P01-010 published in 2004. The MRPI standard allows the certification of materials by registered organisations. In parallel with this standard, a large number of assessment tools have been created, and disseminated to builders and designers.

The housing associations have created guidelines called DUWON quite similar to the French code 'HQE' since their main purpose is to set targets, to manage operations and to evaluate and to monitor performance and the functioning of the building (Sunika 2001).[8] Simultaneously, DUWON intervenes at the first stage in the development of a strategic territorial plan, so making the link between the strategic policy of the housing associations and the application of environmental requirements and recommendations formalised in the NP (Nationaal Packetten).

The requirements of regulations regarding NP have been regularly raised to improve the energy efficiency of buildings and the use of renewable energy.[9] The sustainable development of cities has always been taken into account (densification, recycling of waste, clean transport). The history of being 'a small country captured from the sea' may underly principles of saving resources, of planning, of solidarity and of a consensual way to govern. The academics and the professionals predicted this noticeable evolution of planning, standardisation and regulations. The context of housing demand is clarified by the population figures in Table 8.1. Since 1980, the academic institutions which train engineers and architects have taken into account the environmental and sustainable development approach, wherein professionals have developed a new way of managing projects jointly (see also Chapter 7 by Scheck et al.).[10]

The innovation process is based as much on fundamental requirements for sustainable development as on performance, on criteria for decision-making, on forms of project management and on the content of training. The Dutch world of construction seems to be involved in a virtuous circle of change. About 50 communities and about 100 environmental quality buildings have been completed between 1990 and 1998. Since 1995, VINEX, the fourth national plan for urban planning, was launched with high requirements for sustainability (ADEME/Energie-Cités 2003). However, the

Table 8.1 Population and housing figures

	Netherlands	France	United Kingdom
Population	16 million	64 million	60 million
Density	482 inhab/km^2	113 inhab/km^2	239 inhab/km^2
Number of dwellings	6.75 million	27 million	25.7 million
Social housing stock / total housing stock	35%	21%	21%
Social rental housing stock / total rental housing stock	755	43%	67%

Source: Sunnika and Boon 2002

improvement of requirements in both the new and the existing stock of buildings is being debated, in particular in the context of a neo-liberal government, which emphasises economic topics and promotes immediate benefits for the quality of life and a shorter return on public investment.

The United Kingdom

The neo-liberal policy of the Thatcher government (1979–1990) was distinguished, in the area of housing and cities, by the privatisation of a huge stock of public estates (now owned and managed by private organisations or residents' associations). Between 1990 and 2005 2 million social housing units were sold on the 'Right to Buy' principle. This market emphasis ignored environmental initiatives.

However, in 1990, the Building Research Establishment (BRE, equivalent of the Dutch SBR and the French CSTB: Scientific and Technical Centre for Building) developed a guideline for the environmental and sustainability assessment of buildings (BREEAM).[11] But in the political context of the United Kingdom, BREEAM did not initiate a dynamic in the sector similar to that of HQE in France or of the NP in the Netherlands. After 1991, the privatisation of the BRE implied the commercialisation of BREEAM while the professionals were involved in solving other problems.

At the same time, other 'labels' and other methods for improving construction were published and approved by the government and the professionals. Finally, in this period, BREEAM came in a variety of forms depending on the various types of buildings or construction.[12] With the arrival of the Major government in 1991 and the debates around the Rio Summit, environmental considerations became a current topic. A campaign for regeneration of cities and deprived communities was launched, and a programme of structural reforms of the construction industry was supported by the Latham Report (1994) and lobbying from business. The main objective of this programme was to encourage and improve productivity and the return on investment by the enterprises through the development of groups of public buildings and by the sector working at an international scale and by developing innovative engineering (Winch 2000). This programme, supported later by the Egan Report (1998), did not take into account requirements of environmental quality and sustainable development.

However, national foundations and NGOs (WWF, Greenpeace, Friends of the Earth) have played a major role in disseminating the principles of the Rio Agenda 21, and some architects and consultants have developed private sustainable projects during this period. In the United Kingdom, in opposition with France and the Netherlands, there is no ecology party that can influence the two leading parties, the Conservative and Labour parties. Since 2000, after the election of the Labour government, environmental quality has been linked to quality of life in public policies (Building a Better Quality of Life). A commission for sustainable development was created in 2000, and reinforced in 2006. Public organisations such as Defra (Department for Environment, Food and Rural Affairs), and CABE (the government's adviser on architecture, urban design and public space) are in charge of studies and research on sustainable development and the built environment. Lately, the government and the regional agencies have begun to promote, both financially and legislatively, more sustainable development. New programmes, Acts and regulations have been created: Sustainable communities: building the future (2003), Energy Act (2004), Energy building regulation (2004), Housing: building a sustainable future (2005), Code for sustainable housing (2006) (see also Chapter 9 by Debizet and Symes).

If only a few cities – with the assistance of foundations, architects and consultants – have promoted on the national and international scale environmental experiments such as the BedZED community,[13] these experiments have contributed to making environmental stakes become public stakes, in particular through the media. The movement for 'Sustainable Urban Design' seems to have been initiated.

GUIDELINES FOR SUSTAINABLE CONSTRUCTION WHICH CREATE A DYNAMIC FOR INSTITUTIONAL CHANGE AND RENEW METHODS OF COOPERATION

The creation and utilisation of guidelines for sustainable development in construction structures the collective initiatives of professionals and the management of projects in respect of new requirements, new targets and new methods (Bourdin 2005). This is the case of France and the Netherlands, where the guidelines HQE and NP structure the different stages of projects and the way in which professionals collaborate. These guidelines could be considered as codes that apply across the professions in the world of construction. These guidelines are levers for the organisational and institutional changes that affect professionals.[14] The guidelines have a huge impact in the Netherlands, but rely on the public assessment, public policies, mobilisation of professionals, standardisation and regulations, which are not altogether in line. An irreversible change of institutions has not been yet achieved.

Are we observing a change of paradigm for the design of buildings? Are we shifting from guidelines centred on the building to environmental and decentered guidelines? In a new paradigm, the actors would focus first on environmental factors (natural, urban, economic, social) and then take into account the new requirements (concerning energy, water, air, comfort, climate, transports etc.). Whereas, traditionally, the client and the designers focus first on the financial, aesthetic and functional requirements of the building. This evolution could lead to strong interactions between briefing, design, building and use, to simultaneous innovations in uses, in technologies and sometimes in legislation and policy. We suppose that a process for convergence has been engaged and that this process will be developed in the future especially in the sector of sustainable construction (Ben Mahmoud Jouini and Midler 1996).

The situations are very different for the three different countries we have studied.

The Netherlands

From 1995 to 1998, the Nationale Packetten were created (by the Ministry of Housing, the professions of construction, the industries concerned and representatives of energy and transport sectors) as a way of defining sustainability. A leading consultant has conceptualised sustainability, as shown in Figure 8.1.

In the NP, for each type of building, there are sustainability targets accompanied by both sustainability requirements and/or performances depending on the legislation and by architectural and technical recommendations. Recommendations, for NP Buildings, are related to five main targets: materials, energy, water, indoor environment (comfort) and outdoor environment (nature, landscape, facilities and transport).[15] The recommendations take into account the temporality of the project from pre-briefing to future utilisation, the management of the project and different spatial scales. The NP compensate for the lack of and the heterogeneity of information and knowledge about sustainable construction. The Dubo Centrum disseminates to the public the NP and provides assistance to professionals in their application on projects. The NP are also political and financial tools. Since 1996, in the context of the 'green investment initiative', subsidies have been given to projects which satisfy the NP performance based on the recommendations. In 1998, 61 per cent of social housing planning permissions satisfied NP recommendations; this number should have risen to 80 per cent in 2000, according to the statistics.[16] Quite rapidly, the government, with the professionals, decided to combine the recommendations of the NP with an

Durzaam bouwen has different meanings: robustness, comfort, health of the residents, reliability of the materials, and the integration of the building in its site. Durzaam bouwen is composed of the design quality of the project (longevity) accompanied by social quality (social mix, participatory design, transports), by economic qualities (prosperity, profitability, eco-management) and by global environmental qualities (natural resources, biodiversity, water management, flight against greenhouse effect etc). The representation of Durzaam bouwen is a tetrahedron called the '4P': PROJECT, PROSPERITY, PEOPLE, PLANET (K Duijvestein, 2004).

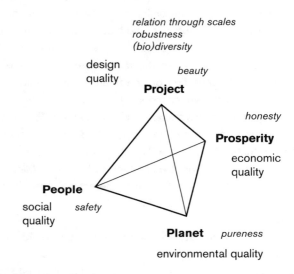

8.1 The Durzaam Bouwen Tetrahedron

Source: K. Duijvestein, personal communication 2004

improvement of legislative performance requirements according to health, security, functionality and energy performance for the whole market for new housing.

As a conclusion, the system of NP has set up a dynamic that goes far beyond the production of buildings. The NP are the hub of knowledge, they set the paths for new competences, they interact with a more collaborative management of construction projects, fix the subsidies and implement the legislation.

From a French point of view, the Dutch have established a large panel of means for implementing a number of actions and these converge on achieving ambitious purposes.

France

The establishment and use of the HQE code is far from contributing directly to sustainable development and to becoming as important in the market as the NP are in the Netherlands. The original division between environmental reasoning on buildings and sustainable development of cities is a French particularity, whereas in the Netherlands sustainable building and sustainable urban design have been linked for ten years. However, recently, convergence between construction, facilities and urbanism has become more important and has led to some experimental projects. Otherwise, construction could be covered only in respect of environmental quality, because the actors, the financing and criteria for decision-making differ from those for facilities and urbanism.

Nowadays in France, the 'Effinergie' guidelines, directly inspired by the Swiss 'Minergie' guidelines, have proved a success with professionals and could bring to the foreground the search for performance. Does the search for high-energy performance mask other objectives such as local employment, local democracy and the search for sustainability at different territorial scales? Indeed, we observed in construction projects both the increasing impact of the developers and town councillors and the deeper involvement of residents and managers. Another tendency is the development of Agenda 21 in territories or housing associations. These Agenda 21 expose several purposes of sustainable development of buildings and cities, they work towards the creation of multi-scale guidelines based on environmental targets (water, energy, air, landscape, transports, etc.) similar to the Dutch reasoning. In this context, building and construction could be managed with guidelines that are different but embedded, or they could be managed together with such guidelines as in the experiment by the SNAL,[17] the association HQE and the ADEME. The HQE was an important action produced by a visionary group of professionals and researchers supported by ministerial and regional politicians, when the government was not interested in sustainable urban development except in respect of transport and waste. The HQE was quickly disseminated within the professionals of the building sector, all the more so since the HQE reasoning is not exclusively concerned with environment. Beyond environment, the HQE has been defined as a quality and management approach (ISO 9000 and 14000), integrating environmental and economic qualities and the quality of life (Olive 1999).

The HQE reasoning also gathers societal interests and individual interests. Thus, for the definition of targets and management, it gathers all the actors of the construction sector, the users and sometimes the local collectivities. Its requiremental code opens debate on the performance to be reached and constitutes a framework for designers and clients and also for the firms to debate, negotiate, validate and share risks when innovating with technical solutions. The HQE reasoning incorporates the principle of post-occupancy evaluation, at least in some of the targets.

The performance of a building is strongly linked to user behaviour. The HQE reasoning (ARENE-IDF 2005) brings these aspects together.

The United Kingdom

The early creation in 1990 of BREEAM guidelines for the concept of sustainable development (environment, economy and society) has produced a tool composed of multiple criteria linked to performance points which depend on chosen solutions. This reasoning was on the model of international reasoning and recommendations of the moment. Contrary to the French context, BREEAM did not emerge from inter-professional debate but was created as a standard assessment tool. The final sum (an addition weighted by criteria points) ends with a qualitative and declarative assessment of the project's quality which can be qualified as: quite good, good or excellent. The assessment is made when the building has been completed; the assessment has no impact on the management of the project or on the relations between professionals. Moreover, in 1990 the BRE was privatised, so its resources have been scattered, which made the BRE commercialise the application of BREEAM when the construction sector was in difficulty. The Labour and Conservative parties were not engaged in sustainable development and environmental quality in the 1990s.

Since 2002–04, the involvement of the government and the regional agencies for development in a policy of sustainable development for housing was reinforced by the Energy Act on energy saving and renewable energies according to the Kyoto agreement. In 2004, a new heating regulation was introduced to reduce consumption (−20 per cent). The Ecohomes code was made mandatory (see Chapter 9 by Debizet and Symes) to improve energy consumption and government plans to increase its construction target from 200,000 to 240,000 new dwellings per year were announced together with a Building Act for 'Sustainable Homes'. It is too early to measure the consequences of this action.

As a conclusion, we observe, at least in France and the Netherlands, the transformation of a method for briefing and design centred on aspects of the building into a methodology focused on urban and global sustainability requirements. The purposes and the process of the project are changing; a change of paradigm is today observable. An organisational and institutional innovation process has commenced. Now, designers focus on diagnosis of the natural, urban and economic environment of the project, and they focus on the search for new solutions: environments which preserve or develop from new requirements concerning energy, water, air, comfort, landscape, climate, transport and so on. This process of change is still at its early stages even if the Dutch approach is the most advanced of those in these three countries (see Chapter 7 by Scheck et al.).

THE ADVANCE OF SUSTAINABILITY, THE CONSTRAINTS ON ITS INSTITUTIONALISATION AND THE PROGRESSIVE LEARNING OF NEW WAYS TO COOPERATE AND TO MAKE DECISIONS

The innovations engendered by the new requirements of sustainability produce unrest within the professions and question the public and professional institutions, their established practices and several criteria of decision-making at all the stages of the construction process. In all processes of change, some actors gain and some actors lose. Profit and loss depend on each particular construction project's context, i.e. the actors, their opinions about the change and about the place of the other actors. Direct links (strong links), indirect links (soft links) and oppositions appear during the projects. Direct links (like locks) are for example legal rules that define a space for negotiations, for autonomy of decision-making between planners, collectivities and residents (present and future). The indirect links often concern implicit choice criteria that are frequently rethought in a sustainability approach. To approach these phenomena we will often refer to the Dutch assessment realised by Van Bueren and Priemus (2002) because the Netherlands is in the vanguard of sustainable development in construction. We will examine the French and British contexts through our observations.

The institutional advances and the institutional constraints

In all the European Member States and in particular in the Netherlands and in France, legislative and regulatory changes have been great since 1992–1994 and very great after 2000–2002. These changes were boosted by European directives – energy efficiency (1993), quality of the products (1998), renewable energy (2001), energy performance of the buildings (2002) – and have sometimes been anticipated by the Netherlands in its national dynamic. France, not so advanced, was characterised by the disruption of public institutions after two periods of decentralisation (1998–2000 and 2002–2004) and by the rise of regions and cities; this context has existed for a long time in the Netherlands and in the United Kingdom.

We are not going to list all the laws, Acts, regulations and standards that surround the professionals. We are going to present some important illustrations for which we are going to describe the point of view of professional institutions.

Regulations

Concerning the regulations, they are not very flexible except when they contradict each other, which often occurs especially concerning the security of people and property. They evolve periodically and are very restricting for architects, engineers and economists. Nethertheless, some professionals go far beyond the regulations by integrating new environmental requirements in an innovative design based on the principle of voluntary action. The performance of basic regulations, according to the HQE code in France and the NP code in the Netherlands, are raised every three or five years and the experimental projects linked to these codes lead the regulations toward stronger requirements. Within this movement and the debate linked to it, a new arbitration should be made between investment and running costs, by anticipating the balance between immediate costs and delayed costs. The process could be slowed down by the professionals who see something to lose or who are unsure of the financial return in the medium term. Today, when professionals and politicians promote, in France, passive buildings (Launch of the 'Effinergie' guidelines in 2006 on the Swiss or Austrian model), most of the people see overcharging and do not see temporary overinvestment. In this context, a carbon audit of projects may help to guide the design decisions better. This is the case in Austria (Vorarlberg) where the finance is more attractive and costs less when the level of energy performance and urban densification increase. In contrast, the British situation does not seem to have this innovative dynamic except in some showcase projects.

Building Acts and contract regulations

Some building Acts and at least some contracting regulations are barriers to innovation and change; they are sometimes visible, sometimes invisible. This is the case in the United Kingdom with the traditional Joint Contracts Tribunal (JCT) contract, and in France, less strongly, with the law of Management of Public Work (MOP),[18] where the traditional contracts do not help or even prevent working together in a large team from the beginning of a project (as is often the case in the Netherlands). The traditional contracts do not facilitate dialogue; they generate drift and frequent additional costs because the architects and the engineers do not properly check innovations. To make contract rules evolve possibly the best way would be to learn from each other and to build efficient cooperation between the client, the design team and the enterprises.

In France, criteria of competence – references in terms of environmental design and management – could be taken into account in architectural competitions and in the way the design team and the enterprises are pre-selected. Regarding the briefing of urban projects which are difficult to set up, 'Study contracts' have been created to build up the brief by comparing and questioning projects by different architect-urbanists. Building the project together to find the best technical solution seems not to disrupt the regulations of professional responsibility. Thus, would it not be better to merge functional briefing and HQE briefing (as is the case in the Netherlands) to produce first a briefing which is not so technical and then co-elaborate the detailed briefing and the design in a larger team with the client, the consultants in sustainability and the design team?

In the United Kingdom, the formal institutional constraints concern the traditional contracting system in which the architect may not cooperate with the enterprise during the design. The Private Financial Initiative (PFI) contracting system allows collaborative design and reasoning in the long term. From experience, uncertainties in the medium and long term do not allow an easy sharing of the risks, thus the negotiations are longer, the design time is reduced and the prices are higher for a facilities quality that is questionable. Moreover, the PFI concerns only big projects for which private competitors are not numerous and have little power in the face of the public 'sleeping partners' (MIQCP 2006). These contracting barriers are all the more so as the projects are performing and innovating in sustainability with new risks which are not controlled and could generate divergences, conflicts and additional costs during the construction stages and during the period of use. In the British contracting system, the design team has to describe, draw and specify all the details, even the ones that are at the interface with the contractor's work, to avoid any complaint from the contractors. To describe, draw and specify all the details is quite impossible when the project is involved in innovation. That the design team has to make these proposals is not desirable because it could be useful to mobilise the knowledge of the enterprises to finalise the detailed design and to achieve the construction. For example, in France the enterprises have kept a strong knowledge-base on which the architects and the engineers could rely, and in the Netherlands the enterprises are often called in during the design of sustainable and innovative projects to give their advice.

Professional institutions

The positioning of the professional institutions in the debate on design evolution, on the role of the new environmental consultants, on the relationships between professionals, could anticipate or constrain changes. We focus on the architectural profession that is, in the three countries, the generalist designer and the leader of the project and is seen as responsible for the project. If the architect is still at the interface of the requirements, he or she could no longer be, as at the beginning of the twentieth century, the 'deus ex machina'. The architect is now one of the important actors in a shared design. In the Netherlands, education in architecture and building engineering are included in a degree course, which is mainly combined. The environmental approach to design was introduced in the universities in 1980. The architectural profession has an important role in collaboration from the beginning of a project, with the client and the engineers. This situation is not a problem, and includes the creation of a new profession: the physics engineer who studies the 'ambience' and comfort, and so deals with acoustics, heating, ventilation, hygrometry, lighting and dimensioning the building envelope. In the context of our research, we could not better the Dutch architectural and engineering professional organisation.

In France, one can wonder if the multiplication of specialised actors and the resulted complexity will be perpetuated? To constitute a new actor for each new function is a French tendency (examples: technical controller, pilot-coordinator, security and health coordinator). This is due to the corporatist 'turn inwards' of traditional professions, which have difficulties in anticipating and training themselves for new knowledge, to take on new competencies.[19] Today, in the context of protection of professional status and especially the legal protection of architects (law on architecture 1977), it is difficult to develop design groups composed of architects, engineers and economists as is the case in the United Kingdom. The regulation of the mission of the design team under the law MOP is a typical institutional structure which constrains or prevents such an evolution. The requirements for sustainability in briefing and design call for competencies and a shared design-process which architects and engineers mainly either do not want to set up or do not know how to set up, even if a few begin to engage in this change. Thus at the demand of clients and of ADEME, three new professions have been created to implement HQE: the client assistant, the environmental consultant (for the design team) and the environmental consultant (for the enterprises). As a result, the actors' games are more complex. A debate on the sustainability of these professions has been launched by 'L'ordre des architectes' and the National Union of French Architects (UNSFA), which feel that they are losing the leadership of sustainable projects. In 1996, the UNSFA and the national 'ordre des architectes' were active members of the association HQE, on the same level as the Institute of the Environmental Consultants for Building (ICEB) which includes client assistants (AMO, HQE) and environmental consultants. The UNSFA and the national 'ordre des architectes' followed the HQE reasoning, but after the first certifications 'HQE reasoning-tertiary buildings' delivered by CSTB and AFNOR in 2005, the national 'ordre des architects' has left the HQE Association. They think that the certifications are technically incorrect, and they claim they are the only designers who have a global approach to the city and the dwelling, who can defend a global approach to sustainable development (social, cultural, economical and environmental) and who are leaders and responsible for a design in touch with the residents and the users. The critique addressed to the HQE Association was that it takes into account only the environmental aspects of sustainable development. The president of the HQE Association answered that certification was only a means of improving, with the help of third parties, the results of HQE projects, that HQE deals also with criteria of qualify of life and with economic criteria and allows the progressive introduction of professionals to sustainable development. In parallel, the UNSFA offered a less severe critique, moderated in tone by the organisation of consultant engineers.

These positions of French professional representatives of the design team are not very favourable to a shared design normalised around HQE reasoning such as the HQE Association and AFNOR promote today. However, the strategies and the interests of professionals are not only led by their membership of a professional group. Some successful projects, collectively led, and with the 'HQE' label, can today be observed (see Chapter 9 by Debizet and Symes and Chapter 10 by Abrial).

In the United Kingdom, professions are strongly institutionalised. The architects, represented by membership of the RIBA, consider themselves as generalists, but they are often considered as specialists in one part of the project. This situation could be accentuated by the development of sustainable construction. In this context, the RIBA has published a report on redefining the profession of architect, suggesting five versions of the profession: regulation controller, client advisor, technical designer and realisation operator, guide for social housing projects, or generalist manager in multi-skilled agencies (RIBA 2005). The debate is open but it is clear that the last version of the profession answers expectations for the design and management of sustainable projects. The reform of the professions could go as far as the creation of an Institute for Construction to which the architects would be affiliated, together with engineers and surveyors (roughly equivalent to economists in France). With the increase of PFI contracts, other professionals, facilities managers for example (see Chapter 12 by Grimshaw), are positioned for the management in the long term and could participate in the management and the design of large sustainable building projects, first in Anglo-Saxon countries and then in continental European countries.

The resonance of informal or underlying institutional rules

Although the research we have conducted gave us only partial information, this information made us formulate a hypothesis that we chose to cross-reference with the evaluation realised in the Netherlands by Van Bueren et al. (2002).

Innovation

Resorting to innovation for answering the new sustainability requirements reinforces the idea of a divergence of opinions or contradiction of opinions between actors. Then the divergence of opinions or contradiction of opinions can lead to a compromise in order to allow the project to be completed. In France and the United Kingdom, these compromises could be observed even in the projects in which the teams did not have good specialised design or management skills. Major efforts had to be made by the clients and their assistants, and a debate, which included simulations and analyses of technically risky solutions, had to be engaged in order for the risks to become shared.

*   The risks concern essentially the achieving of technical performance, but other risks are thrown in: financial risks, risks of lack of quality in the studies or in construction, risks of late modification of the project, risks of unexpected delays

or costs, risks of dissatisfaction by the users. The problems are selected according to actors and according to context, and so a design process of a 'constructivist type' (Martin 2000) and recursive is initiated. This process finds a positive end only after exchange and sharing of the selection criteria for problems and solutions.

• Are the criteria of decision-making fixed in function of their real value (example: carbon criteria and/or financial criteria for the choice of a solution for energy supply) or in function of their value for the actor and so always questionable? Are the criteria debated one by one according to the sustainability and functionality of the building and then classified without ignoring the risks taken by each actor? And when there is refereeing, is it fair with regard to the management of financial pluses and minuses?

In a minority of British and French case studies, we have observed huge tensions between the client and the design team. These tensions have finally been resolved in compromises that satisfy most of the initial sustainability requirements and most of the members of the project team. In both the countries, the driving targets, sometimes in conflict, are the control of energy (which has an impact on the architectural and technical design), the comfort of the users (Summer and Winter comfort) and the economy of the project. The other targets have more limited impacts both in France and in the United Kingdom. However the management of water is very important in the Netherlands.

Financial feasibility criteria, legal criteria of the projects and the organisation of decision-making

The analysis of Van Bueren and Priemus (2002) in the Netherlands sets out the financial and legal criteria and the difficulties of integrating them in the project and optimising interaction between actors. With our reading of their analysis and our observations, we can sketch some generalities.

There is a heart of traditionalism in contractors, who do not see how the sustainability approach can be profitable for them, whereas there is a huge enthusiasm from the designers. Simultaneously, the coordination of the project is often deficient, according to a large number of actors, and there is a lack of motivation.

The choice of a site for the project is dependent on urban planning which does not take enough account of future projects; also the choice of density and type of infrastructure could be better planned.

The urban design process, the legal planning, the land planning and the planning of delivering a planning permission do not take sufficient account of sustainable construction projects. In addition, the designers of buildings, in particular social housing, do not take sufficient account of feasibility studies, of the different motivations of the actors, of the briefing requirements and of plans for realisation.

Paradoxically, the strong decentralisation of public initiatives implies a fragmented process of decision-making, limited views of the stakes and of the targets to reach, so several projects satisfy only the lowest standard or the quality prescribed by regulations.

Within housing associations, there is a different point of view based on the uncertainties concerning reachable performance and the overinvestment which may be associated with them. The differences are all the more so since only a small part of the construction overinvestment can be transferred onto higher rents. So overinvestment is taken on by the funds of the organisation, but on the other hand the running costs are expected to be decreasing.

In the particular case of housing intending for sale, the final user is not sufficiently or not at all implied in the process of decision, the influence of the consumers is still very limited. In general, the property developers make their financial calculations without taking into account the costs in use. The realisation of small operations reinforces this tendency as unit costs increase, especially if innovative materials are used. Van Bueren and Priemus (2002) underline the question of sharing of pluses and the minuses during decisions taken for reasons of self-interest and without taking into account the point of view of the other actors: a recurrent phenomenon of a lack of shared understanding. The unequal distribution of the pluses and the minuses in the discussion and the classification of sustainability targets is a supplementary factor that influences the actors and often leads them to evaluate in an unrealistic manner the costs and the benefits. These estimations are all the more so since the evaluation is made on the prices of the market without taking into account environmental costs.

Finally, even in the Netherlands, the process is still much too fragmented in many stages which have their own rules, their own actors, their own market and so decision-making is both insufficiently shared and decentralised. Decision-making is strongly influenced by professional codes and private targets of profitability.

CONCLUSION

The Dutch, French and English experiences seem to underline perceptions that the principal initiative comes from national and local political power, even if change is being initiated through a silent revolution of professional practice, of ways of managing projects and of decision-making criteria. Otherwise, the place of the professions in the market is governed by political, public financial orientation as well as by civic regulations, initiatives and obligations, which follow from scientific research and the sway of opinion for a more sustainable development.

The protection of the environment has been overtaken by sustainable development. Sustainable development is now a business, in which huge investments have been made (in 2006) at a global scale.[20]

Government policies focus on a more integrated and a better-controlled economic, urban and social development. Thus the Dutch model of sustainable urban design should be generalised, more coherent urban and building studies should be initiated together with new models of interaction. These initiatives, coming from public action, involve several actors and more and more private-public partnerships.

Due to the increase of experimental sustainable projects and sustainability initiatives, the organisations and institutions should be able to capitalise on the results of these projects and initiatives to improve and to build a strong market for sustainable building and urban development.

We suppose that multi-actor organisational learning (Argyris and Schön 1978) is the principal vector of a change process for development, which has begun in all the European Member States.

The taking into account of sustainability targets changes the context of projects. Time scales (from short to long term) and spatial scales (from the community to the planet passing by the city) are considered differently. Research, experimentation and professional practice are not any more strictly separated, all of which is essential for the model of organisational learning. This model is linked to models of the capitalisation of experience and of continuous improvement.

The setting up of the model of organisational learning is difficult because it questions customs, decision-making criteria and everyday professional practices, all of which are centred on the building rather than on the links between the building and its environment and its social uses. The building-and-community design model is transformed by the requirements of these diagnoses. In the everyday and institutional context, this off-centred model could engender creativity but also perpetual tension.

Repeated experiments in sustainable design, the creation of tools (to cooperate during the different stages of the project or to evaluate the building during the project or a posteriori) and individual and collective learning could validate a change of contractual and institutional rules.

The observation of sustainable building projects reveals a strong will for technical and organisational change and a questioning of the actors about the sustainability of their actions.

Agenda 21 is based on the notion of 'thinking modernity' developed by Ulrich Beck (Beck 2001; Vandenberghe 2001) and is a form of thinking about society by itself.

Choices and technical decisions question, in a political way, the risk that industrial capitalist society may destroy itself; as well as the elected politicians, experts, professionals and residents/citizens should be worried about it and take it on.

We suppose that the institutional constraints we have observed during our research will be progressively and continuously questioned, whereas the new guidelines will become essential and will be disseminated. Urban developers and social housing developers are at the 'avant-garde' because they are in a direct relationship and have an account to give to the two key actors in this change: the residents and the local elected politicians. This hypothesis is supported by several research and experimentation projects quoted by Van Bueren et al. (2002). These projects stress the strategic character of multi-actor learning and the development of this learning by proximity networks, by cities and regions. Within these projects, multi-actor learning seems to be the essential component of community renewal and social housing. These authors compared housing associations in France, in the Netherlands and in Germany; they highlighted the same global social and environmental approach, the similarity of social problems and inventoried the conditions of success or failure for multi-actor collective learning. These conditions of success or failure were: new financial means to find or to mobilise private funds, the requirement of competence and sophisticated information and training systems, the complexity of interaction in the relationship and organisational system, the huge length of time for change (at least five years), the tools and management methods are not independent and finally the type of management which could facilitate or constrain the assimilation of new methods. In most of the large projects, the model of management which is developing is composed of a piloting comittee, meetings for planning and validation at different stages of the project, thematic meetings, training in techniques and communication, the development of feasibility studies, risk analysis, strategic plans for the long term and for maintenance. Finally exchanges about experiments are undertaken more often whether within one organisation or between organisations.

NOTES

1   The research we have conducted focuses on the effects of the more and more frequent applications of the sustainable development principles to the construction of buildings in three European countries: United Kingdom, Netherlands and France.

2   Such as laws, decrees (laws of definition of the responsibilities, of the missions, of the relationships, etc.), Acts (urbanism, building, environment, markets, etc.) and regulations (accountancy, tax system, techniques, energy, security).

3   PUCA (Plan Urbanisme Construction Architecture) is a ministerial organ dependent on the Ministry of Urban Planning.

4   AFME became ADEME (Agency for the Environment and for Energy Management) in 1992. In 2006, ADEME was composed of 820 employees among which were 350 engineers. Its budget was about 310 million euros, of which 75 per cent was for spending on research, development and subsidies. ADEME is a French example of the preference to concentrate expertise at the centre and to disseminate it locally after. This preference does not have an equivalent in the United Kingdom where the technical expertise is located at the level of regional agencies and local government. The Netherlands combine both, on the one hand a central expertise and strong national plans and on the other hand local expertise and subsidies of councils and cities.

5   ARENE-IDF is the Ile-de-France Regional Agency of the Environment and New Energies. CERDD is the Nord-Pas-de-Calais Regional Center of resources for sustainable development.

6   The AIMCC is the Association of the Industries of Construction Products. AFNOR is the French Association of Standardisation.

7   CSTB is the Scientific and Technical Centre for Building.

8   DUWON is composed of a management tool (strategic plan set up step by step) around which are decision-making tools. DUWON's precise indicators allow a discussion about requirements at different steps of the project and finally help to define the environmental impacts. DUWON proposes targets but not recommendations. There are three levels of ambition from the highest regarding a long lifetime of facilities to the lowest regarding a short lifetime and a small budget.

9   In 2000, the target EPC (Energy Performance Coefficient) for energy consumption in new buildings was −40% of that in 1996 and −60% of that in 1990. These figures are to be compared with the −25 per cent from 1996 to 2006 in France whereas the production of renewables was multiplied by 10 from 1995 to 2002.

10 They created, in particular, the functioning of the project as a building team.

11 BREEAM is the first assessment method of environmental impacts in housing. It was developed by the Building Research Establishment on economic, social and environmental criteria, on the model of sustainable development as was promoted by the Bruntland Report in 1987.

12 BREEAM Ecopoints = urban scale, BREEAM Ecohomes = housing, BREEAM for offices = offices.

13 BedZED, the Beddington Zero Energy Development, is the UK's largest carbon-neutral eco-community – the first of its kind in the UK. BedZED was developed by the Peabody Trust in partnership with Bill Dunster Architects and BioRegional Development Group, environmental consultants.

14 These guidelines are applied as standards, i.e. on the voluntary action principle. They are efficient only if the professionals advance together and if the guidelines are in line with the legislation.

15   There are different 'packetten' for buildings: housing, offices, industrial buildings, educational buildings (the 'packetten' are different for new buildings or rehabilitation) and also for planning projects and for civil engineering projects.

16   The results were not so good because the subsidies from the government have paid for the overinvestment whereas the buildings did not always reach the performances and the housing association did not think in terms of global cost. The government is now stressing the role of municipalities and residents to set up their own projects (Van Bueren and Priemus 2002).

17   SNAL = Syndicat National des Aménageurs Lotisseurs (National Union of Housing Developers).

18   The law of Management of Public Works defines the contractual relationship between the public procurement management and project management. It defines the role of the architect in the execution of a project from the initial sketch stage right through to the handing over of the keys. Gradually this law has been twisted, and the actual stages of design and site management have ended up in the hands of engineers and technical consultants, leaving the architect as the artist of the facades.

19   In France, the academic faculty system is based on the distinction between architects, engineers, economists and so on in contrast to the countries of northern Europe.

20   According to studies led by PNNUE (National Program of the United Nations for the Environment), the investment of the industrials in sustainable development is about $100 billion (Newspaper *Le monde*, 13 July 2007).

REFERENCES

ADEME/Energie-Cités (2003) *Mesure des performances énergétiques des collectivités (EPL) aux Pays Bas*. Rapport d'étude. Paris: ADEME.

ARENE-IDF (2005) *Les Compétences de la HQE*. Paris.

Argyris, C. and Schön, D.A. (1978) *Organizational Learning: A Theory of Action Perspective*. Reading, MA: Addison-Wesley.

Beck, U. (2001) *La Société du risque: Sur la voie d'une autre modernité*. Paris: Champs Flammarion.

Ben Mahmoud Jouini, S. and Midler, C. (eds) (1996) *L'ingénierie courante dans le Bâtiment*. Paris: PUCA.

Bornarel, A. and Akiki, E. (2003) *Qualité environnementale des bâtiments: Manuel à l'usage de la maîtrise d'ouvrage et des acteurs du bâtiment*. Paris: ADEME.

Bourdin, A. (2005) Dynamiques de la maîtrise d'ouvrage urbaine et mutations du contexte local. In J. Frébault (ed.) La Maîtrise d'ouvrage urbaine. Paris: Le Moniteur.

Gili, R. and Courdurier, E. (2000) *Le Retour du politique dans la maîtrise d'ouvrage*. Paris: PUCA.

Godard, O. (1994) Le développement durable: Paysage intellectuel. *Natures, Sciences, Sociétés* 4(2): 309–322.

Hetzel, J. (2003) *Haute Qualité Environnementale du cadre bâti*. Paris: AFNOR.

Klijn, E.H. and Koppenjan, J.F.M. (2000) Public management and policy networks. *International Journal of Research and Theory* 2(2): 135–158.

March, J.G. and Olsen, J.P. (1984) The new institutionalism: Organizational factors in political life. *American Political Science Review* 78(3): 734–749.

Martin, C. (2000) *Maîtrise d'ouvrage et maîtrise d'œuvre: Construire un vrai dialogue*. Toulouse: Octares.

MIQCP and Centre de Recherche sur l'Habitat (2006) *Evolution de la politique PFI concernant les bâtiments publics en Grande Bretagne*. Paris.

Olive, G. (1999) *ATEQUE: 5 ans de travaux (1993–1998): Aide au développement d'outils d'amélioration de la qualité environnementale des bâtiments*. Paris.

RIBA (2005) *Constructive Change: A Strategic Industry into the Future of the Architects' Profession*. London: RIBA.

Rialhe, A. and Nibel, S. (1999) *Quatre outils français d'analyse de la qualité environnementale des bâtiments*. Paris: PUCA.

Schmitt, P. and Debergue, S. (eds) (2006) *Réussir un projet d'urbanisme durable: Méthodes en 100 fiches pour une approche environnementale de l'urbanisme AEU*. Paris: Le Moniteur.

Sunnika, M. (2001) *Policies and Regulations for Sustainable Building: A Comparative Study of Five European Countries*. Delft: DUP Science Delft University Press.

Sunikka, M. and Boon, C. (2002) *Housing Associations and Sustainable Management: Environmental Efforts in the Netherlands' Social Housing Sector*. Delft: DUP Science Delft University Press.

Van Bueren, E. and Priemus, H. (2002) Institutional barriers to sustainable construction. *Environment and Planning B: Planning and Design* 29: 75–86.

Van Bueren, E., Bougrain, F. and Knorr-Siedow, T. (2002) Sustainable rehabilitation in Europe: From simple toolbox to multilateral learning. In M. De Jong, K. Lalenis and V.D. Mamadouh (eds) *The Theory and the Practice of Institutional Transplantation*. GeoJournal Series. Dordrecht: Kluwer Academic.

Vandenberghe, F. (2001) Introduction à la sociologie cosmopolitique du risque d'Ulrich Beck. *Recherches* 1(17): pp. 25–39.

Winch, G. (2000) *The Contracting System in British Construction: The Rigidities of Flexibility*. Rapport d'étude, Groupe de Bagnolet. Paris: PUCA.

9

Expertise and Methodology in Building Design for Sustainable Development
A Franco-British Comparison
Gilles Debizet and Martin Symes

Sustainability introduces new goals in building design and requires new skills and project management methods. These include environmental assessment methods, the choice and use of which often has a marked impact on the outcome. Comparing the use in practice of the French evaluation system HQE and that most often used in Britain, BREEAM, permits the identification of shared trends in these two countries but also suggests that one of the reasons for a variety of outcomes lies in the structure of these assessment methods. To some extent, these depend, too, on national traditions of development, and of governance.

After a description of the differences in context, the chapter reports case studies of a number of construction projects in France and in the south-west of Great Britain. The cases illustrate the impact of introducing Environmental Evaluation methods while taking account of the fact that bringing Sustainable Development into play differs between the two countries. The two groups of cases, taken together, suggest that the initial goals of a development team cannot be maintained throughout a project without compromises to meet the needs of local communities and politicians. In addition, they suggest that the new roles to be played by the various professions are especially problematic for architects and engineers. To some extent the outcomes differ from country to country because of the different frameworks of professional responsibility.

USUAL STRUCTURE OF BUILDING DESIGN SERVICES

Building design requires attention to qualities of use and the ability to maintain them against foreseen and unforeseen turns of events. Design also takes into account the financial limits and the balance between investment and working costs. Design mobilises many types of knowledge (architecture, mechanics, energy, chemistry, hydraulics, economy, law, project management and so on); these organise the professions of building design in each country. Of course, relationships between the professionals vary according to the project. But design activities and specific professional contributions seem to be also circumscribed by usual national arrangements.[1] We will first focus on differences according to the country.

A simple arrangement in France with a sequential process

French history has left its mark on the building sector. Political centralisation created both a powerful group of state engineers and a prominence of creativity and art in architectal education. Some laws precisely define the roles as between developers and designers, and between architects and engineers. According to law, developers are presumed *non sachant* (unknowing), which means that they are supposed to ignore technical rules and the art of building. However, in the case of state or community paid buildings, developers (public authority or agency) must define their needs in a briefing session before choosing the design teams in competition. For example, the type of heating system is defined by the briefing. The briefing stage should be very scrupulous because a change of requirements by the developer during the design phase could cause contract annulment. The contracts between private developers and design teams are more flexible; the partner can negotiate most of the items. However, both practice and jurisprudence distinguish the responsibility for definition of needs (briefing to be done by the client) from that for design.

Apart from small buildings like a house, design teams contain at least an architect, a structural engineer and often a thermal and electrical engineer. These professionals working on the same project usually belong to different companies. According to the building size, developers have to introduce other kinds of professionals: structural and fire controllers, a quantity surveyor and later, a working site planner and a working site safety controller. Large office and commercial buildings usually require other specialists, for instance a computer system network engineer, a lighting engineer, an aerialist engineer, a fire system designer.

Regulated by rules, these professions are structured in small and specialised firms. Architects actually first create the form and the structure of a building on their own. After developer confirmation, the structural engineer checks the forecast structure and eventually modifies the size of wall, beam or floor. After approval of the detailed plan by the developer, the thermal engineer assesses heating and air conditioning load and defines most of the elements of the system. Then, the design team members set up the writing and the drawing of the technical prescriptions for builders; so they also set up the responsibility of the future building performance according to the specification writing. Technical specifications are inspired by public standards that in fact organise the division of work between many building trades such as bricklayers, carpenters, plumbers, joiners and so on.

Regulations and jurisprudence are based on (and also organise) a traditional division of activities between the client and the design team members. Even for private projects, contracts and jurisprudence are largely inspired by public project regulations. So briefing and design respect usually the same sequential process as they have for many years. The profitability of design firms, converges with this routine process. Architects invest much effort in the outline form and the facade and less in frameworks (or thermal behaviour). Then, engineers precisely design framework (or thermal system) and guarantee performances. However, building design is regularly confronted with new aims, which require more cooperation between architect and engineer. Environmental quality and thermal performance requirements could dominate the building design process in the coming years.

A variety of arrangements in the UK

History has also left its mark on the British building industry, but so has the legal system, which is not based on Roman law but on cases (precedents determining the likely outcome of any dispute) and provides for considerable flexibility in practice. Some would say this allows rapid response to changes in the market for construction services.

UK architects train by taking the examinations of the RIBA (granted a Royal Charter in 1837), or by obtaining exemption at a recognised School of Architecture, and are then qualified under the Architects Directive of the EU. This permits them to use the title architect, and requires them to conduct themselves in a professional manner and to carry insurance against professional liabilities. However, the function of architectural design is not protected by law (as it is in France) and it is not uncommon for engineers (such as Arup) to lead a design team. The argument that architects' standing should depend on their creativity, and that professionals should have the freedom to practise however they think best, is still taken seriously.

During the 1980s, the period of 'Thatcherism', government initiated a reappraisal of the privileges accorded to many of the established professions. Architects lost the ability to prescribe their fees, and official studies of procurement methods in construction (see Chapter 8 by Henry and Paris) recommended the use of various new types of contract, partly in the hope of reducing the uncertainty which was associated with innovation in architectural design. These are often administered by specialist project managers (usually surveyors). So architects now see themselves as generalists and leaders in building design, but often are treated as if they were only specialists contributing to the definition of construction projects. Whether design for sustainable development is a general requirement of architects or the preserve of specialists, is thus an issue of major interest for the professions and the UK cases in this chapter will throw some light on current practice.

The standard form of contract for construction projects (JCT) treats the architect as being appointed by the developer (building owner) and acting on the developer's behalf during the design phases, up to and including the specification of details and the obtaining of tenders (costs), this last activity normally being competitive (Willis 1981). During this period, the architect will recommend the developer appoint consultant engineers and surveyors to work with the architect (if the architect's firm does not already employ its own in a multidisciplinary team) under the architect's instructions, so an integrated design can be proposed at all stages. After tenders have been received, the developer appoints a construction firm and the architect's team changes role. At this point the team members become administrators of the contract and should deal fairly with complaints (for example about lateness of information) whether received from the builder or the developer. This system is thought to work well for medium-sized projects, but to be unsuitable for very small buildings (where it is better for developers to act as their own builder, employing trades people as direct subcontractors). On very large construction contracts, use of the traditional system has been thought to lead to the contract administrator receiving enormous numbers of complaints (requests for variations) and then to immensely long legal procedures, after construction has been completed, being needed to resolve the final account (the total cost). This situation led both to client dissatisfaction with the process and to 'offers' by other professions to take over the architects' role (they may have little skill in this area and have to pay high fees for insurance cover). Hence the growth of management contracts mentioned above.

Management contracts come in two broad types: in the first, a construction firm takes on the project management role after a preferred tender has been accepted, and thus cuts the architect out of his or her contract administration role during the construction period, and in the assessment of final cost. In the second type, the construction firm is appointed (competitively if thought appropriate) at the same time as the design team and works alongside it from the beginning, being therefore implicated in all decisions made at this time. A variation on this method is known as Design Build, in which the construction firm employs the architects and other design team members, offering a one-stop service to the developer. Sometimes the latter will also employ a surveyor to monitor cost implications of decisions as they are made, thus overseeing both contractor and by implication, architects in their employ. A further innovation has been the development of 'partnering' in which all members of the design team share some of the financial risk.

The most recent innovation in construction procurement in the UK is the Private Finance Initiative (MIQCP 2006), a new methodology for designing, building and operating buildings in the public sector. In these contracts, the builder (not the developer) raises the finance required and then owns the building for an initial period of its operation, leasing it to the user organisation until the time comes for ownership to be transferred back to the developer (in fact a government department set up specially to act as its property arm). In principle, PFI and associated types of contract should make the achievement of sustainable development easier, as all relevant factors can be taken into account, and the long-term time scale is explicitly included. However, PFI has been criticised for giving too much weight to purely financial constraints. One of the UK case studies in this chapter is based on a PFI project.

NEW ENVIRONMENTAL ASSESSMENT METHODS IN FRANCE AND THE UK

Since the 1990s, some environmental assessment methods have been developed in France and the UK. In each country, one 'movement' has given rise to new frames of reference (see Chapter 8 by Henry and Paris). In France, the Haute Qualité Environnementale (HQE) Association put forward a single new approach to building briefing and design (see Chapter 8). In the UK the Building Research Establishment (BRE) developed an approach to environmental assessment methods; various versions have been created for use in different circumstances.[2]

France: HQE®

HQE® is a registered trademark that can be used by developers to qualify a building, particularly the approach of briefing, designing and working. Currently, three types of building can be certified as an HQE project: offices or schools, housing blocks, and single houses. In addition, the HQE approach inspires much project management for other building types. Most of this is neither assessed nor certified.

An approach defined originally by environmental requirements and a management system

The HQE approach had been originally defined by two guidelines in 2001. The DEQE (Définition Explicite de la Qualité Environnementale) proposed roughly 150 architectural and technical prescriptions or requirements, which could be assessed.[3] These requirements were grouped into 14 targets, here in four main types:

- relationship between building and immediate environment, choices of construction process and materials, low nuisance construction site
- energy management, water management, waste management, repair and maintenance management
- hydrothermal comfort, acoustic comfort, visual comfort, olfactory comfort
- sanitary conditions of indoor spaces, air sanitary quality, water sanitary quality.

The SME (Système de Management Environnemental) was based on ISO 14000 standard.[4] It described when, how and what kind of performances should be checked at the different stages of the construction process.

Current certifications

Based on these two texts, the HQE Association and CSTB (Centre Scientifique et Technique du Bâtiment) worked with AFNOR to built up certifications.[5] Two are currently used in France.

'NF bâtiments tertiaires – démarche HQE' certificates offices and schools. This certification has been tested in 2004. The protocol settles on many requirements grouped into 14 targets. Requirements concern mostly performances rather than technical solutions. Evaluation defines a level of satisfaction by target. At least 3 targets should be assessed very efficient, 4 should be efficient and the other 7 could be standard. First the developer chooses the satisfaction level of targets. The building project is assessed at three stages: end of briefing (briefing), just before building work contracting (design) and delivery. Usually the assessor (licensed by the certification organisation: see Chapter 8) converses with the developer and design team during the project process. In May 2007, 7 buildings were definitely certified, 31 succeeded at the design stage and 33 the briefing stage;[6] most of them are situated in the Greater Paris area and started by private real estate companies. Certification including assessment costs 12,000 euro (less than 1,500 square metres) to 40,000 euro (over 45,000 square metres). Because of its high cost, this certification does not actually interest small office buildings. The penetration of certification is low, even if we consider only large office building projects in France.

'NF maison individuelle – démarche HQE' certificates a contractor and then the houses, which satisfy the protocol. Contractor agreement is inspired by ISO 9001 standard. After agreement, the contractor is allowed to use the brand and offer clients an HQE house. A part of 175 requirements deal with the means to brief (e.g. site investigation), design (e.g. checking methods) and delivery (e.g. instructions for use). Most of the other requirements are performances or technical prescriptions and gain credits. Hundreds of credits could actually be allocated but 30 suffice to satisfy certification. Roughly one hundred contractors are allowed to offer HQE houses in France. They register an HQE house project to a certification organisation and send some information during the construction process, one house in five is actually assessed on the spot. This certificate is not very particular about environmental quality, it is firstly about quality management. It is useful to improve the transparency in the relationship between client and contractor: national regulations aimed at satisfaction with new individual homes should be at least important progress especially about energy efficiency and environmental quality.

The HQE approach has an important influence over local authorities and consequently real estate companies and developers. The keen interest by local authorities and housing companies is not reflected by the low number of certificated buildings. In February 2005, the HQE Association listed six hundred projects announced by their developers (Association HQE 2005). However, a large majority of them did not enter in a certification process.

CERQUAL, a building quality certification organisation, offer a new label. 'Habitat et Environnement' inspired by the DEQE documents (cf. above); it describes checking and calculation methods but the requirements are less numerous and not grouped into 14 targets, energy management takes over from other HQE items. The protocol does not combine an environmental management system. The certification process is much easier. This certificate is well received by housing trusts and home real estate especially in the west part of France and the Paris area.[7] Even if it is in a minority among new housing, it could be considered as a main development for this traditional activity. Note that as CSTB and HQE Associations prepare a new certification ('NF bâtiment d'habitation – démarche HQE'), other certification organisations could be in competition with CERQUAL for licensing housing: this type of building is the main building construction sector.

Development of the methodology

We identify two new protocols which could be very influential in the coming years. The HQE Association prepares a protocol for developments: it answers an HQE controversy about the difficulty to improve environmental quality if the project is limited to the building. Conversely, a new label will soon be created by the main building economic stakeholders to promote only energy efficiency. 'Effinergie' will look like Minergie and Passivhaus.[8] Straightforwardness and low cost of certification will be its strong points compared to the HQE approach.

The UK: BREEAM

Sunnika (2001: 69) summarises the UK approach to managing sustainable construction as follows: 'The government has invested considerable effort in promoting sustainable building measures, but the level of ambition is not very high and implementation is mainly voluntary'. She concludes that there are no economic measures and no relationship with social aspects, although our analysis suggests that there are few such characteristics rather than none at all. As reported by Henry and Paris in Chapter 8, the British National Strategy for Sustainable Construction has two main components: regulatory (modification of the Building Regulations and other laws) and advisory (the issuing of a variety of Guidelines, including BREEAM). A Land Fill Tax was introduced in 1996 but fiscal approaches are not generally favoured, except in respect of social housing. In addition, mandatory codes are in the process of introduction for rating the performance of all new housing .

Topics, links with design process, certification

Sunnika's review of the controls aimed at sustainable construction summarises the regulatory component as having four main branches: measures for the control of pollution (Environmental Protection Act 1990), for water conservation (although the Water Resource Law 1991 deals only with ground water protection, not the use of water), for the use of materials and the management of waste (this being a voluntary standard: BS 7543) and for energy saving. The Environment Act 1995 established an Environment Agency and a Sustainable Environment Protection Agency and was accompanied by a Home Energy Conservation Act requiring local authorities to plan for an improvement in the levels of carbon dioxide and other emissions.

The structure of the main Building Regulations (Act of 1984) illustrates the flexibility of the British approach to legislation. They are divided into a number of parts, of which Part L, dealing with the conversion of fuel and power, concentrating on methods of saving energy and providing a number of methods for calculating these savings, has been updated a number of times. The most recent addition is the Energy Performance of Buildings Regulation of 2007.

It is noticeable that the guidelines for housing have been introduced separately from those for other building types. This is partly because the housing construction industry operates as a separate sub-industry from that concerned with the majority of commercial and public buildings, and partly because the housing industry has a diversity of other control systems in place. Public (or social) housing is financed by the Housing Corporation, which uses its own Housing Quality Indicators and has implemented ISO 14001, but until recently has considered sustainability to be a community issue, not a technical one, and relied on bringing its influence to bear on Local Agenda 21 processes. Private housing is by and large left to 'the market' which varies considerably from one part of the country to another. The Building Research Establishment (BRE) produced a voluntary environmental assessment method called EcoHomes (its use being a main topic of one of our case studies) and has encouraged the use of the Green Guide Specification for Homes to promote the choice of green materials.

At the time of writing, this situation has changed (see RIBA 2006). The present UK government seems to be moving towards a policy of regulating performance. EcoHomes has been adapted to create a Code for Sustainable Homes to be applied to new homes voluntarily in England from April 2007. The plan is for the Code to become mandatory for new homes from April 2008. However, a distinction is drawn between the different housing sectors. Private developments will have mandatory assessment only to begin with, but social housing will have to meet a certain standard (known as Level 3) for water consumption and carbon emissions immediately, the Housing Corporation applying this to the next public funding round. Other aspects of the Code (building materials, surface water run-off, pollution, health, ecology and management) are to be rated but specific performances not required provided that the correct overall score is met. The energy component of the new standard will become the level for revised Building Regulations two years later, applicable to all new housing, but the government maintains that for private sector sales or leasing there will be no new financial implications, an Energy Performance Certification system, with similar standards, having already been announced for June 2008. The plan is for energy standards to be gradually raised over the next few years, reaching zero carbon-emissions for new housing by 2016. A consultation document on the introduction of water efficiency in new homes (as well as in commercial buildings) has also been released. Interestingly for the theme of this book, for the housing sector improvements, a network of licensed assessors will need to be established to provide Code certification.

The principal Guideline considered in the remainder of the UK case studies is that introduced by the BRE in 1990: BREEAM (BRE Environmental Assessment Method). At the time the BRE was a government agency, but it has since been privatised and is now a trading subsidiary of a research charity called the BRE Trust. BRE trains, examines and licenses organisations and individuals to become qualified Assessors under the BREEAM Schemes. Assessors pay for training and licensing and clients pay assessors for the assessment service. BRE is the independent certifying body accredited by UKAS (United Kingdom Accreditation Service), which provides the examination of assessors and the quality assurance and certification of BREEAM assessments.

BREEAM proposes various simple measures, with each positive measure gaining 'credits' which, following a weighting procedure, count towards the overall score. Overall judgements are provided using the terminology Pass, Good, Very good, and Excellent. BREEAM is not officially certified in way that HQE is in France, but there are firms who act as assessors, under licence from BRE. Some of these are architects seeking a new line of business. The case studies in this chapter show how flexible the application of BREEAM has become.

Development of the methodology

Versions are updated regularly (they are intended to have a ratchet relationship with increasingly demanding Building Regulations) and different versions have been created since its launch to assess various building types.

These versions essentially look at the same broad range of environmental impacts:

- *management*: overall management policy, commissioning site management and procedural issues
- *energy use*: operational energy and carbon dioxide issues
- *health and well-being*: indoor and external issues affecting health and well-being
- *pollution*: air and water pollution issues
- *transport*: transport-related carbon dioxide and location-related factors
- *land use*: greenfield and brownfield sites
- *ecology*: ecological value conservation and enhancement of the site
- *materials*: environmental implication of building materials, including life-cycle impacts
- *water*: consumption and water efficiency.

Credits are awarded in each area according to performance. A set of environmental weightings then enables the credits to be added together to produce a single overall score. The building is then rated on a scale of Pass, Good, Very good or Excellent.

BREEAM exists currently (May 2007) for nine building categories: Schools, Retail, Offices, Prisons, Multi-residential (e.g. elderly people's homes, hostels or student residences), Industrial units, New homes, Existing homes and Courts. Requirements depend on category. Any building type that is not covered by a standard BREEAM version can be assessed under a special system called BREEAM Bespoke. BREEAM can now be used to assess any building type anywhere in the world using the Bespoke system.

As shown below the numbers of assessments made varies from fifty to many hundreds. No doubt, this is partly a result of different volumes of building in each sector.

Different assessments can be carried out according to building categories. The main types are:

- *Design and procurement*: at the design stage for new build or refurbishment projects.
- *Post-construction*: first assessment or second one to ensure that BREEAM issues specified are implemented according to design and procurement assessment.
- *Management and operation*: while building is operational assessment considers policies and procedures in addition to existing building and fabric layout.

In the case of new buildings, the developer pre-assesses credits score and requests usually a licensed BREEAM assessor during the design stage. BREEAM Office checks assessor assessment before delivering building certification to the developer and adds details of developments to the BREEAM Database (unfortunately not available for public inspection).

Outside standard BREEAM categories the developer requests an assessor first to develop a bespoke method in accordance with a BREEAM consultant and second to assess the design or the construction. Bespoke BREEAM experiences help to develop new standards.[9]

Many government offices, local authorities and housing corporations request Very good or Excellent rating for their own development or on the land they have sold. So a wide majority of offices or industrial unit assessments satisfy these ratings. BREEAM has spread widely in the United Kingdom since 2000 as the statistics in Table 9.1 show.

Bartlett (2005) argues that 'for sustainability to be successfully taken into account . . . there must be a client-driven agenda . . . a means of measurement and the use of tools'. An illustration of the significance of this proposition (and the difficulty of achieving it) is given by government procurement experience. In 2002, the government body concerned introduced a requirement for the achievement of an Excellent rating by all newly procured buildings in the government estate. However, it would appear that only a minority have been offered for assessment and few could

Table 9.1 BREEAM Assessments

Certified assessments

UK / No. of assessments	Offices	Industrial units	Ecohomes (projects)	Ecohomes (units)
2000	50	11	1	1
2001	66	2	9	319
2002	97	26	32	1018
2003	84	20	94	2842
2004	94	29	549	13583
2005	100	50	1152	24186
2006	132	55	1224	29444
Very good or Excellent	83%	74%	23%	25%

Registered assessments (including not yet certified projects)

UK / No. of assessments	Offices	Industrial units	Ecohomes (projects)
Since 2000	1091	249	9736

Source: Unpublished statistics provided by BRE Global Ltd. October 2007.

satisfy the rating specified. Some of our UK case studies discussed below show factors leading to success and failure in this respect.

To support the use of BREEAM, the BRE has developed BRE Environmental Profiles (based on information regarding Life Cycle Analysis (LCA) and with Ecopoints giving a reference on materials and components which may be used), ENVEST (a design tool, also using LCA). These combine guidelines and checklists. The case studies will show that BRE has been flexible (and opportunistic?) in collaborating with the major public agencies responsible for building procurement to develop versions of their guidelines to suit the needs of these agencies.

HQE and BREEAM: main summary of the comparison

When designers, developers and their clients (if they are represented) discuss environmental performance, the environmental assessment methods are, in both countries, often considered to be a new standard language. According to their instigators (Association HQE 2005; Birtles 1997) this is an important reason for judging these two methods to have been successful.

BREEAM is currently more widespread than HQE. It started earlier, and it gives a score while HQE gives yes-or-no. Requirements are usually less numerous. It assesses the result of design and construction and not the process as does the HQE approach. Both have been applied to different building categories. Both BREEAM and HQE consider the main environmental items impacted by building. They both care about global, local and indoor quality.

TEN CASE STUDIES OF THE IMPACT ON THE DESIGN PROFESSIONS

To understand how the needs for considering sustainability and for the use of environmental assessment methods modify the roles of developers and design team members, we have observed the course of a number of building projects (see Table 9.2). Studies were made of the promotional and institutional documents defining each project or its developer, together with a selection of working documents produced and used by the project team members. Main project team members, including those directly concerned with the environmental aspects, were interviewed.

We singled out projects with respect to these criteria:

* a size sufficient to justify the resort to a specialist in environmental management
* a project in which the environmental ambitions were reasonable from an economic point of view and so repeatable in other projects
* a project progress sufficient to be sure that building design would be definitive.

Table 9.2 Case studies in France and the UK

Building project	Locality	Type of Contract or contracting	Cost M€	Purpose	Dates (Design to Delivery)
Résidence OPAC38	Bourgoin-Jallieu Rhône-Alpes	Public contract after Architectural Outline competition	5	Housing	2002–2003
Hôtel de Ville (City Hall)	Echirolles Rhône-Alpes	Public contract after Architectural Outline competition	15	Public office	2002–2006
Halle des sports	Voiron Rhône-Alpes	Public contract after Architectural Outline competition	5.3	Sport hall	2003–2006
Hôtel de Ville (City Hall)	Les Mureaux Ile-de-France	Public contract after Feasibility Studies competition	7.5	Public office	2002–2005
INEED	Alixan Rhône-Alpes	Public contract after Architectural Outline competition	6.3	Office	2003–2006
Building 270 EMGP	Aubervilliers Ile-de-France	Design private contract (negotiated)	14	Office	2003–2005
Ecohomes	Langport	Traditional	3.8	Housing	2003–2005
Architecture Studios	Bristol	Design and Build	4.3	Higher Education	2000–2002
NHS Trust	Swindon	Private Finance Initiative	200	Hospital	1999–2003
Whitehall Place	London	PFI/JCT	43.7	Office	2001–2005

Source: Based on Henry et al. 2006; see also Acknowledgements (pp. xix and 227).

For each operation, we intended to interview at least four professionals: developers or project manager, architect, thermal engineer and, where applicable, environmental manager. Research resources allocated by the 'sleeping partner' (PUCA) allowed us roughly fifty interviews. Finally, we chose ten projects: four in the UK and six in France. In each country, we avoided projects where the phase of design had not ended. During the investigation period, some buildings were finished while others were under construction. We tried to select both public and private projects in spite of a relatively small number of private ones.

Six case studies in France

All the French case studies involved an HQE approach; however these projects began before the certification existed. Three had been assessed by HQE certified assessors (actually during design stage). Two of them were finally certified (Les Mureaux City Hall and 'Building 270' EMGP Company), they were the first five 'NF bâtiments tertiaires – démarche HQE' certified buildings. So, these cases could be considered as in an experimental process.

Description of the cases

Located in Bourgoin-Jallieu (24,000 inhabitants, 40 km from Lyon), this five-floor Residence OPAC38 contains sixty flats. L'OPAC38 is a housing company depending on the Isère District (Conseil Général de l'Isère, France); this public company was several times distinguished for innovation in renewable energy use. The client chose ADRET Consultancy as AMO-HQE from the beginning; they adopted the HQE approach.[10] They focused attention on:

- materials (e.g. brique monomur, doors and windows in wood)
- energy management (solar sanitary water, PV, reinforced insulation etc.)
- water management, thermal comfort (wide wall inertia)
- low nuisance construction (noise, waste management).

This project began before certification appeared. Brickwall was the main difficulty during design and, above all, during construction; the masonry contractor spent much more time than forecasted. Neither architect nor contractor had any experience with this material.

Located in Grenoble suburb, the Hotel de Ville in the new centre of Echirolles city (35,000 inhabitants) was created around the new tramway line (since 1987). The new City Hall groups the municipality council and the headquarters (200 persons, 6,000 square metres). Two three-floor office buildings are linked by an atrium. The deputy mayor in charge of environment persuaded the city council to adopt an HQE approach. The programmiste (who writes the briefing for the client) and AMO-HQE had been chosen together. An architectural outline competition was based on both functional and environmental briefs that defined environmental priorities. High performing targets were:

- relationship between building and immediate environment
- low nuisance construction site (site waste management mainly)
- energy management (new underground air cooling/preheating, cooling by groundwater, heating by city rubbish incineration etc.)

- repair and maintenance management (footbridges in front of the facades, easy access to piping and wiring, easy to remove partition, revetment resistancy etc.)
- hydrothermal and visual comfort (no windows on west and east faces, mobile and semi-automatic sunshade on south face and over the atrium, individual modulation of temperature, thermal inertia by concrete floor etc.).

The main controversy inside the project team (client representatives and designers) concerned the air conditioning. During the competition, designers announced a heat pump. However at design stage, the client refused an 'electrical solution' and preferred to use the city heating network (produced from rubbish incineration) in winter and a direct cooling by groundwater in summer. Designers considered that groundwater cooling could not satisfy the required internal summer temperature: the thermal engineer strongly opposed this nature-dependent system (which depends on groundwater flow and temperature) and the conseiller environnement (see p. 215) carefully studied thermodynamic building behaviour. Finally, the client agreed to ease temperature requirements: ten days a year the internal temperature could be over 28°C and the heat pump was not installed.

Briefing and design stages were successfully assessed by HQE assessors; however, the city of Echirolles refused to pay for the certificate, so the third stage (delivery) was not assessed and the building is not HQE-certified.

The Région Rhône-Alpes included a sports hall when restoring the Lycée Ferdinand Buisson during the period 2003–2011 after long discussions and studies that began in 1996. Located inside the nineteenth-century school park, the hall was destroyed and rebuilt by the Communauté d'Agglomération du Pays Voironnais (CAPV).[11] One large exhibition hall, three training rooms and some technical and office rooms have to be used by pupils and the many sport clubs located in Voiron. The programmiste, who had already worked for CAPV in 1996, proposed an HQE approach for this project in 2002, so he was also the AMO-HQE of this project. According to the brief, the high performing targets were:

- relationship between building and immediate environment (to balance parcel narrowness and other buildings' proximity)
- energy management (energy saving)
- acoustic comfort (internal adsorption and external insulation especially during a public competition).

During the competition, the designers announced solar PV, vegetative roof, heating floor and new underground air preheating. However, the designers (and then the client) underestimated architectural outline and energy-saving solutions, despite AMO-HQE notifications. During the design stage, architects did not agree to amend the architectural outline and the client refused to overspend, so he finally gave up solar PV and underground preheating. He did not commit to HQE certification.

A new Town Hall is located in the centre of Les Mureaux City (a new suburb 40 km from Paris built around an old village during the 1960s). The old city hall was too small and the central square inappropriate for a city of 32,000 inhabitants. An urban regeneration project was decided in 2001. City administration wrote a pre-brief and the council invited tenders for a briefing and design contract.[12] After selecting three teams, the client chose to apply the HQE approach as the environmentally responsible deputy mayor put forward. Each team drew a specific architectural outline in relationship with client representatives (energy manager, maintenance manager and general manager); they developed the brief in the same time. A young architect, engineers, project planner and a programmiste, who was already HQE experienced, formed the winning team. The building was already basically designed when the client decided to certify the project and recruited an AMO-HQE.[13] Five high performing targets had been chosen:

- low nuisance construction site (because of location in city centre)
- energy management (saving, water/water heat pump, solar sanitary water)
- water management (rainwater use for garden and toilets, saving water taps)
- waste management
- repair and maintenance management.

The Chambre de Commerce et d'Industrie de la Drôme developed the INEED office building in Alixan to welcome innovative companies, some regional foundations in relation to biology, wood and sustainable building and a training centre. The project (3,600 square metres, three floors) is located close to the TGV railway station of Rovaltain (80 km south of Lyon). The developer and AMO-HQE (who is also the programmiste) focused on:

- choices of construction process and materials: wide brick wall (combined with concrete porticos), mixed floors (concrete and wood), natural earth coating
- energy management: insulation and thermal inertia with wide brick, variable double flow ventilation, underground air pre-heating/cooling, solar PV, heating regulation
- water management: vegetative roof, rainwater used for toilets
- hydrothermal comfort especially in summer: sunshade, climbing vegetation, desktop computer banning, nighttime ventilation.

A concrete structure was already summarily designed when the developer required using wood for the structure. Many studies and an extension of time were necessary to introduce a wood floor. In discussions the developer (especially AMO-HQE) opposed the design team (especially structural engineer and architect). The developer did not start a HQE certification process.

EMGP Company is a private developer of Building 270 EMGP. The company specialises in office and commercial building. It owns many parcels inside an old industrial area very close to Paris city (Aubervilliers). Building 270 consists of seven storeys: welcome offices (8,400 square metres), a ground floor (1,000 square metres) and 128 parking spaces on two basement levels. A first building licence was obtained in 2001; it concerns the usual concrete structure with glass facade. In 2002, this company decided that 'Building 270' will experiment with an HQE approach especially to reduce the use costs and for marketing reasons. The project manager (developer representative) turned to an AMO-HQE to modify the initial project: with the architect and the engineers (structural and thermal), they formed a real project team. Architectural form was preserved but walls and coating finally changed. This building was one of the first five HQE certified projects. Six targets were assessed as highly performing:

- relationship between building and immediate environment because of the proximity of Paris peripheral highways
- energy management: variable double flow ventilation, variable lighting controller, highly thermal insulation
- water management
- waste management: rainwater use for garden and toilet (however, governmental sanitary administration did not actually allow using rainwater in toilets inside Building 270, unlike Les Mureaux City Hall)
- repair and maintenance management: ability to access and repair wiring and piping
- hydrothermal comfort: air conditioning.

Environmental topics and performance requirements

As described above, developers can choose their priorities among topics related by the assessment method. They have to answer two questions that are somewhat related. Which topics should have priority over the others? What level of performance should be defined?

A developer is cautious about these choices. First, some of the environmental topics are actually opposed: they cannot be completely satisfied together;[14] a developer has to find the balance between two or more topics. Second, topic requirements usually have repercussions on building costs: most of the topic combinations can either be achieved with just monetary sacrifices or by restraining architectural freedom. Therefore topic choice and performance requirements could be considered as part of the building design process, even if choosing the designer's team happens after them.

We will discuss later the conjunction between topic choice and requirements, budget for project and professional roles. First, we shall explain the main factors of topic choice and then we will describe the topics that have been deeply studied and disputed between designers and developers.

Factors influencing the choice of environmental topics

In France, the HQE target choice is determined by the thematic priority of the developer. The most usual aims concern internal comfort and energy conservation. These aims could be considered antagonistic but they are often explained together. Then, maintenance facility, surrounding relationships and weak nuisance worksite worry developers secondly. The other aims, still important but not so usual, concern the resources and construction materials: the use of local ones seems to be an unofficial priority.

These choices are conditioned by developer organisation. Pre-existing internal skills prompt developers to focus on some topics. Inability to be understood by decision-makers (the client) or high construction costs prompt developer to remove topics.

Then, the facility to respect some HQE requirements (vice versa difficulties to reach other requirements materially) encourages the developer to balance between his own needs and the luck to get an HQE certificate in economic conditions.

Particularly disputed or deeply studied topics

During design, any requirements that prove too costly or too difficult are combined. That could cause tension within a design team. The official design team leader (usually the architect) normally decides to respect the initial requirements and proposes costly solutions. Therefore, the final decision belongs to the developer. He balances between lower performance and higher investment or higher functioning cost.

At this stage, the environmental assessment method plays an important role in the project process.

In France, the HQE method makes explicit requirements before the design team begins to work. Design teams have to assess the environmental performances of their own design; developers ask them if they do not. Only a few topics have truly been deeply studied and discussed among designers or between them and the developer:

- Heating production means are often compared and optimised: global cost during the life period of the heating system is the first criterion, carbon dioxide emission is also an important criterion.
- Use of natural heating resources is also discussed: it concerns solar power for domestic hot water and heating, preheating of external air by underground circulation and, of course, bioclimatic design. A thermodynamic computer simulation of future building is often made to verify and optimise reliability and profitability.
- Equilibrium between luminosity and summer overheating requires factor calculation as well as thermodynamic computer simulation, especially in the case of a wide building with central atrium or an east–west oriented building.
- An innovative system with interference in both frontages, structural and/or thermal compartments pulls designers to long discussions about calculation hypothesis, reliability and economic effects.

Two other important topics that do not involve the designer much are the size of the car parking area, which is discussed at length within the developer's company, and the waste management, which needs fine and detailed definition with the contractors.

Roles in building design team

Environmental assessment methods introduce new topics and new methods in the construction process. They modify both the decision-making inside the developer's company and the design process. However, situations and developments seem different according to the country.

In France, new professionals appear among the project team. One helps the developer to choose priorities and to look after environmental performances during design and construction stages. He has been named AMO-HQE (Assistant Maître d'Ouvrage Haute Qualité Environnementale). Another professional (conseiller environnement) works inside the design team.[15]

Roles of AMO-HQE and conseiller environnement in France

AMO-HQEs are recruited by clients from the briefing till the end of construction; sometimes they have to assess two years after the building comes into service. The AMO-HQE helps the developer directly and does not have any official or contractual relation with design team. During the design stage, the AMO-HQE prepares and takes part in regular meetings between developer and designers. We identify five roles for the AMO-HQE:

- A *passer*, who brings knowledge and methods, first to the developer and then to the design team. He or she may give any document end references to the design team.
- A *mediator*, who in case of divergence between departments of developer company or authority, reaches a compromise and finally acts as a catalyst for environmental performance requirements. Sometimes, the AMO-HQE proposes methods to go to a compromise between developer and design team.
- An *expert*, whose skills guarantee some performances or, vice versa, call an announced performance into question. Considering the diversity of environmental topics, the AMO-HQE refrains from pronouncing on every topic.
- A *monitor*, who looks after the respect of environmental performances expected by the developer all over the building process. The AMO-HQE notifies the developer of any risk of failure.
- An *embellisher*, who makes a building project seem environmental friendly, sometimes more than it really is. The AMO-HQE advises developers to present the best environmental aspects of the project.

These roles are mentioned in chronological order, although they can exist simultaneously especially during the design process. According to context, developer organisation and also the skills and willingness of designers, the AMO-HQE plays to varying degrees the different roles. The AMO-HQE should be not only an expert on environmental impacts but also a thematic consultant including strategy and training. If they do not, he or she prompts the designers (especially architects and engineers) to work more together. That is also the job of the conseiller environnement.

The conseiller environnement is recruited by the design team to complete the team skills. His or her experience in sustainable building or environmental oriented design is useful to win the race (in all the case studies, the client required HQE skills). Like thermal engineers and structural engineers, he or she negotiates his or her income with the design team leader (architect usually). His or her contribution is limited to design stage. We identify four roles:

- A *passer*, who brings physical or chemical knowledge and technical solutions to the design team. If thermodynamic computer simulation is required by the developer or necessary to guarantee any performances, the conseiller environnement makes or subcontracts it, and suggests the calculation hypothesis to structural or thermal engineer.
- An *expert*, who guarantees some environmental performances or at least the methods to assess them. Because of the high diversity of HQE requirements, he or she is used to resort to specialists of other environmental topics.

- An *embellisher*: in the case of architectural outline, the conseiller environnement makes building outlines seem environmental friendly, then advises the designers to explain the environmental advantages.
- A *designer*, who contributes to design but does not usually draw or write specifications for contractors, unlike architects, thermal engineers or structural engineers.

The most HQE-competent among the design team, the conseiller environnement naturally becomes the 'interlocator' of the AMO-HQE with whom the relationship is usually antagonistic. He or she interferes in the traditional relationship between architects and engineers.

Transformation of role of the architect and engineers

Relationships inside design teams were more numerous and more fertile than they are for usual projects. During design, the prospect of assessment forces team members to exchange data and to question usual technical and architectural solutions. When monitoring environmental requirements, the AMO-HQE contributes to broad cooperation inside design team. His contribution is relatively delimited by the HQE® approach even if his skills and his relationship have an impact on the cooperation scope.

HQE approach requests design team members to deliver hypothesis data and layout sheets during design (and not only after design in comparison to BREEAM). Relationship between architect and engineers could be both controversial and cooperative. We identify four main factors:

- *Income*: designers originally forecast a number of working days for the project. During design stage, they spend over time to improve the project if they expect a long-term benefit (e.g. emblematic building, learning by cooperation, satisfaction of a powerful client). Otherwise, designers avoid changing of methods and technical solutions because that spends time.
- *Legal responsibilities*: usual design team members carry on the responsibility of a type of requirement according to regulations, jurisprudence and, sometimes, contract in case of private development.[16] An innovative solution increases usually the risks of being unsatisfactory; designers are careful especially when they have to write the technical specifications.
- *Skills in relation to environmental requirements*: some environmental preoccupations like carbon emission or indoor-air quality are relatively new. Knowledge and experiences are currently very heterogeneous among architects and among engineers. Knowledge and individual experiences help to assess

the risk of unsatisfactory requirements and contribute to clarify responsibilities and cooperation.

- *Conseiller environnement roles*: conseiller environnement seems to be very soon involved in architectural design. However neither regulation nor jurisprudence delimits precisely his individual responsibility, he is officially an adviser. So, according to his relationship (that depends on his income, his reputation making expectation, his skills and his nature), he contributes to collaborative or controversial working methods.

Conclusions of the French cases

The six French cases show a transformation of project process in comparison to the usual sequential process. Innovative solutions were introduced, new professionals appeared (AMO-HQE and conseiller environnement), cooperation increased inside the design team, developer requirements and design choices were explained. We observed that this transformation varies according to the cases; client representatives and design team cooperate highly in case of a private contract or during or after a feasibility studies competition in the case of a public contract. Solutions were more innovative in case of public development. If we consider the satisfaction of interviewed professionals, a successful HQE building project depends on:

- initial and constant willpower from the developer
- AMO-HQE competence, rigour and tact
- knowledge and skills inside the design team (usually brought by the conseiller environnement but sometimes by another team member)
- desire to learn and progress of all the team members.

The permanence of this transformation is still a question. Is necessary cooperation generated by environmental assessment or by introduction of unusual aims? Would AMO-HQE and conseiller environnement still be useful if environmental friendly knowledge would be spread through building professionals?

- Conseiller environnement utility depends on his being ahead in comparison to other team members. As they progress, he will likely specialise: e.g. thermodynamic behaviour simulation, life cycle materials analysis etc. His contribution could become occasional during the design process. An eventual conseiller environnement profession could be permanent only if national regulation and jurisprudence give him any responsibility inside the design team, which is most unlikely.
- AMO-HQE knowledge could trivialise. However, his contribution as mediator and monitor would be indispensable to a developer especially for non-recurring

projects. Actually the outsourcing trend favours this 'new profession'. It does not need any regulation because an AMO assists the developer: their relationship is only contractual. Moreover, the AMO-HQE could advise sometimes only a design team (and so become a conseiller environnement of some projects in which he is not involved as AMO-HQE).

Four case studies in the UK

To understand the rather different context of British practice in sustainable development in more detail, four detailed case studies were carried out. These were broader based studies than those undertaken in France, not focusing only on the use of the BREEAM assessment methods, which in a number of the cases had not been introduced when the projects were initiated but were introduced at a later stage in the process.

The following questions were considered:

- How does the organisation of the work on a project respond to sustainability objectives and how is their achievement evaluated?
- To what extent does the political context, including economic constraints and legal structures, lead to a better understanding of how to improve outcomes?
- How do the professions have to adapt and what differences are developing in the roles of client and design team leader?

The following sections also emphasise cross-cutting issues. The first section introduces the scale and complexity of the projects and reports on the environmental evaluations to which they were subjected. The second explores the effects of developments in policy, especially those connected with new contracts and associated new methods of financing investment in the public sector. The third can then go into further detail of the commissioning, design and construction processes, and emphasise the reorganisation of professional roles.

Description of the projects

These projects were all located in areas of southern England which favour growth, investment and innovation. They are drawn from both public and private sectors. It was not possible to include social housing, nor to deal with the problems of the former industrial zones of Northern cities.

The first project is an example of private housing development (Ecohomes), the second and third are major investments in public services (Architecture and Planning Studio is in Education; NHS Trust Swindon in Health). The fourth project (Whitehall Place) is the refurbishment of a building of historic interest.

Ecohomes cost £2.6 million. It consists of 8 houses, 4 flats and a number of common facilities. The site is in the southwest of England, a highly desirable area. Design work started in 2003 and construction lasted from 2004 to 2006. Architecture and Planning Studio had a total cost of £2.9 million, and contains 9 studios, a workshop, a laboratory, seminar spaces and offices. It is on the main campus of a 'new university' in the west of England. A feasibility study was undertaken in 1998 and construction was completed in 2002. NHS Swindon is much larger: a 550-bed hospital with parking for 1,100 vehicles, and the construction cost was £135 million. It is on the edge of an expanded town which has had a high level of growth in jobs and homes, beginning in the 1960s. Discussion of this project started in 1993 but the new building was not opened until 2003. Whitehall Place is between the two scales: requiring the demolition of most of an out-of-date office block, of which the main facade was listed and had to remain unaltered. The interior was rebuilt and the construction cost came to £29.5 million. Whitehall Place is in the centre of London. This project also took ten years to complete, with a feasibility study in 1995 and occupation of the new offices in 2005.

Evaluating sustainability

All four projects were evaluated in accordance with BRE norms, these norms having sufficient flexibility to be applied to many building types. These valuation processes were linked to design objectives and had an influence on the running of each project.

In the case of Ecohomes, the client's project manager was a certified auditor of the BRE Ecohome evaluation kit. So he acted as an adviser to the architect on construction techniques, the choice of materials and selection of subcontractors. The main client for the Architecture and Planning Building was unwilling to pay for a formal evaluation to be undertaken, but the user group made an informal evaluation themselves. This showed the building to be 'Very good' on the BREEAM scale for office buildings. In developing the Swindon hospital, the NHS Trust's design team developed its own evaluation tool, NEAT (Environmental Assessment Tool) in cooperation with the BRE. Whitehall Place was graded 'Excellent' against the BREEAM criteria.

Finance and contracts

Policy influenced the financing of Ecohomes but not its contract. The regional development agency, a government body, had as a goal 'to promote the three pillars of ecological development . . . an ecological approach, consultation with the local population and a contribution to the local economy'. The agency had a particular interest in one of the common spaces of the project, a refurbished warehouse, and that new jobs be created there. A part of the finance was therefore guaranteed, as was another part by the county council, which pursued the same aims.

For the construction phase, a conventional JCT contract was used. In the interviews, it was reported that 'despite this choice, the budget was only exceeded by 10 per cent and the contract period only had to be extended by three months'. It was also said that one of the lessons of the project was 'not to use this form of contract: the risk is too great . . . it does not encourage the partnership approach which is needed'.

The Architecture and Planning Building demonstrated modest innovations, in finance and in the contract. The source of part of the construction cost was another government body (Higher Education Funding Council), which wished to support 'research projects which included the use of information technology and led to practical training outcomes'. As for the contract, the university used a special form of JCT contract (Design and Build). This transfers responsibility for the final cost to the contractor (allowing for agreed variations only) and allows 'much better financial control'.

It is therefore of particular interest to consider the other two case studies, as both used innovative Private Finance Initiative (PFI) contracts. This approach, dear to the New Labour governments, requires there to be a partnership between public and private organisations for the delivery of new public services. The private organisation is expected to shoulder the risk in return for favourable financial terms.

Thus with the NHS project, the Trust retained ownership of the land, but a hospital company (of which the contractor was a major shareholder) financed the construction over 3 years, and has taken responsibility for maintenance over the next 27 years. The Trust pays a monthly rent to the company and settles the accounts for services used (electricity, water etc.). Those involved said the construction went well, being completed on time and to budget. In addition the contractor was able to show that the cost was not much above that for similar projects. The main problem arose later when it emerged that energy consumption was 30 per cent higher than might have been anticipated. And it appears that the contract did not give priority to meeting the goals of sustainable development. There was no objective figure included for energy consumption, and no method laid down by which energy use would be managed. A Trust representative maintained that 'the responsibility is shared' but it is the Trust which bears the unexpected expense: there is no penalty for the contractor (Carillon).

Even at Whitehall Place, these innovations were not completely adopted for the contract was only partial PFI (JCT type). It covered finance, the design, construction and renovation of the building, but not the facilities management required when it was brought into use. One of the consultants involved also said that 'it would have been preferable to define the environmental specification clearly and precisely at the beginning of the project'. In the event, the owner client did not hesitate to give appropriate financial support on occasions when the specification was altered during the running of the contract to meet client needs. And since they completed their work on this project, the architects involved have been unable to persuade more conventional clients to make ecologically sound design choices when adverse cost implications would have followed.

The adoption of new partnership-type contracts clearly does not guarantee avoidance of the conflicts of financial interest which can arise in design for sustainability.

Adaptation by professionals

The goals of sustainable development and the new expertise required was partly introduced by the client for Ecohomes as the project was initiated by the Somerset Trust for Sustainable Development, the main developer, whose mission statement is 'to make sustainable construction the norm by 2010'. The project manager had undertaken a number of training courses which led in this direction, including one on building conservation. The consulting engineers had previous experience of sustainable construction, as did the 'quantity surveyor', and the construction company had already worked on a 'dynamic house project' which included active insulation. However, the architect had no prior knowledge of design for sustainability. Some of the gaps in knowledge were supplied by the Trust, which had a library of technical specifications which focus on ecological construction.

However, in the case of the Architecture and Planning Building it was the representative of the future users (Professor Colin Fudge) who first thought of it as having to respond to the needs of the environment. He had acquired a strong interest in environmentally conscious design while working in Australia in the 1980s then deepened his knowledge by carrying out various studies for the European Commission in the 1990s. The client who would own the building (the university's Estates Department) became involved with sustainability issues only at the end of the briefing phase. The choice of the main contractor (Willmot Dixon, who was also responsible for design under the Design and Build Contract) was also unconventional, as some of the other tenderers were persuaded to withdraw when it became clear that they were unhappy with the ecological design approaches required. Then a further member of the future users' group (Lecturer Craig White) monitored the detailed design, working with a firm of engineers (Buro Happold) who had acquired considerable skill in this area, especially in design for energy conservation. Other measures considered included the reuse of rainwater, the choice and treatment of timber, the use of solar panels, and the calculation of air movements (so that natural ventilation became possible). There were some conflicts between the users (teachers) and owners (university authorities), but most decisions were resolved with reference to a 'value engineering' approach, which took long-term costs into account.

At Swindon the NHS Trust did not specify a sustainable development in the early stages, but the Trust's interest grew when it became clear that this was a national concern. Neither did the contractor selected (Carillon, also designer under the PFI system) use sustainable design as a selling point. Nonetheless this firm took advice from a specialised consultancy (Natural Step), who convinced Carillon that a sustainable approach could limit its financial risks, especially at the margin. In order to obtain the contract, Carillon had had to develop a 'business case' and a 'public sector comparison' for the final cost of their propositions. They included: control of water use, recycling waste, choice of materials and relationships with suppliers. The building economist undertook research, established a database of good practice and a record of lessons learned from experience.

Whitehall Place was also a special case, as priority was given to retaining the principal facade. It also appeared impossible to introduce natural lighting or to use solar panels, both architectural strategies which would have made a substantial contribution to energy conservation and hence sustainability. The owner client was the Crown Estate, but the users were to be the Department for Environment, Food and Rural Affairs (Defra) who established the detailed brief and clearly had a strong interest in sponsoring a building with minimum environmental impact. Defra set out a 'Sustainability Charter' which was accepted by the contractor (who had design responsibility), architects and engineers. At the end of the day the building was classed 'Excellent' on BREEAM, account being taken of such factors as the use of materials, insulation, waste treatment and lighting controls. One of the most important decisions taken was to install an ammonium-based cooling system, as this does not destroy ozone. For one of the architects involved 'ecological design is an apprenticeship'.

Conclusions from the UK cases
The conclusion drawn from the British case studies was that a new structure of professionalism is in the process of being defined and that this has consequences for architects working in the UK construction industry. Innovations in the technical performance of buildings are clearly at the heart of design for sustainable development. Our case studies suggest that in practice aimed at achieving this, British architects have to adapt to

* finding a context for construction where long-term investment is encouraged
* introducing design evaluation systems suitable for the building type
* understanding that new objectives may be introduced by any of the actors

- learning from experience throughout the project
- seeking financial support from all branches of government
- responding to requirements for new contractual arrangements
- solving conflicts of interest at the earliest possible moment.

THE FUTURE OF THE PROFESSIONS AND OF ASSESSMENT METHODS

The following comments are drawn from the information gained in undertaking the case studies, as well as on the reviews of institutional arrangements which preceded them.

The professions

In the UK and in France, those involved in the promotion and design of environmentally assessed developments have a better understanding of the context in which construction will occur, in order to identify and solve conflicts of interest at the earliest possible stage. This could be an adaptation which is long overdue. Sustainable development is a goal which should lead in this direction. Thinking about environmental impact, about future patterns of use and about the financial provision to be made for external costs, is fundamental to this approach but has rarely been correctly implemented in the past, as construction is an activity in which short-term thinking has tended to prevail. The new professional skills demanded by the call for clear assessments of sustainability will make the former more likely to happen. So there is bound to be pressure on planners, architects, engineers and, in the UK, surveyors, to obtain, and offer to the market, the knowledge which is required. In France it seems that a new professional activity (oriented towards the client body and sometimes towards the design team) is emerging. In the UK, the more probable scenario is that certain members of the existing professions will compete to claim 'ownership' of this knowledge. As a consequence, some architects and engineers may become highly skilled in this area, but others will find the investment required is not viable.

The existence of assessment methods, in both countries, makes the latter problems less likely to arise. In France it is well established that there are new technical requirements which must be addressed, and for some professionals (those accustomed to objectifying their design choices), this may not necessarily call for a change in behaviour. But the locus of responsibility is changing in design, with architects taking a smaller share of design decision-making and some technical support teams (thermal and environmental BET) having stronger roles. In Britain the much more widespread arrangement of design firms as multidisciplinary companies, in which architects and engineers (some very specialised) become accustomed to working together, may facilitate the use of evaluation tools and speed up their introduction to normal 'everyday' practice.

In our view, the probability that new objectives may be introduced to a project by the client and other actors in (or around) the development team (users, neighbours, AMO-HQE and so on) is highly significant. The British cases make this abundantly clear: there is often no fixed brief or immutable set of requirements to be met. In the instances where the client is not naive (as in France the client officially has to seem!), and when the knowledge-base is developing rapidly, such flexibility can have very positive effects. The importance of taking true account of environmental impacts was shown to be stressed by a number of different actors and at different stages in the development process. The general public (users in the long term) also has a role to play in promoting better accountability. Voluntary bodies, the well-educated pressure group members, those taking up legal or political positions, can all take over what up till now has always seemed the prerogative of the professional. How far this kind of action will spread to France in the coming years, remains to be seen. In the UK, the focus of professional legitimacy appears to be changing; in France it may have to as well.

A process of professionalisation involves the development of innovative technologies (including low-tech and social innovation), the search for a market to which this new knowledge can be offered, and the influence of government in promoting and supporting an emergent and specialised approach. These conditions are arising in practice from the diffusion of concern for sustainable development objectives. The traditional design process in which the architect, in taking the brief from the client, also takes the lead in introducing new ideas, persuading others to adopt them from the beginning and to follow them through to later stages of construction, is no longer valid. The traditional system of authority in the construction industry no longer holds. One of the most fundamental aspects of design authority, that of setting the aims of the project, seems to have been dispersed among the actors and over the life of a project. The move towards sustainability in building design seems to imply that architects, in France as well as in the UK, can no longer be certain that they will set the agenda for their work.

The environmental assessment methods

As is clear from the text of this chapter, the development and the use of evaluation methods is highly dependent on the national context. The environmental management system (EMS) is specific to the HQE approach in comparison to BREEAM: it comes under the national context. The variety of arrangements in the United Kingdom does not allow a single EMS; anyway, the very detailed terms of a building contract built up an implicit management system. Besides, the gap of training between architects (oriented on architectural design) and engineers (analytic skills) in France makes more necessary a common approach and not only an assessment method. Thanks to HQE, the client forces it on design team members. However, client and designers need a lot of time to apply a new management system during a HQE certified project, whatever its size. The benefit of a fixed EMS is uncertain for small projects. This could be one of the causes of lower spread of the HQE certification than BREEAM.

Another cause is the temporal gap. The first developments of BREEAM began roughly ten years before HQE. Most of these years were dedicated to developing and testing the British method. HQE approach benefited: from international experiences especially for the environmental specifications, its development stage could be shorter. Even if it is too early to assert, we presume that HQE approach is spreading in France two to three years later than BREEAM has done in the UK. The question is the scope of the asymptote. In the UK and a fortiori in France, certified buildings are currently still a minority among the new constructions. The number of certifications is growing both in France and the UK. It seems likely that the asymptotic scope will be higher than it is today, but different because it is highly dependent on the national context.

It is also clear that there is, within these national evaluation systems, a fair amount of freedom for practitioners to select variations in the factors to be measured and the standards to be applied. So a major question is to understand whether the particularities of each situation are so specific that comparison between results is impossible. Are the standards to be achieved in different countries (in this case UK and France) similar? Or is one national jurisdiction always more exacting than another? To answer this question, it is necessary to know whether the units of measurement are the same (or easily translated) and to determine the answer to this problem, it is necessary to understand where the measurements made are objective and where they are subjective, involving not scientific information but human judgement.

Our case studies, and contextual investigation, show that there is a large element of judgement involved, especially in the UK evaluation systems. There is a choice of aspects to measure and a selection of criteria by which satisfaction or achievement can be determined. The only aspect which is consistently included is that of energy use and the ways in which that can be measured are allowed to vary. There is a possibility that the level of carbon dioxide emissions will become a universal criteria in the near future, for new building, but this is not normally applied to the operation of the existing stock.

So we come to the broader basis of comparison. Can we say that doing an evaluation is a good thing, and if so, equally good in all national conditions? Those professionals we have interviewed (engineers, architects, surveyors) think so. Almost without exception they have let us know that they thought that working against explicit sustainability criteria was a good thing: something they would do again, whenever professional circumstances allowed (or forced) them to do so. But this does not mean that even using such assessment methods entirely systematically would have truly increased the sustainability of all the buildings we studied. The only real test, in the long term, of the effects of using these assessment methods, is on the results in use of the buildings concerned. More information, about what actually happens in each country in the later stages of use, will be required before this can be fully determined.

ACKNOWLEDGEMENTS

This work was partly financed by a grant awarded by Ministère de l'Equipement (Plan Urbanisme Construction Architecture) to Eric Henry at Laboratoire PACTE Politique et Organisation of Université de Grenoble. Invaluable support was given by Marie-Cecile Puybaraud of Johnson Controls International. Research assistants in the UK were Julie Codet-Boisse and Adrian Boots. In France, the other team members were Magali Paris (CRESSON-ENSAG) and Stéphanie Abrial (PACTE).

NOTES

1   Design activities include estimation of needs during briefing, imagining form and building structure, choosing between technical systems and materials, checking the building performance, drawing prescriptions for builders, and overseeing the building site.

2   Development of BREEAM predates the privatisation of BRE and hence the establishment of the Trust.

3   Association HQE, Définition explicite de la qualité environnementale Référentiels des caractéristiques HQE, Document 5–15 November 2001.

4   Association HQE® – Référentiel du système de management environnemental pour le maître d'ouvrage concernant des opérations de construction, adaptation ou gestion des bâtiments, 23 November 2001.

5   CSTB is a French public establishment similar to BRE in UK. AFNOR (Association Française de Normalisation) is the French correspondent of the International Standard Organisation.

6   Certificats NF Bâtiments Tertiaires – Démarche HQE® – Mise à jour du 16/05/2007, Certivea, 5 pages. Certivea is a certification company depending on the state agency CSTB.

7   148 buildings were certified and 300 in progress according to CERQUAL website (www.cerqual.fr/pro/habitat_environnement/programmes.php, accessed June 2007).

8   Minergie and Passivhaus were originally developed respectively in Switzerland and Germany. They care only about energy saving and renewable energies.

9   School BREEAM started 2004: 11 buildings had been assessed on 16 March 2007. Retail BREEAM started 2003: 4 buildings assessed.

10   SME and DEQE written by HQE Association in 2001.

11   CAPV is a local federation of 50 municipalities around Voiron City (80,000 inhabitants together).

12   The 'Marché de Définition' is an exception to the sequential process described above (imperative distinction between briefing and design stages). If a local authority identifies a need but is not able to define precisely the nature and the scope of the project, the law allows it to invite a tender for both briefing and design (according to a very imprecise pre-brief). Two teams at least should be selected to design urban and architectural outlines, then the winner team continues the next design stages alone.

13   In 2003, HQE Association invited developers to experiment with the new 'Bâtiment tertiaire – demarche HQE' certification.

14   Thermal comfort could be easily expected with high energy consumption that produces carbon dioxide; luminosity in deeper rooms requires high windows that could cause overheating.

15   In fact, the same environmental (or sustainable building) specialist works either as AMO-HQE or as conseiller environnement, but never both in the same project.

16   Individual design team member responsibility is linked to the writing of the building work technical specifications. For example thermal engineer becomes responsible for the comfort temperature achievement in winter because he designs the heating system.

REFERENCES

Association HQE (2005) Le mouvement HQE® dans les Régions, 4ème Assises HQE Reims, 10–11 March 2005.

Bartlett, H. (2005) Understanding the implementation of sustainability principles in UK educational building projects. PhD, Cambridge, Cambridge University.

Birtles, A.B. (1997) Environmental impact of buildings and cities for sustainability. In P.S. Brandon, P.L. Lombard and V. Bentivegna (eds) *Evaluation of the Built Environment for Sustainability*. London: E&FN Spon.

Henry, E., Abrial, S., Codie-Bisset, J., Debizet, G., Paris, M. and Puybaraud, M. (2006) Expertises, competences, et gestion des projets de construction durable. Unpublished report following research financed by Plan Urbanisme, Construction, Architecture, Ministère des Transports, de l'Equipement, du Tourisme et de la Mer, Paris.

MIQCP (2006) *Evolution de la Politique PFI concernant les bâtiments publics en Grande Bretagne*. Paris: MIQCP et Centre de Recherche sur l'Habitat.

RIBA (2006) Practice Bulletin 378, 14 December.

Sunnika, M. (2001) *Policies and Regulations for Sustainable Building: A Comparative Study of Five European Countries*. Delft: Delft University Press.

Willis, A.J. (1981) *The Architect in Practice*, 6th edn. London: Granada.

10

New Professional Leadership in France
Stéphanie Abrial

The growth in the concept of sustainable development threw up a number of new economic, political, environmental and social dimensions at the end of the 1980s, hard on the heels of forecasts of the exhaustion of natural resources and climate change. European construction professionals had to integrate these new ideas into the way they designed and built (see other chapters in Part II). In France, the growth in environmental concerns led to the emergence of new ideas and practices around this issue which, in a fairly unique way, gave rise to the HQE (high environmental quality) movement.

In this chapter, entitled 'New professional leadership in France', the idea is to analyse the concepts of this unusual notion using as a reference the perceptions, positions, thought patterns and know-how of the professionals directly concerned. The French case stands apart somewhat, in the sense that it reveals a particular type of actor (unlike the case of England where the approach seems less unified), referred to as the 'founders' of a movement whose starting point lies in the pioneering work of the ATEQUE workshop (workshop on the assessment of environmental quality in buildings 1992).[1]

'FOUNDERS' OF THE MOVEMENT FOR INCREASING SUSTAINABILITY

Emergence of a conviction that environmental quality matters
In France, at the beginning of the 1990s, under the political influence of the minister delegated to housing, Marie-Noëlle Lienemann, the first work on environmental assessment in buildings began. This work was primarily coordinated by the PCA and ATEQUE.[2] Professionals, industrialists, researchers and personalities such as Olivier Piron, Gilles Olive, Bruno Peuportier, Roland Fauconnier, Pierre Troadec, Sylviane Nibel and Hubert Penicaud found themselves adopting a common environmental approach which came about, among other things, through government-sponsored experimental solar energy programmes.[3] This was the beginning of a group of pioneers that we deliberately choose to call the 'founders'.[4] The name 'founder' was used in our research to designate pioneers involved in the professional construction sector

and part of a movement interested in sustainable development in the same field (see Table 10.1). Our hypothesis on the coherence of this group is that beyond the sharing of a certain number of environmental concerns, these 'founders' represent the beginnings of a movement which has helped new modes and forms of collaboration to emerge. The name 'founders' seems less suitable in the United Kingdom to the extent that actions linked to 'sustainable building' were few and far between and were little or not at all encouraged by the Thatcher government at the beginning of the 1990s. The 'founders', as we call them in our survey, can thus be part of different professional groups (architects, engineers, researchers, industrialists, etc.) and share a specific vision of environmental quality in connection with their respective professional identities.

First of all, it is worth noting the combination of several levels of discussion: the profession, the line the development is taking and professional choices (individually) are all operating in conjunction in the light of strong, fairly generalised citizens' concerns about the environment (collectively).

When the French founders described their professional activity, they justified their initiative on the basis of the urgency of the environmental issue. Consequently, the scope under consideration goes beyond the construction sector and includes a broader reflection on all phenomena relating to the planet's environmental balance. Global warming, pollution, nuclear power, waste and policies are all common themes which made those surveyed feel that they belonged to a 'movement' with an environmental conscience in France. The actors in construction, beyond their own specific technical skills, feel they represent a form of reasoning based on the desire not to be left behind on what is an international issue. Shared convictions around a sort of environmental credo brings them to the conclusion that 'nobody can be against the environment'. On that basis, the promotion of their professional activity is found in references to individual experiences, meetings and personal motivations that are not always directly linked with the building sector:

> when I got involved with HQE, it was with Gilles Olive in 1999. We were sure that it was not a new profession: I am an architect and for me, it is quite normal to be interested in the environment. You can't do anything in architecture if you don't take some interest in the environment. I felt that the environment held everything together: sociology, space, resistance of materials. ... Whether in Venezuela, in Africa or on a boat, with an environmental approach you address a problem and your approach will be just as good as mine. ... On boats, there is real passion and I find the same thing in environmental projects.

In this respect, we observe a fairly humanist set of representations and values which are shared by those surveyed who gravitate, get know each other and live as

Table 10.1 French 'founders' who took part in semi-directive interviews

Interview	Name	Body and status	Interview date
END01	Olive, Gilles	Founding chairman of D2C, former peer of ATEQUE and HQE.	01.05
END02	Piron, Olivier	Infrastructure ministry, former Secretary-General of PUCA, civil engineering	01.05
END03	Schnaidt, Alain	Architect, HQE-AMO, partner in 2DKS	06.05
END04	Bidou, Dominique	Secretary-General of HQE association, civil engineering	01.05
END05	Peuportier, Bruno	Researcher at Ecole des Mines, Paris	04.05
END06	Charbonnier, Sylvie	Isover Saint Gobin	03.05
END07	Fauconnier, Roland	FFB	01.05
END08	Bousseyroux, Daniel	Syntec ingenierie	06.05
END09	Chautard, Guy	Secretary-General of HQE association	01.05
END10	Nibel, Sylviane	CSTB researcher, Marne la Vallée	01.05
END11	Rigassi, Vincent	Grenoble architecture school and Ecobatir, architect and engineer	02.05
END12	Troadec, Pierre	AIMCC	03.05
END13	Amadon, David	Head of PO1E AFNOR	03.05
END14	Patte, Emmanuelle	ICEB	06.05
END15	Brindel, Beth Sophie	CM3E, HQE GT rehabilitation association	03.05
END16	Poupin, Daniel	CICF Secretary-General	05.05
END17	Gamba, René	CICF environment manager	12.05
END18	Pénicaud, Hubert	Architect-engineer, member of several environmental architecture groups, HQE-AMO	03.05
END19	Sénior, Gérard	UNSFA	03.05
END20	Nossent, Patrick	CSTB certification	07.05
END21	Sidler, Olivier	Enertech, Isolons la Terre group	12.05
END22	Gobin, Christophe	GTM construction, former Secretary of the Bativille association	03.05

Source: Based on Henry et al. 2006.

Note: The text of this table has been translated by Neil Draper.

if they belong to the same ideological, professional 'community', in connection with the environment. The phenomenon of leadership à *la française* is part of the shared notion of a conscience which goes beyond the professional scope, with a wider mission encompassing the environment.

> Environmental quality is an ideological basis for compromise, for dialogue . . . nobody can be against it . . . clients want it.

> It is a spatial and temporal convergence of people who meet and who believe in something at a given time and who want to give it to the public. The HQE approach and sustainable development have to be collective . . . it can't be any other way.

> The idea we had over there was to say that sustainable development is something which concerns us in our everyday lives, and the objective was to see that each of us could represent and embody sustainable development in *our* everyday lives.

> It is because at the outset, we said that environmental quality is deployed around man . . . it is a little bit that: ecology starts with man.

> I am not defending something personal, I am defending something which will help us get a better world, something that is in the public interest.

> The objective is to say: 'at the end of the day, climate change will lead us, whether we like it or not, by force or by consent, 40 years down the line i.e. tomorrow . . . to design buildings with zero consumption in terms of environmental impact and in terms of the extinction of resources, materials and greenhouse gas production'. If we don't create a set of laws for the next 40 years to address 3 billion m^2 which generate 100 million tons of CO_2 a year, at the rate we were at last year (we have already created 4 per cent more emissions) – this year we are breaking all records with the 20 days of cold weather – we are not going to be able to survive at these levels of CO_2 concentrations, health-wise.

In this 'movement of founders', reflection crystallises around these people's ability to group together and to invest in tools, methodology and the skills of their professions to face up to new environmental issues.

> At the outset, we need a common thrust, we need to find the answers to the questions: 'How is sustainable development methodology developed? What will it change for us? How do we apply it? What are the skills that are needed?'

It means moving from discussion to action. In order to do this, the discussion must open up internationally and allow us to compare the approaches of other countries, in Europe in particular (HQE, LEEDS, BREAAM, and so on). The 'founders' describe what is done abroad, compare their experiences with the experiences of others and analyse the situations described. They talk about their relations with other professionals and emphasise what, in their view, works better elsewhere. We note that they are very keen on what happens abroad (Germany, UK, Canada, United States, etc.) and give the impression that France may be falling behind.

> Internationally, the environment is all about innovation. Today with HQE, at GBC [Green Building Challenge], the HQE gives us a knowledge transfer platform to compare with LEEDS and BREAAM. In HQE, rainwater recovery is now part and parcel, but the technology comes from Germany. In reality, it comes in the form of transfers: how do you do it? What are your performance levels like? We are going to have to have different approaches.

> We go to trade shows to see what's going on . . . we go to trade shows in Germany. We work with Otto Wak, with engineers with 15 years' experience in this field. The Nordic countries are 15 years ahead of us and in the United States, architects have been talking about it for ages. It is developing rapidly in the private sector, in big companies. There are a whole lot of people who are really committed to the environment in the US.

> The Anglo-Saxon system is a pure assessment system with thresholds. . . . We use an association which manages the system with whatever they want . . . and we work on a consensus basis . . . and if there is a really big obstacle . . . we stop . . . to sum it all up, just look at the Paris bid for the Olympic Games, 'What did they promise?' Well, LID (Low Impact Development) . . . the American system!

However, at the same time, for example, those surveyed seemed to be reasonably satisfied with the way that the HQE approach works: unlike others, the French seem to think that they are setting up a proper environmental quality initiative through the HQE tools. Even though they are not perfect, the approach seems valid. Thanks to this approach, discussions, reflection and workgroups arrive at negotiated positions which are not forced through without consultation.

NEW SKILLS AND IMPROVED FORMS OF COLLABORATION

Bringing together existing and emerging actors in the construction sector

When we look to analyse the impact of growing environmental demands in construction on professions involved in environmental quality (QE) projects, various phenomena of professional redefinition and reorganisation emerge. On the one hand, the traditional professions – surrounding the contracting authority and principal contractor respectively – are adapting to a more complex world, requiring greater integration of qualification, expertise and skills from all and sundry. With QE, architects, engineers and contractors need not only to acquire a specific type of knowledge in respect of the environment, but also to use a new skill which can be identified in the forms of collaboration and compromise needed to work on such projects. The development of QE seems to question each of these fields on their own professional and inter-professional capacities.

Also, in something of a satellite situation and as an interface between these traditional professions,[5] new professions are taking an increasingly strategic role in the emerging market of environmental quality in construction. This primarily concerns two categories of professions: AMOs (assistants or supports to the contracting authority) and environmental consultants. The progressive emergence of these professions within HQE projects is closely linked to the contracting authority's growing needs given the new project elements that have to be included and the pressure placed upon the principal contractor to complete highly demanding construction programmes. The use of AMOs and/or environment consultants is due to the need for technical assistance and QE legitimacy. This results in the addition and juxtaposition – sometimes in a single project – of skills that are required of people who do not all have the same training, the same representation or the same level of knowledge in the environmental field.

In Figure 10.1, three professional groupings represent the actors involved directly in the construction process in France. Two other groupings gravitate around

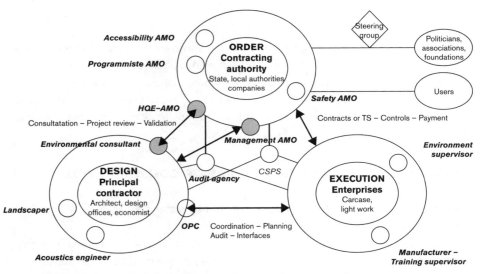

10.1 Old and new construction actors in environmental management

Source: Henry et al. 2006

Note: text of figure translated by Neil Draper

this issue of sustainability: political regulation and industry practice. The professional groupings are responsible respectively for the order, design, implementation and construction of the building. Within each of these circles are the traditional professions who are involved in the different phases of a project. Peripherally – sometimes more integrated, sometimes on the margins of these zones, with the emerging 'HQE' professions in grey – we show the professions emerging in the face of rapid development of sustainable development demands. The multiplicity of links which join them together reflect the density of the new forms of collaboration which are being set up in this polarised network. On the basis of this model, several remarks – in connection with the general issue of QE development – can be formulated.

Repositioning the contracting authority in its relationship with the purchase order

On the subject of orders for buildings, public contracting authorities – as currently exist in France – seem to have to adapt themselves to some very real pressures due to the increase in the socio-political desirability of environmental issues and sustainable development, and a clear lack of skills in terms of the manner in which such projects can move forward. Announcing the construction of an HQE town hall or secondary school gives the commune or the region placing the order a strong image, an identity which it thirsts after because of its communications value.[6] The challenge for the contracting authority therefore becomes more complicated. It is not a traditional construction project, but one that integrates environmental and sustainable development dimensions, perhaps without the necessary skills being available. As we will see further on, in more detail, this issue of the balance between the desire at the outset and the resources available also goes hand-in-hand with the financial and managerial resources allocated to the project. In general terms, however, the HQE approach at the starting point implies a repositioning of the contracting authority's role in terms of its skills and its relationship with its political masters and those who will use the building. The 'fashion' effect, which make it more or less part of the public conscience, will generate a varying level of commitment and involvement on the part of the contracting authority in its leadership role and in the definition of forms of collaborations employed.

> HQEs today are a real mixed bunch. It's true that the first HQE projects involved people who were really committed, but today half of the contracting authorities who talk about HQE couldn't care less. Fashion comes into it, but they have their obligations to the politicians. There will always be a Green Party member who will say, 'But why don't we do HQE?' because of the image they want to give themselves. It just looks good to look green. Of course, it's clear that in every other HQE project today, the contracting authorities are pulling in their horns.

Today, what I notice is that the contracting authorities want HQE assistance and that our design offices have a big card to play if they can provide it.

There is also the question of technical complexity – in a meeting with VAD, I met a contracting authority from a small commune in the Rhône area who tried to get through the first tertiary certification process but gave up because it was much too heavy for them to handle . . . not financially, but with the questions they were asked, the system of management that it required and so forth.

Because, to my mind, the main part of the work is with the contracting authority. To get through most of the work – because having people who can follow this sort of dossier within their teams doesn't mean a secretary or someone hidden away in a corner, or an engineer who can do all that on his own. Indeed – you need a motivated team which can put the resources in place to achieve it.

The problem of the levels of training of contracting authorities goes beyond the simple question of environmental awareness. 'The most important thing is steering the project. You have to know that the contracting authority always has the last word', said a founder we surveyed. To lead a construction project which meets environmental quality requirements, as several people questioned have said, the decision-maker has to be able to make the most appropriate choices for the political request formulated, for the use to which the building is to be put and for the technical possibilities of actually building it. Observations made in our survey are pretty conclusive: the way contracting authorities are organised today, does not make them particularly competent in the start-up and supervision of HQE projects. The lack of knowledge and skills on methods of design, materials or indeed HQE-approach techniques is at odds with the decision-making power the contracting authority has. This is what some people surveyed mean by 'new challenges':

Those who think about environmental quality honestly, and there are no more than 20 of them . . . 20 no more . . . and contracting authority people are traditionally not properly trained.

You have to train the contracting authorities because there are no qualifications, nothing at all.

What we know is that the more you cut it up into different phases, with different actors, the more you need highly competent contracting authority management.

Nowadays, decision-makers ask sustainable development questions . . . it's a technical thing they don't quite understand.

> I think mostly about contracting authorities on public projects who are often considered as people who don't really know much but have loads of power . . . they delegate without putting what's needed into it.

> In my view, the contracting authorities really need the skills, or to be able to get them from outside.

There also seem to be difficulties in the forms of collaboration that prevail in sustainable design and HQE. This change operates around two main dimensions: on the one hand, the contracting authority seems to find it difficult to remain managerially independent in terms of the definition and leadership of the project. On the other, it seems to have to be part of a much more complex negotiation process both internally, with the programme development phase, and externally in its relationship with the designers.

On the first point, the environmental and sustainable approach leads the contracting authority increasingly to look for guarantees from experts who are not necessarily experts in construction. Non-experts are, as often as not, users. This means listening, taking expectations and comments of inhabitants, citizens and consumers into account, because they are the best placed to talk about the uses of a building. It is of course they who, once the building is finished, will judge the result. In the repositioning of its skills, the contracting authority must therefore be able to integrate this type of external entity and make a place for them through the specification process. The quality of their leadership throughout all the stages of the project seems relatively dependent on the contracting authority's ability to interpret the expectations of end-users. The challenge is combining local expectations with consultation processes. A contracting authority faced with an HQE approach is one who succeeds in translating the non-expert message to experts, without necessarily being involved in the assessment itself. As a result, the legitimacy of an HQE project is no longer simply based on the traditional arbitration of the contracting authority but on the meeting and exchanges between users and experts. The 'hierarchical' paradigm is being replaced by a 'negotiated' paradigm.

The use of experts – as a support to the contracting authority's team – changes the dynamics when the brief is being put together. The decision-making body faces difficulties when faced with environmental and sustainability demands because it must find some of the skills required outside, if not available internally. To put the project together, you need to call on outside expertise, in the form of HQE AMOs and environmental consultants. This is where there is a change in the way of operating and the way leadership of the project is delegated. This separation undoubtedly makes some issues such as the choice of reference set and selection of targets even more visible, but also applies to going for certification or not. With growing environmental demands, there is an additional requirement: not to make a mistake with the 'combination' of professionals involved in the project. The choice of the number, complementarity and even compatibility of these QE specialists is a decisive stage in the balance between functional programming and HQE programming.

Working in the most integrated way possible in construction project management

The second grouping shown in Figure 10.1 comprises the principal contractor's team. We note that while there are big changes and real difficulties, the environmental issue has raised more important questions in practices that are part of the French construction tradition, marked by relatively hierarchical relationships.

On the principal contractor side, any *architect* dealing with an HQE project is first of all confronted with a situation which requires an additional skill for which he has not always been properly trained. The HQE approach is a major challenge because it specifies the expectations of the contracting authority – and often elected politicians – in the form of targets.

> We said to ourselves: 'It's very important for architects to put themselves in the frame, because, on the one hand, it's part of their job and also because they have the best overall vision at the beginning and at the end of the project, and only the architect has that . . . and therefore, is the best placed to manage all the teams. We are not saying he should do everything, but it is he who can coordinate everyone. So it's just the architect's normal mission plus an extra component'.

Whether they are trained or not – we will see that this is a recurrent problem – architects have to take into account the fact that the construction market is defined with this environmental and sustainable angle in mind. One person questioned summed up this way of seeing things very clearly: 'if the architects weren't involved, the project would work against them . . . they quickly understood working with regular clients that they had a card to play'. Thus, the key impact of HQE on the profession is that they cannot ignore it.

> What is interesting from the point of view of our profession as architects, and I wonder how it will turn out, is that now architects have to get involved, because if they want to sign certain deals, they have to commit to the HQE approach requested by the contracting authority.

> And now, we ask ourselves questions like: 'How can the HQE be an asset to French architects abroad?' We need qualifications, things we can demonstrate with a method . . . and we don't necessarily have to copy the method from Japan or elsewhere . . . but show that it has created new expertise among our architects and designers . . . we have to show

that it has given rise to a culture that will help deal with environmental problems as they are raised in other countries.

I find that it's a real pity that the Order of Architects has resigned from the HQE Association nationally,[7] because once again, we're cutting ourselves off from what could help us move forward and from a new emerging profession.

While this reality cannot be ignored, it may nevertheless raise a number of reactions, and not ones of approval or compliance. Among the comments made during our survey, we know that concerns – and sometimes downright refusal – do exist in respect of the development of environmentally responsible design. The arguments advanced revolve around three categories of fears: the HQE is a very complicated approach for professions who believe they are already working to respect the environment; the HQE shifts the relationship with design because it imposes a reference set, standards and the possibility of restrictive certification; finally, if the architect wants to get training or use HQE specialists, this means a phase which is costly in time and in money and therefore often seen as dissuasive.

On the first point, it seems that the environmental and sustainable approach as described through the HQE has led to difficulties in building design. The technical and detailed nature of the approach – those questioned talk about 14 targets – outlines a framework which is sometimes seen as restrictive and incompatible with the creative freedom of the designer. While before, architects saw themselves as the professional best-placed to manage all phases of design (the architect is a generalist), we observe that today's approach focuses on actors with complementary missions and a distribution of the different work sequences. The hypothesis on 'distributed' and 'negotiated' design therefore becomes central. The use of environment experts (as shown in Figure 10.1) means greater separation of know-how and skills.

> Where we're going to have to change is where before we used to say: 'There are our constraints and, at a given point in time, we convert those input data into spatial composition'. And from this spatial composition, we would say to the engineers: 'There, I've finished the drawing, I've done my building, now you can do the thermal engineering, the acoustics and so forth'. I think that that's all in the past: the HQE approach in general doesn't allow it, and by and large, it's not a good thing, because the environmental approach requires a number of skills during the design phase that we don't have, or at least don't have enough of . . .

This idea comes back in many answers.

As a second point, we note that people's concerns are structured around constraints expressed in terms of norms and the relationship with certification.

Architects, when they get into an HQE approach, have the impression that their approach and their work are going to be more strictly governed by standard- and regulation-related recommendations, imposed in particular by the contracting authority. With the development of HQE, the question is: 'to what extent do changes triggered by growing HQE demands lead to creating skill gaps within the profession (trained architects and more traditional architects) and affect their ability to work with briefs (between more HQE-specialist architectural firms and others)?' The professional identity of the architect is changing because he now works in a project context which requires him to think in a more integrated manner faced with the issue of the environment. 'In France, architects have a fine arts background', explained one person questioned. Dealing with standards and certification reflects this change of paradigm. The profession is changing, requiring constant dialogue and negotiation with all those involved: the contracting authority, the AMOs and the contractors. All of a sudden, we seem to be finding ourselves in a slightly paradoxical situation with more demanding contracting authorities – in terms of targets and certification – and professions which are aware of it and seem to approve the approach but are not ready and/or willing to meet the contracting authorities' demands.

Faced with this situation, we note an adaptation which has led to French designers working in a less traditional manner. Architects and engineers, for example, have greater need to design together and consider the way they coordinate the different phases of the project. We observe that the work of the engineer and that of the architect is changing, requiring flexibility and adaptability as imposed upon them by the contracting authority in the day-to-day running of an HQE programme. Some points need addressing in relation to *engineers and design offices* in this context of growing environmental demands. The messages put across show that stereotypes are attributed to engineers, marking a stated cut-off between the creative design universe – the architect's world – and that of calculation and technical feasibility. Representations are formed via a comparison suggesting the work of the different parties should not be mixed while, paradoxically, the need for better complementarity between the different phases of the project comes through strongly. This paradox is interesting because it clearly illustrates – and this applies too to the message of the founders of the HQE movement – the culture shock resulting from the confrontation between a traditional, permanent model of construction and a more integrated vision which we see emerging from the environmental theme. Here, there is a real sticking point for construction in France.

> In the construction industry, we have this problem of the separation between the architect and the design office . . . having worked in England, I find that their design offices are much more involved in the early part of the design – in the sketch phase. When we tendered for

jobs, we worked with the structural engineer and the fluids engineer on the form of the building. We would say: 'This form is going to be very good for air circulation because the form that you were looking at . . .'. The engineers gave us input during the sketch phase when we were creating together, and the same applied to structures. While in France, at least from what I've experienced in the agencies where I've worked, they are consulted late on in the process, making it less interesting for them and therefore for us and, what's more, we're calculating after the event while everybody is allowing for a margin of error in their own bits of the process.

Engineers are described by the founders as 'people who thrive on energy', who make 'models' and 'develop tools' without really worrying about the overall environmental design of the building and who have 'a tendency to use software as a magic wand'. The relationship with calculations, measurements and technical aspects seems to be perceived as an obstacle to professional rapprochement and reinforces this dubious division of the various professions.

As for criticisms on the 'level', the 'lack of creativity' and on the 'tendency not to see each other' there are also some remarks about the degree of charisma of the engineer who is always compared with the architect: 'The leader is often the architect because engineers are not very good at presenting, speaking, etc.'. In people's answers, a distance is established and maintained through these differences in assessment which give a fairly instrumentalised character to the architect and design office relationship. Following this approach, engineers are perceived as having to be at the architect's beck-and-call. At the same time, while these two universes are compared, we observe that value is given to what engineers can bring to the environmental project. And again paradoxically, engineers are stereotyped because of the traditional nature of their training and the social representations attached to them, but they do enjoy recognition for their know-how and skill in the roles they are perceived to play in the QE approach. This practical vision of a new level of complementarity required for successful HQE calls for tender seems to override long-standing disagreements between the professions.

The struggles between design offices and architectural firms, in spite of this mix of individuals with different professional identities, seem to be part of a 'before' period where a general model for construction equated to a rather rigid and partitioned type of relationship. This model continues to exist but we note that as the contracting authority's processes become more professional, there is a more formalised demand for environmental quality and they are surrounding themselves with experts in the project planning phase. This change is being operated in the way the design process is organised. The principal contractor too must also adapt to these new rules. It must adopt an internal operational mode which is more highly integrated and impose a 'common vocabulary'. Indeed, one of the conclusions of the survey is that this change is in progress. The outcome of the teaming up of architects and engineers is no longer simply dependent upon the need for identity affirmation by one group in relation to the other, but upon both parties' changing relationship with the specification order.

Companies and manufacturers facing a complete set of new requirements

As the third skills grouping to be considered in the French construction process, industries and contractors are also having to deal with the development of HQE and sustainable development. Two major aspects feature in people's answers on the subject: first, we discover high levels of acceptance of the environmental issue, based primarily on the desire to innovate and find a key place economically in a booming market; second, we note the progressive adaptation of companies to techniques and materials and their involvement in the management of HQE operations. This would include committing resources such as environmental trainers and supervisors. Thus, contractors are an integral part of what is happening in the HQE field. They too are making their own adjustments internally and externally in terms of know-how and forms of collaboration.

We note that professionals from the industrial sector are identified as stakeholders of the new environmental challenges because they have economic and political interests over the long term. These interests are reflected in products, innovation and the need to bridge the training gap between the major groups and their subcontractors. They include the HQE reference set but do not stop there. On a pragmatic note, the theme of investment in this field including the AIMCC's (Association of Construction Products Industries) registration of the HQE trademark is indicative of its importance.

> In industry, it's fair to say that for high product performance, a good industrialist must limit energy consumption, offer the best performance for the lowest material/energy consumption possible . . . this is one theme . . . . if I were an industrialist I would manufacture in such a way to earn the best possible margins.

The second point concerns resources that companies buy in to support their work in the sustainable development and construction sector. Here, we are talking about strategies implemented to meet environmental demands effectively. During interviews, these are primarily to do with two themes: being members of bodies which act directly upon standards and regulations; which means grassroots circulation of information – especially given the great difficulties faced by companies on the ground – and organising training for small companies and subcontractors.

This applies in particular to management, waste-sorting and the environmental quality of materials.

> It would be untrue to say that we the industrialists have nothing to do with it. Because for us, standards are tools which we have been using for a very long time. We are certainly going to be more involved than others who are put off by standards. For most architects it was a pretty scary thing, while for us, given that standards entail defining a common nomenclature, it's something we're comfortable with. But having said that, I wouldn't say that the AIMCC was the only one.

> There is a review with contractors before starting the construction, but I think that's very important. I would say that in the HQE process, we are a bit less repetitive than we were. Clearly, companies are now more familiar with materials and techniques they didn't know before, as well as new working methods and environmental requirements. They need time to put new working methods in place.

On the subject of the use of new materials and introducing new types of worksite organisation, contractors need to adapt and they are doing so. Thus, we realise that companies have to reorganise internally and externally to address the new difficulties they face on the worksite. Several founders questioned explained that some of their professional mission is dedicated to the transfer of knowledge to companies.

> In general, we now have 20 or so technical training CD ROMs made by industrial partners, and the self-employed craftsmen come for an afternoon from time-to-time, whether or not there is a contract at hand, to explain and discuss the problems that they meet in their trade with training and demands. We give them the possibility of meeting all GTM BATIMENT managers and reciprocally, we want to hear their difficulties. As we speak, there are over 20 technical training CDs available from suppliers. Of course, contractually, they are sub-contractors, but I think they have a broader vision than that nevertheless.

> Our role is to offer them stuff, run sessions for them . . . both awareness-raising and training on the new approaches . . . as much from a technical and technological point of view as from a management point of view. When we train people like that it's really a small step forward. We cannot oblige our companies to do it, we are there to raise awareness and it's up to them as to whether they choose to come and be trained or not. We offer the tools and the companies choose whether or not they use them.

Using the diagrammatic representation in Figure 10.1 of the old and new actors in the construction sector involved in environmental management in France, and the analysis of the changes occurring in the three different professional groupings, we will now look at the more detailed points raised on the emerging HQE professions.

FROM BRIEF TO DESIGN

Non-conventional career pathways and personal implications of newly recognised goals

On the subject of contracting authority support and environmental consultancy, we note first of all a degree of confusion in names and definitions given to these professionals and their relationship with the environmental dimension – AMO, AMO-HQE, programmiste (the brief specifier, i.e. the person detailing the content and schedule of a construction project), HQE programmiste, environmental consultant, environmental supervisor – those questioned used the terms haphazardly and with combinations of names which shows that the identity contours of these professions are not properly established. We also notice some vagueness in the description of missions identified as being attached to those roles.

These difficulties in pinning them down come on top of concerns with the skills of those experts in their contribution to projects for which the contracting authority wants to be seen to be exemplary environmentally speaking and their skills in negotiations with other actors. This also applies to the visibility of their work at the interface of the three groupings of our construction model. On these three points, the messages we received indicate that major challenges are shadowing these emerging professions.

In the choice of a HQE and sustainable development approach, the contracting authority will, in a different fashion for each new project, engage with a reflection on the integration of a new actor into the decision-making team. From the word go, questions are asked as to the legitimacy of this choice and the type of collaboration: is it worth using an HQE-AMO? What financial resources are available to make it work? How will this environmental professional find his place in the development of the brief? Do there have to be separate functional and HQE briefs? How is the AMO positioned during the project follow-up phase and in his relationship with the principal contractor? These questions are all part of a set of representations which put the HQE-AMO in a situation where, even though the AMO is from the outside, the AMO has to show his or her worth within the contracting authority team and provide a successful interface with the project designers. This means that the onus is on the contracting authority to communicate on its environment-related needs to internalise the know-how gleaned outside (which has not always been the case). In the same way, the HQE-AMO must as clearly as possible understand the content of the requirements stipulated on the one hand in order to successfully transform knowledge into skills and on the other, to adapt the level of his or her work to the way that the other professionals work.

The French 'founders' emphasised first that the use of an HQE-AMO meets an explicit requirement of the contracting authority which cannot fulfil the environmental requirements on its own. As one person questioned observed: 'the contracting authority favours these conditions because it's reassuring to them'. The idea of 'reassurance' is interesting because it returns to a theme previously addressed: the need to call in an expert to lend legitimacy to the approach. In this context, the missions allocated cover a whole range of activities whose common denominator is communication and teaching targeting the decision-makers: defining project orientations together, formalising needs through the production of documents, explaining targets and the impact of their choices, making their networks and previous experiences available to the client and maintaining people's interest in the HQE approach.

> We work on the definition of the project, the setting up of the project, its orientations and the passive aspect . . . as it's a competitive call for tenders, we talk a little bit about energy and we prepare illustrative documents which explain how the building works, present the building as a biotope . . . this is very easy for people to understand. We prepare a little document . . . the contracting authority asks for it . . . we organise ourselves to be able to answer his demands. We keep ahead of the game because we only work with HQE project reference sets. In terms of demands, we draw up an environmental profile by proposing CSTB performance levels. We think that by promoting this reference set we will move things forward. You have to keep close to HQE I think.

The issue of brief and the involvement of the HQE-AMO in the scheduling phase is, undoubtedly, one of the most important and most controversial aspects of these interviews. On the basis of the brief, the project can be brought to life: 'On these operations, the brief has to be very precise, we cannot do an HQE operation without a brief', specifies one founder. From that point on, reflection is based on the degree of participation of the HQE-AMO in the preparation of the functional schedule. It seems that at that stage, for the contracting authority, it is important to clarify the positioning of the different parties in respect of this collaborative approach. Without it, there is a risk of what one person questioned describes:

> You have some HQE-AMOs who fall out with the AMO and say 'If we are asked to do HQE, we don't need to have an HQE specialist' and others say: 'Why are they doing our job when they haven't got the skills to do it?'

This kind of situation is by no means isolated. It reflects a real difficulty in exercising the mission of assistance to the contracting authority and in the conditions of the brief-specifying phase. The examples provided by the monographs of our survey complete this approach and show that several situations exist around these professional combinations.

If you take the example of the construction of Echirolles town hall, we note that the contracting authority's team – in this case, the municipal team – very rapidly voted for HQE targets. The decision to adopt a HQE approach and to have an environmental approach in the brief was taken from the very start (in 2001). On the other hand, the issue of whether this HQE brief has to be distinguished from functional brief does not necessarily hold for everybody at that stage in the project. The fact of having two programmers is referred to. Arguments then began within the contracting authority's team because of the additional cost incurred by this option. Very quickly, without actually questioning the choice of targets, a call for programme tenders was launched which specified the association in the same team of brief specifying, HQE and economist skills. The result was that two different teams came together. There will be a functional programmiste and an HQE-AMO programmiste. We now understand the difficulty in formalising a single way of functioning in the initial stages and also of integrating actors who, each bringing their own skills, will play an individual and collective role. Finally, on the town hall project, the HQE brief is much more detailed than the functional brief because it provides information on the site, the environmental objectives and the targets.

To take another example, that of the town hall of Les Mureaux, we observe that the way the operation was put together and the idea of including outside support to the contracting authority were different. On this project, which is a renovation project (a town hall building already existed), a very light pre-brief (around 10 pages), was drafted by a programmiste. After that date, the town hall launched a call for definitions which served to establish the brief at the same time as the project was being designed. At first there were two programmistes (from the same company), one of whom had an HQE background. This situation is quite different from the previous one, since the project is finally dreamt up at the same time as the functional brief and the HQE. The result of this is that the programmiste functions together with the architect, a solution which is highly favourable to shared, convergent design.

Through these two case studies, we know that there is no ready-to-schedule idea associated with the HQE approach and that each operation corresponds to a particular way of including the AMO. The challenge is both in the skills that each one brings to the project and also, and more particularly, in the knack of getting them all to work together.

Beyond this issue of the brief, we note that there is a difficulty of identification and visibility of those professions associated with support to the contracting authority. This uncertainty comes from the diversity of profiles and careers of those professionals. As the people questioned insisted, the HQE-AMOs come from very different horizons and sometimes from worlds that do not always cross over: the AMO, a researcher, architect who is self-taught, militant, seems to have a wide range of careers which make it impossible to identify a typical profile, a professional identity defined by the structures of diplomas or specific experiences. This complex identification process is further exacerbated by questions of understanding and identification of frontiers between HQE-AMO and architect. Since it is an emerging profession – at the interface between the forces of control and of implementation – the HQE-AMO is going through a process of adaptation to the professional sphere of the principal contractor, which does not always see such associations as positive sources of complementarity. There is also the challenge of the various responsibilities of the different parties.

> Without wishing to be cruel, there are loads of HQE-AMOs who are contracting authorities who haven't made it, and it's interesting to see how architects receive AMOs . . . it doesn't generally go very well .

> Because, most of the time, what we see is assistance to the contracting authority 'HQE' who does design, excludes certain things and so guides technical choices which are not the domain of the contracting authority. There, there is a pathology which appears, and of course there will be expertise, there will be disputes . . . that's quite normal. We're going to end up seeing a contracting authority taking on HQE-AMOs who are not insured for the mission. 'Why isn't he insured?' Because he's only covered for straightforward civil liability, not the 10 year guarantee; but as my projects feature elements to do with technical regulations, we are covered by the 10 year guarantee. Since these choices have been made by the contracting authority, liability will be with he who has advised: he will be liable and won't be insured. Such disputes are bound to happen . . . which is logical, since we are going to touch on questions of money, consumption, commitment to results which are not honoured, etc. Of course, they will go back up the ladder and they will say, 'Hang on, we didn't recommend that, it was the support function to the contracting authority who said that . . .' It's a big danger. On the other hand, a programmiste and an AMO and HQE skills are crucial.

To complete this chapter, we return to our initial hypothesis that the French 'founders' were at the origin of a 'movement' which introduced skills, new directions and new ways of working together in pursuit of environmental quality. This professional reality is taken from the 'negotiated' design model; it is real yet ambivalent. It is based on values (the need to commit to a project for the planet) shared by all actors but which at the same time, cause problems of identity repositioning. Architects arguing with the HQE can no longer think of their relationship with design as they did before. They no longer – or should we say, they no longer only – embody the image of the free creator. In the same way, the arrival of the HQE-AMO and environmental advisers on the professional services market turns the power struggle on its head in the sharing of responsibilities and the legitimacy of the project. As a result, traditional professional identities are thrown into question by the emergence of strong environmental concerns. In this context, the question of leadership *à la française* in construction is not the same: it is now for each activity area (contracting authority, principal contractor and industrialists) to take the part of the environmental pie that suits them best. Without that, and with operations on a certain scale, it will lose its power, both in carrying the project and its political statement of ambition.

ACKNOWLEDGEMENT

This chapter was translated by Neil Draper (neil@gocommservices.com).

NOTES

1   Initiative supported and financed by the state, which gave rise to the creation and validation of a reference set registered with the trademark 'HQE'®. Because our work is to do with expertise, skills and collaboration between professionals and our research concerned more with the implementation of environmental quality in a sustainable development sense rather than a practical one, we will use the term 'HQE' as a concept and an approach, in reference to interviews we have had with various people.

2   PCA is the construction and architecture plan which subsequently became PUCA, the planning, construction and architecture plan.

3   We are thinking, for example, of the '5000 solar houses' competition launched by the Industry Ministry and the Infrastructure Ministry in 1980.

4   We surveyed a group of 22 'founders' who were willing to be interviewed as part of a university research study entitled 'Expertise, skills and management of sustainable construction projects', jointly led by the CRISTO/PACTE laboratory of Grenoble and Bristol (University of the West of England, UWE) in May 2006 under the supervision of Eric Henry and Martin Symes. The results presented in this chapter are the fruit of that research.

5   It should be noted that we were not able to take the professions and actors linked to certification audits into account because auditors were not authorised to take part in the survey because of the confidential nature of audits requested by the CSTB.

6   For example, the visibility afforded to the HQE approach in Echirolles' (38) town hall construction project, if the municipality's website is anything to go by. It is striking to see the extent to which the construction of a new building gives rise to explanations, worksite photos, a chronological slide-show, a description of the materials used and a specific section on what the HQE approach is. We note the importance of the 'shop-window' effect and the impact of communications (a theme we will address further on) for a project of this scale as soon as the environmental dimension is present: http://www.ville-echirolles.fr/rubrique51.html.

7   This resignation was linked to criticism of the HQE in the name of cultural development as a component of sustainable development.

REFERENCE

Henry, E., Abrial, S., Codie-Bisset, J., Debizet, G., Paris, M. and Puybaraud, M. (2006) Expertises, competences, et gestion des projets de construction durable. Unpublished report following research financed by Plan Urbanisme, Construction, Architecture, Ministère des Transports, de l'Equipement, du Tourisme et de la Mer, Paris.

11

Sustainable Building in Italy
The Rules, Professions and the Market
Marco Filippi and Enrico Fabrizio

In the first part, the Italian real estate market is analysed and how issues of sustainability are related to it is discussed. Then, the main regulations and tools to rate sustainable building in Italy are presented and the similarities with other foreign tools are highlighted. The theme of regulations leads to the subject of local authorities, where the interventions undertaken by them to achieve the objective of a sustainable building construction are emphasised. Finally, the attitude of public and private owners is discussed with the reference of some case studies, and the developing professions of the future in Italy are suggested.

THE REAL ESTATE MARKET AND THE CULTURE OF SUSTAINABLE BUILDING

Real estate investments in Italy totalled 186 million euro in 2005, 44 per cent of which in new buildings, 39 per cent in building renovation and the remaining percentage in maintenance; 45 per cent of the new buildings are residential, 32 per cent are non-residential, and 23 per cent are infrastructures (CRESME 2006).

According to the analysts, the construction market grew steadily in 2006, and was characterised by lower growth rates than in the past. The new house building industry has been continuing to grow, but a slowdown in terms of transfers and prices has been registered in the real estate market, renovation has hardly taken off, while non-residential building seems to be regaining its importance in the industrial sector, and even more in the tertiary sector and in some commercial building types.

Quality, both in terms of performance and attractiveness of a building, is an important strategic matter. Recent years have seen an innovative development of building products and materials, but not an improvement in performance and attractiveness of finished buildings or in their ability to fulfil and adapt to the social and economic changes of residential and non-residential demand.

Survey results show that only 43 per cent of Italian families are satisfied with the quality of their own houses, while 16 per cent explicitly complain about low building quality. A focus on the critical aspects of building quality has highlighted the following five categories (CRESME 2005):

- A new mentality is needed to overcome planners' and builders' resistance to innovation.
- The small companies dividing the market have small competencies (that means less qualification) and small resources (that means less innovation).
- The perverse connection between rough design, product innovation and bad installation has to be removed.
- The centrality of prices causes the detriment of construction quality because, where only prices count, an extreme competition is produced and the builders adjust their prices restraining quality levels and innovation margins.
- There is a lack of guidelines and incentives, no industrial policy in building, and insufficient attention given to qualification.

In the light of these critical aspects, a decisive factor to win the challenge of building quality is the change of planners' and builders' mentality, that is a different approach to the way of producing and tackling the market.

While the building production world (products, components, materials) is aware of the need of change, those who design and build continue to work in accordance with traditional models and with strong profit-oriented logics, without paying attention to the new knowledge, or without being able to recognise the importance of change in demand (i.e. more technology, more safety, more attention to health, energy saving). We see modest projects not keeping abreast of the evolution of products, materials and technologies, and planners who do not keep up to date. We see builders who tend to choose cheap materials and carry out inadequate work aiming for a maximum saving.

Moreover, this happens in the presence of end-users who are not yet capable of measuring or evaluating building quality.

In this respect, the culture of sustainability can be the keystone of change. Sustainable building somehow represents the transformation of the collective consciousness about building quality into reality.

A sustainable building

- respects the environment in terms of soil use and landscape integration
- preserves the local building traditions
- saves energy and water
- exploits local climate resources and renewable energy
- does not pollute and is built with recyclable materials

- is healthy, safe, and comfortable for the occupants
- is equipped with user-friendly advanced technologies
- is easy and less expensive to manage.

The problem is to determine how such a culture can be shared by end-users, builders, producers and planners, and moved from book pages to design drawings and from design drawings to the actual construction, up to influencing the daily management of the building.

In Italy the culture of sustainable building has found some regulation and incentive initiatives by a few isolated local authorities, and has received a certain attention from some major public and private owners, but it is not yet widespread.

Some focused actions from the government, in compliance with the 'Directive 2002/91/EC of the European Parliament and of the Council of 16 December 2002 on the Energy Performance of Buildings (EPBD)', have helped to draw increasing attention to the specific themes of energy saving and exploitation of renewable energy sources within the context of public owners and small private owners. These themes are related to building energy sustainability.

In general, however, we can say that in the Italian real estate market, where the owner, the builder and the end-user mostly have divergent economic interests, it is hard to turn sustainable building (in all its meanings) into a widespread reality.

The prevailing behaviour is to minimise the 'prime cost' (that is the cost related to the building construction) instead of minimising the 'global cost' (that is the sum of 'prime cost' and building system management costs for an adequate number of years) which takes into account the future and, therefore, building sustainability.

Generally, there is a tendency to strictly select the possible interventions. The logic is to undertake only the interventions which imply a precise evaluation of the building from the buyer's viewpoint, and therefore, which hold an individual rather than a social value.

In this kind of real estate market, it appears that the culture of sustainability can't grow without any focused regulation, certification procedures concerning both design and building, qualified professionals and builders, or, last but not least, well-informed owners and end-users, who are willing to incur higher investment costs aiming for economic benefits in the future and to give clear proof of positive or negative results achieved using the buildings.

VOLUNTARY AND COMPULSORY ASSESSMENT TOOLS

Italy does not currently have a national regulation, either compulsory or just technical, concerning the theme of building sustainability as a whole. There are some compulsory rules concerning the energy performance of buildings, i.e. the Legislative Decree 192/06 and the Legislative Decree 311/06, and the Italian Institute for Standardisation UNI (Building Commission, WG 10) will issue a standard including a rating procedure to be used at the design stage, similar to the well-known BREEAM, LEED and Green Building Tool procedures, and based on:

- a requirement for a performance approach aimed at identifying the indicators to be rated
- a positive score for each indicator accounting for the level of ecofriendliness of the project with reference to current practice or standard performances (where existing)
- a multiple and hierarchical weighting method to calculate total scores.

However, some procedures proposed by public authorities and professional associations are being spread in Italy. The most common procedures are as follows:

- ITACA Protocol
- iiSBE Italia Tool
- ANAB SB100 Checklist
- INBAR Certification
- CasaClima Certification.

The first two tools (ITACA Protocol and iiSBE Italia Tool) originate from the Green Building Tool (GBTool) procedure that was tailor made for Italian building technologies by work carried out at a national level by a group formed by the Environment Park of Turin along with the Institute for Building Technologies of the National Research Council (ITC-CNR), the National Environment Protection Agency (ANPA), the Italian National Agency for New Technologies, Energy and the Environment (ENEA), the Piedmont Region, the Augusto Rancilio Foundation (FAAR) and some universities (Politecnico of Milan, Politecnico of Turin, University of Genoa). These organisations joined the Green Building Council (GBC) in 2000 with the intention of customising the GBTool for the Italian state of construction and building technologies.

Tools that closely refer to a national context, such as BREEAM or LEED, were discarded and the preference was accorded to the GBTool since, as a result of an international collaboration, it is a comprehensive and generic assessment tool that can be customised by national users. The customisation activity was carried out by successive application of the tool on a number of case studies including a residential village in Vinovo (Turin), a building at the University of Pavia and a residential building in Padua. These case studies were presented at the Oslo International Sustainable Building (SB) conference in 2002. Following this, the tool was tested on other case studies including the Mediapolis Park in Ivrea (Turin) and the 2006 Olympic Italgas Village presented at the Tokyo SB conference in 2005.

ITACA Protocol

With regard to the environmental sustainability assessment of residential building, the customisation of the GBtool led to the ITACA Protocol in 2004 (www.itaca.org/). This is a result of the regional public authorities' will to adopt a method to make differentiated choices, aimed at encouraging the construction of buildings, which prefigure a collective interest by applying solutions more respectful of environmental values.

An interregional working group on bio-architecture of ITACA (Federal Association of the Italian Regions and Self-Governing Counties) decided to use the GBTool as a base for a new sustainable building rating system which was being drawn up. Two years later the result of the GBTool customisation in the Italian residential building context led to the so-called ITACA Protocol officially approved by the Conference of the Presidents of the Italian Regions. Since 2004 many regions have adopted it as a reference rating system, albeit in different forms: the Tuscany, Friuli Venezia Giulia and Basilicata regions have adopted it as Guidelines; the Marche region has adopted it as an energy and environmental certification tool (in compliance with the European Directive of energy certification of buildings), and the Piedmont region has applied it in the Piano Casa 2006–2012.

The protocol (Moro 2005) is made up of 70 assessment sheets, each one referring to a requirement where satisfactory evaluation is necessary. Requirements are grouped into seven areas as follows:

- environmental quality of exterior spaces
- resource consumption
- environmental load
- indoor environment quality
- service quality
- maintenance quality
- transports.

Each assessment sheet contains control indicators or parameters to evaluate requirement satisfaction, regulation references, and scoring indications. The performance score ranges from −1 to +5. A negative score is assigned when the performance indicator is below the target of local regulations or current practice. A score of 0 is assigned when the performance indicators equal the benchmark. Total building score is determined by a weighted sum, where weight is the relative importance of the performance requirement. The scores can be modified by local authorities to customise the method to the local context.

Given the complexity of the method, two simplified ITACA Protocols have been drawn up, consisting of 28 and 12 assessment sheets respectively, and contain the essential requirements for sustainable building. These simplified methods are intended to be used in the case of small-scale building interventions and during the early design stage, when it is not possible to give substance to all the requirements of the 70 assessment sheets.

There have been a few problems in applying the protocol. The protocol, designed for dwelling evaluation, does not in fact take into account the energy requirements for the cooling of space that is now becoming common practice in the Italian residential sector. Another problem regards performance indicators that need a quantitative assessment through calculation or measurement. In this case the protocol requires extremely specialised software or technologies and instruments that may not be available to the professional using the assessment tool. To overcome these drawbacks an update of the ITACA protocol is currently being developed.

Many applications of the ITACA protocol have been carried out in Italy, but it is difficult to find data about the results of the implemented assessments.

Beccali et al. (2007) applied it to two residential buildings in the county of Agrigento. To achieve the assessment, it was necessary to make a determination of performance indices not only from construction documents but also from in situ measures of some environmental parameters. They also compared the full-length protocol to the simplified protocol in order to check if there was any difference between the two versions that gave slightly different scores.

The most important potential of this tool appears therefore to be its use as a design support tool to assist architects with environmental evaluation of different design alternatives: in fact from this point of view the protocol contains a comprehensive amount of energy and environmental scenarios and suggestions for consideration when starting to design a building.

Recently, for the first time in Europe, a large banking group has launched a funding promoting construction according to sustainable building criteria, offering preferential rates and conditions both to building contractors with regards to instalment loans, and to private buyers as regards the mortgage concerning the mortgage split and contract. The group has adopted just the ITACA Protocol as an evaluation basis for the incentive allowance of sustainable building construction policies.

iiSBE Italia Tool

The GBtool customisation for environmental sustainability assessment of all buildings except of dwellings has been carried out by the Italian section of iiSBE (http://www.iisbeitalia.org/), the International Initiative for a Sustainable Built Environment, created in 2005 by the Environment Park of Turin and the ITC-CNR of Sesto San Giovanni (Milan). The scope of this no-profit organisation, located in Turin, is to provide policies, methods and tools for a sustainable built environment through networking activity, to support the GBC activity and to hold a register of accredited advisors (Moro 2006). Since 2006 iiSBE Italia provides also the scientific and technical support to maintain and update the ITACA Protocol.

The customisation activity (Lollini et al. 2006) regards:

* definition of building environmental sustainability assessment phases using the GBTool
* applicability testing of the assessment tool in different design phases and for different buildings
* definition of the methodological approach when using the GBTool as a certification tool
* contextualisation of the tool.

Given that the assessment phases are as follows,

* assessment checklist definition
* assignment of relative weighting factors
* definition of benchmarks for every performance indicator
* evaluation of design solutions with respect to the benchmarks
* calculation of building overall score,

the customisation considered the definition of an assessment checklist tailored to Italian constructive typology, for different building uses and the assignment of weighting factors and the definition of benchmarks. All these activities tailored the tool to national, or even local, construction practice and standards of the building location.

In fact, benchmarks have been defined taking into account:

* first, compulsory Italian national or regional standards, if present
* then, literature benchmarks when no standards were available
* finally, simulations performed by the working group when no standard or literature information were available.

This activity then involved a detailed study, especially regarding buildings for special use (e.g. cinemas, retail outlets).

The final score obtained by the assessment can lead to a rate certificated by iiSBE International (Piccoli 2007). There are mainly three different uses of the tool:

- design solution assessment
- support to design (from feasibility studies to construction documents)
- voluntary certification.

In case of an existing building the assessment can be used to demonstrate the actual performance of the building. The certificate will expire after five years.

The iiSBE Italia tool was adopted as an assessment tool in the Ex-Ansaldo Area design competition in Milan (see later in the chapter), in the design of the new Mediapolis Park (Ivrea) and to perform an operational energy and environment assessment of the IPERCOOP Shopping Centre of Sesto Fiorentino (Florence). The tool proved to be applicable to different design stages and to different building uses.

ANAB SB100 Checklist

The SB100 (Sustainable Building in 100 actions) is a building environmental sustainability tool (http://www.anab.it/SB100/) drawn up by the Italian National Association for Bio-Ecological Architecture (ANAB) in partnership with the Ecopolis Research Institute (IRES). It consists of three parts: guidelines, a positive list and a checklist. The guidelines define 10 targets. The positive list is made of 100 actions that lead to the 10 targets specified in the guidelines (energy, water, materials, waste, safety, comfort, context, information, costs and management). For every action a sheet is supplied which explains the action and indicates bibliographic references and standard references. The checklist is used to assess the building environmental performance through a scoring method and to count the score, on the basis of which the building is given a merit class ranging from 1 to 5. The assessment is based only on a qualitative check of the presence/absence of an action in the project.

A software tool is available on the website of the National Counties and Town Councils that have adopted it. Up to now the counties of Bologna, Perugia, Piacenza and Rimini and some town councils are going to use this tool, but there is no public evidence of the outcomes achieved.

INBAR Certification

The Italian National Institute for BioArchitecture (INBAR) has developed an energy and environmental quality trademark (http://www.bioarchitettura.it/). This certificate is intended to attest the sustainability of the entire building construction process from the design stage to the building management stage. The certification process is divided into three parts: the first, known as decision process, is intended to provide the assessment during the environmental pre-feasibility study, site analysis and design phases. Then design covers all phases, from preliminary design to construction document preparation and safety management on the building site. At each stage also documentation is sent to an INBAR assessor.

INBAR certification is outlined as follows. In the first stage (step 1), a certification request is addressed to INBAR that replies assessing the environmental feasibility of the project on the basis of general data provided by the real estate agent.

In the case of positive advice, the certification process continues by defining an integrated design team capable of dealing with all skills that a sustainable design involves (step 2). In this stage, INBAR can advise building owner professionals to join forces with the design team if some skills are lacking.

Then (step 3), a detailed analysis of the site is performed on documentation sent to INBAR by the project team. Successively, the assessment is similar to the one provided by the other tools during design phase and is organised in assessment sheets grouped into the following five areas:

* outdoor environment and relation to the context
* rational use of resources
* minimisation of environmental loads and wastes
* optimisation of indoor environment standards
* space quality and building systems management.

In this stage (step 4), all construction documents must be sent to the certification organisation before presentation of construction permit to local authorities. This allows INBAR to judge whether the certification process should be continued or not (requiring a minimum score of 30 out of 45).

In the stage of building construction (step 5), INBAR checks the tender and construction documents.

Lastly (step 6), the INBAR inspector visits the building site and carries out the test. Subsequently (along with any additional tests that may have been necessary) INBAR presents the certificate according to the inspector's report.

The certification process can be dealt with using a tool available online after submitting the registration fee. In this case also, there is no public evidence of the outcomes achieved in the applications carried out.

CasaClima certification

This is a tool for assessing the energy performance of a building through the optimisation of the building envelope thermal insulation and the exploitation of solar gains (Lantschner 2006). A spreadsheet, which can be downloaded free from the net, is available to perform the energy calculations of a general dwelling. Energy calculations refer partly to the European standard on energy need for heating (EN 832) and partly to the German Passivhaus standards.

It is based on a consumption classification, from letters A to G like the European certification scheme for household appliances, according to the net energy need for heating. The superior limit of Class A is 30 kWh/m^2 per year (that is the double of a Passivhaus, where that parameter has to be lower than 15 kWh/m^2 per year); therefore, an additional class, called A Gold, has been defined for buildings whose consumption is within the limit of 10 kWh/m^2.

In the county of Bolzano the certification is issued free of charge by 'Aria e Rumore' Office, 'Agenzia provinciale per l'ambiente' (County's Agency for the environment, http://www.agenziacasaclima.it). Recently its application became compulsory for all the new buildings.

The rating is made only after on-site instrumental surveys have been carried out (thermographies, blower door test) and not on the basis of the project documents. CasaClima certification has been created in the county of Bolzano where it is now deep-rooted after the issuing of certifications for 1,800,000 m^3 (10 per cent falls within class A and 0 per cent falls within class B), and where moreover it has been compulsory since 2005. It is now being spread throughout the national territory also, thanks to a strong promotional and informative activity during numerous technical meetings and fairs. An international fair focused on this subject, Klimahouse, took place twice (the second time in 2007) in Bolzano. A specific quarterly review, called *Casa&Clima*, has been published since March 2006. It is intended to spread the culture of low consumption dwelling-houses, of installation technologies and of innovative materials related to them. Besides, it illustrates the most significant buildings certified CasaClima.

The limits of such an approach, based on the German literature regarding the passive house (Passivhaus) and therefore focused on the building interventions closely related to the type of passive house, are evident. Moreover, the evaluation is essentially based on the determination of the net energy need for heating. In order to overcome the first drawback, the CasaClima[più] certification has laid down a series of quality requirements to be fulfilled in addition to the energy assessment. A CasaClima[più] building must have a thermal requirement lower than 50kWh/m^2 per year, and also exploit renewable energies, use building materials which are not dangerous for environment and health, and undertake at least one of the following interventions: photovoltaic panels, thermal solar collectors, rainwater collection, green roofs.

ACTIONS BY LOCAL AUTHORITIES

The number of local public authorities (town councils, counties, regions) producing town planning and building regulations aimed at sustainable building is increasing more and more in Italy. Moreover, they play an important role in promoting the culture of building environmental sustainability, overcoming what for a long time has been considered a tendency or a model of behaviour for few experts. Their actions have attracted the interest of builders, the real estate market and the building material and component production world, which, through updated and technically advanced innovations, has to fulfil a demand which is more exacting, qualified and aware of the specific themes of environmental sustainability, and also economically encouraged.

Already in 1998, when building sustainability was not yet common, the Italian National Agency for New Technologies, Energy and the Environment (ENEA), in partnership with some national associations of architects, engineers, building contractors, and some town administrations, laid down a 'Code for energy and environmental quality in the built environment'. This document, also in accordance with the French initiative of Haute Qualité Environnementale (HQE), defined, in terms of recommendations, the objectives to be achieved by local authorities within the context of interventions on their territories, use of energy and environment resources (water, air, soil, green and energy), and incentives to private individuals. In addition, it defined the principles to apply while drawing up planning documents (with particular reference to mobility around the building, acoustics and aerodynamics of the urban structure), and the energy-environmental criteria concerning intervention: designs, building management, health and comfort.

The aim was to involve a large number of local authorities, companies, institutions, and associations capable of giving the information to fulfil the principles included in the Code, and therefore to set up a network of knowledge and competencies about the matter, incite the public administrations to control pollutant emissions, implement energy plans, exploit renewable energy sources at least in public buildings, and establish building regulations in accordance with the objectives of high energy and environmental quality.

The Code initiative did not have a significant result, but starting from 2003 some local communities have been integrating their own building regulations with performance requirements aimed at sustainable building. In some cases, the theme was addressed only in terms of energy aspects (and starting from 2005 those decisions have been supported by the legislative measures in accordance with the above mentioned European directive EPBD), while in some other cases it was tackled in depth, as regards general quality of building and urban systems, and resource consumption (not only energy).

The innovative building regulations for the small town (13,800 inhabitants) of Carugate, near Milan, and the 'Energy and Environment Attachment' to the building regulations of the city of Turin' are two examples of this way of operating.

In the first case, the town council has adopted a prescriptive approach to guide the territory's development towards environmental sustainability principles, by adding a series of compulsory or optional interventions in the new building regulations (applied for new buildings). The compulsory interventions include the improvement of building envelope energy performance, of thermal and electrical installations, the improvement of indoor thermal comfort in summer, thermal solar installations for domestic hot water production intended to cover at least 50 per cent of the energy requirements, and drinking water consumption control. The optional interventions include green roofs, low temperature terminals, bioclimatic components and photovoltaic solar installations. Thanks to the adoption of the building regulations, the primary energy savings expected for 2010 range from a minimum of 12 per cent to a maximum of 24 per cent, according to the impact of renovation interventions on the existing real estate.

In the second case the urbanisation charges are reduced as far as 50 per cent for interventions on the building (i.e. increase of daylighting and thermal insulation and decrease of cooling loads in summer by shadings) and on its technological equipments (i.e. use of thermal and photovoltaic solar panels, rainwater collection and use, condensing boiler installations, low temperature heating systems, and individual regulators and counters for the delivered thermal energy).

Whether they liked it or not, almost every regulation text which was produced fell into the prescription logic, imposing performance limits and the use of a particular component or a particular technological system, without tackling the theme of sustainability in terms of 'sustainable income', 'ecological integrity', 'inequality, institutions and environmental impact', 'participation and sustainable well-being' or 'alternative ethical approach' (Hatfield Dodds 2000). However, their positive stimulating effect remains in a more conscious demand for sustainability.

THE ATTITUDE OF PUBLIC AND PRIVATE BUILDING OWNERS

Even when aware of the social value of sustainable building and sensitive to sustainability, the major public and private building owners are confused: they understand the potential of sustainable building and see the demonstrative value and image benefit, however they cannot define the features of a green building construction or attribute a management or economic benefit to it.

They are willing to incur extra construction costs, aiming for a long-term capital recovery, but

- in the absence of compulsory requirements related to sustainable building, and of expertise in the matter, they do not know who to refer to
- they have to deal with local authorities with no competence in the matter, who often discourage them by applying compulsory urban planning rules and obsolete building regulations
- they cannot get precise information from architects about the improvement of the sustainable building performance in comparison with a non-sustainable building
- they find difficulties in estimating the extra construction costs they have to incur
- they cannot know the operational cost of a sustainable building, or compare it with a non-sustainable building.

They often end up relying on architects who propose steel and glass architectures (with a strong urban impact) as sustainable, even though these actually just agree with the standards of a contemporary architecture ruled by technology.

Frequently the public owners entrust the carrying out of good projects to inadequate tender procedures for the construction works (i.e. contracts based on the maximum reduction of auction base price) and therefore they lose control of the building process.

Often, the public and private owners are not aware of the choices they are making, and consider the theme of sustainability as restricted to the design stage, as if it was exclusively a design value. They don't realise that sustainability is a value which has to be preserved during the building operation, by adopting consistent management methods.

Many intelligent and innovative projects, properly carried out, fail at the post-occupancy stage, when the facility management adopted by uninformed service companies (which normally apply conventional or economically rewarding management techniques) do not respect the principles according to which the building has been conceived.

As regards the relationship between public contracting agents and sustainable building, a recent case in Italy is worth citing as a significant example: the planning (Filippi and Mellano 2004) and construction (Filippi and Mellano 2006) of the Olympic villages for the 2006 XX Winter Olympic Games.

By the time Turin had become a candidate for the Olympic Games, the Torino 2006 Organising Committee (TOROC) had already submitted a document entitled *Green Card*. This document contained concrete guidance for designing and constructing the Turin sports facilities and infrastructure and handling the affected environment. It also contained the Agenda XXI implementation process of the Olympic Movement.

While considering potential sites for the games and assessing the technical characteristics of the structures, TOROC drew on the guidelines in the document entitled *Strategic Environmental Assessment*. This document analysed the long-term environmental and socio-economic effects of the Olympics on the surrounding areas, looking at critical aspects, situations requiring further study and constraints. Crucial themes were energy, water and soil, biodiversity and landscape, mobility and transport, and sustainable local development. Plans for mobility, safety of workers and the population, prevention of natural risks, water system management, handling of inert substances, and continual monitoring of changes in the environment were drawn up in the light of the *Strategic Environmental Assessment*.

In 2002, TOROC entrusted the Agenzia Torino 2006 with drafting the *Preliminary Planning Statements* document to lay down guidelines for the design of the sport facilities (ice rinks, ski jumps, bobsleigh run, ski-lifts, competition ski runs), the roads, snow production plants and Olympic villages.[1] At that time, no directions or instructions on sustainable building had been devised by either TOROC or by Agenzia Torino 2006. Sustainability had been referred to only in the feasibility studies as a general service but not as a design objective. To respect international agreements on the subject of sustainable Olympics, the decision was taken to highlight this theme, above all in the construction of the Olympic villages that would host the athletes and journalists (TOROC 2003).

Because no validated methods on sustainable building rating and certification were available in Italy or indeed in Europe, Agenzia Torino 2006 entrusted the Politecnico di Torino (www.polito.it) with developing a document concerning the sustainable building. The *Guidelines for Sustainability in Design, Construction and Operation of the Olympic Villages* were then prepared and adopted as a reference handbook for design and engineering services competitions related to the six Olympic villages.[2] In order to give substance to the policy of sustainable architecture in such design competitions, the Agenzia reserved a significant share of the proposal score (18 per cent) to sustainability of the building.

The *Guidelines* were organised in requirement classes concerning utilisation of climatic resources, environmental quality of the exterior spaces, integration with the environmental context, consumption of energy and water, environmental loads, quality of the indoor environment and quality of service. The requirement class cards were classified within the *Guidelines*, in relation to sub-requirement classes and to single requirements. For each requirement, the card specified the goals, qualitative and quantitative requirements, reference strategies and technologies, essential bibliography, standard and regulations, as well as control tools and control indicators during the design, construction and operation stages. Control tools were defined and based on the check of technical documents, design drawings, numerical simulations, results of measurement performed in situ or in the laboratory and of the monitoring results (Filippi et al. 2002).

Ten Olympic villages were built, some parts completely financed and others the result of private–public collaboration (TOROC 2004, 2005). After the construction phase, looking through the as-built documentation and visiting the sites, it can be seen that the *Guidelines* did not reach the ambitious goal that had been fixed: to build significant examples of sustainable architecture in the urban environment (Filippi 2006).

The planners and designers in charge of the projects generally showed unsatisfactory capability of integrating micro-urban design with building design, and building design with installations design, may be due to the limited available time or to insufficient information or to inadequate amounts of the funds available. They preferred to concentrate the 'weight' and the image of sustainability in some isolated building and installation components, such as thermal insulation materials based on natural fibres or solar shading, thermal solar collectors, heat recovery systems.

Construction works were entrusted to concessionaires and building contractors who were interested in putting the buildings on the post-Olympic real estate market, so, in order to control investments and to overcome the pressure of numerous functional changes during the working process, the few components considered as qualifying at the design stage were soon neglected. In conclusion, despite the principles stated, only a modest result has been achieved from the technical point of view.

The situation resulted in the case of the XX Olympic Winter Games is definitely the example of a building process strongly influenced by circumstances beyond the design intentions (Figure 11.1), but we cannot say that it is unusual when the owner is public. Generally the entrusting of the assignments related both to engineering services and construction works are mainly aimed at obtaining the minimum job price and no rewards are acknowledged for a good quality (therefore a sustainable building). Moreover, the functions in charge of project examination and validation, and in-process and final inspections are too weak and do not enable a proper management throughout the whole building process.

An exemplifying case of behaviour of a major private owner is the International Design Competition Ex-Ansaldo Area, Milan (Figure 11.2). The international design competition on invitation was launched in October 2005 by Pirelli Re and Morgan Stanley. The aim was to plan a building complex to be used for office and retail purposes in an area of 58,800 m^2, with a building footprint of 13,500 m^2 and a gross floor area of 59,700 m^2. In the competition guidelines, the client had required maximum flexibility and adaptability of spaces, energy efficiency and long-term sustainability. One of the major reasons for interest and innovation in this design competition has been the adoption of an environmental sustainability assessment tool.

11.1 Former MOI Olympic Village in Turin (architect Benedetto Camerana and Partners)
Source: Enrico Fabrizio

11.2 Ex-Ansaldo area in Milan (Pirelli Real Estate)
Source: Photographer not identified

The tool adopted by Pirelli Re was a customised version of the GBTool, prepared by iiSBE Italia. The participants were asked to respond to the 70 requirements of the tool and to do preliminary self-assessment producing evidence to justify the score. Then iiSBE and ITC-CNR organisations verified the assessment of the projects and assigned the final score.

Two projects, ex aequo, were selected as winners: Archea Assocati and Michael Maltzan Architecture. The two winners have been invited to cooperate and draw up a new project that will not simply be a merger but will retain the best features of both winning projects in a new concept.

The environmental sustainability assessment was however particularly burdensome to the participant project teams, partly because of the short term of the design competition and partly because of the redundancy of the requirements of the tool used, that in many cases was too detailed to be applied in a preliminary design competition or not consistent with the building function (for example a positive score is assigned to the production of domestic hot water completely from solar collectors even if the building function is office or retail). In this case, sustainability has been definitely a positive characterising element of the competition announcement, but the tool used to examine the project results turned out insufficient for the required design level, and in some parts inconsistent.

Even at a smaller scale there is a strong interest in sustainable building. A pilot construction project of single-family row houses in Fiano Romano (Rome) is currently at the design stage (general contracting is EuroAEdifica).The project, called Ecovillae, is presented to be the first sustainable construction project in Lazio, and will be built over a land area of 30,000 m² located behind the A1 motorway. The eco-friendly design of the 105 residential units for a gross floor area of 10,000 m², was oriented not only to achieve a high degree in energy performance but also to guarantee high quality of communal areas (gardens, play areas) and integration within the natural context. A preliminary assessment of project sustainability has been made through the ITACA tool and the project was assigned an overall score of 4 out of 5. The ecological footprint of the project has also been calculated and it is equal to 2.5 hectares per capita.

Two further examples worth being cited are the private residential area of Central Park in Schio (Figure 11.3) and the public nursery school of Arcugnano, both in the county of Vicenza. They were designed with a particular stress on building energy performance through the minimisation of the energy demand for heating and cooling (thermal insulation, sunspaces, use of natural ventilation and night cooling) and the exploitation of renewable energy resources. The Central Park will also be the first ever zero heating homes in Italy.

It is remarkable that in these cases, even though one of the major energy

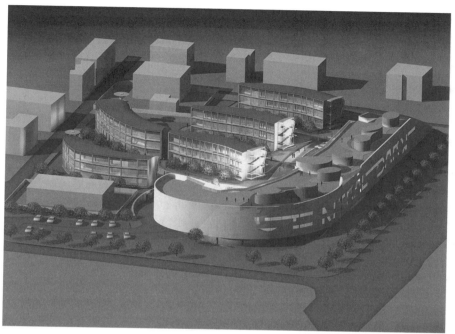

11.3 Residential area of Central Park in Schio (FONTANAtelier: architect Luisa Fontana with ARUP Italia)

Source: FONTANAtelier (architect Luisa Fontana) with ARUP Italia

consultancy firms, ARUP Italia, was entrusted with the design development of building physics, building energetics and building services, no rating tool was used to assess (and recognise) building sustainability.

The above mentioned examples show that the public and private owners, despite their efforts to promote a culture of sustainability, are still inexperienced and need to be supported by an encouraging professional and entrepreneurial world which does not apply the logic of sustainability only at the design stage.

OLD AND NEW PROFESSIONS

Building design is in itself a compromise between requirements which are sometimes conflicting. Sustainable building design is even more than that. It requires an integrated approach characterised by a combined analysis of all the project variables and the search of optimal solutions through comparisons between all the professional competencies working on the project: building owners and/or tenant, project managers, architects, interior designers, landscape architects, mechanical engineers, electrical engineers, energy consultants, facility managers, commissioning agents and, if possible, construction contractors.

The integrated approach has to be applied starting from the beginning of the project, when the sheet is still blank and the project manager has to encourage every possible form of communication, in order that the design intentions of all the competencies around the table can proceed in parallel and then converge in an atmosphere of strong collaboration. During the design project, numerous options must be created to be then analysed by precise tools in terms of environmental impact, resource consumption, construction costs, operating costs and so on.

From the economic point of view, only an integrated design process shared with the owner can overcome the prime cost barrier, and lead to the concept of life cycle economics in order to demonstrate the effectiveness of the investment.

In Italy a very small number of engineering companies are capable of offering all the competencies mentioned above. In addition, the inflexibility of the professional categories and of the respective pricelists for the professional fees hinders the creation and growth of multidisciplinary competence groups.

Small and medium sized projects are entrusted to architects or construction engineers who are normally supported by mechanical engineers and electrical engineers, only in exceptional circumstances by interior designers, landscape architects and energy consultants, but never by facility managers or commissioning agents.

In the recent years, only for relevant projects (in terms of image, or social value, or economic value) entrusted to famous architects by international tenders, have we seen more advanced professional competencies, supported by methods and tools able to face the matter of sustainability project and to provide innovative technological solutions (Grumman 2003).

Therefore we can say that today's construction professionals are unaware of the criteria for making their choices, and that they are led by the market and industrial production. A generation of architects who are victims of green rhetoric are being created. They try to insert eco-materials, green materials, passive building tech-nologies, sustainable equipment, renewable energy (sun, wind, geothermal) into their projects without any awareness of the internal coherence that a building project requires or of the concepts of integrated design: it is obvious that narrow ranges of thermal comfort are not consistent with natural ventilation and free cooling techniques; a substantial energy demand cannot be satisfied by renewable energy sources alone; an equipment is sustainable only if associated to systems that work properly.

In order to create a conscious design of a sustainable building it is absolutely necessary to add new professional skills to project teams. With reference to sustain-able construction the professional skill most required today is a designer that, in an holistic relationship, supplies the architect with the most advanced knowledge in building physics, building technologies and equipment, also be able to model the phenomena of the building as a whole and as components. The new professional figure should be able to

- assess the environment in which a new construction has to be inserted
- analyse and evaluate the behaviour of a building envelope with reference to building physics: thermal inertia, daylight, solar shading, window system concepts, building envelope functioning
- evaluate energy savings of passive heating and cooling strategies and of natural and hybrid ventilation strategies
- simulate the energy demand of buildings and building services on an annual basis
- verify indoor environment comfort conditions: thermal comfort, acoustic comfort, visual comfort, indoor air quality
- analyse the project in the context of its life cycle
- look for opportunities and find incentives for sustainable buildings and promotion programmes
- apply green building rating procedures.

These skills should become part of the cultural baggage of new professional designers coming from Schools of Architecture and Engineering. This moves the debate onto the formative pathways that must mark out the new professionals.

Now that a study reorganisation is going to affect the Italian universities, it is under discussion whether the above mentioned new professional figure should come out: from a degree course in polytechnic architecture, from an engineering degree course in energy technologies or, better, from a postgraduate course dedicated both to architects and engineers.

Waiting for the definition of these new formative paths, nowadays the mechanical and electrical engineers, who for a long time have been charged with the design of energy systems, central plants, mechanical and electrical installations, appear to be the professionals within the design team that are able to deal with most of the technological themes concerning sustainable construction. However, owing to their academic training, these engineers have the least knowledge of building construction and are not able to work in an holistic relationship and to conceive integrated design solutions.

Moreover and paradoxically, their engagement turns out to be a work of minimising the economic incidence of the mechanical and electrical components and of transferring the cost savings obtained to the 'competing' different building components, with obvious negative consequences for their professional fees.

TOWARDS THE SUSTAINABLE BUILDING

Sustainable building should not be seen as an objective by itself. It is part of a wider action plan, aimed at the sustainable development of the planet. Moreover, the strength of local, regional, and global impact of the built environment on the available resources (air, water, territory, vegetation, and fauna) is considerable, and therefore any existing opportunity to influence the way of constructing buildings deserves particular attention.

In Italy the conditions that support sustainable building are not yet available. The design teams do not include all the needed competencies; compulsory requirements related to sustainable building are lacking, as is a commissioning process that can ensure that all building systems are performed interactively according to the design intent and the owner's requirements. Contract forms allow builders to change design specifications during the construction phase and no culture of facility management exists capable of guaranteeing duration over time of the construction.

Nevertheless, in Italy, as well as all over Europe, a considerable demand for sustainable buildings is growing. These buildings are seen as buildings that save energy and water, exploit renewable energies, are healthy, safe and comfortable, are equipped with user-friendly advanced technologies and are easy and less expensive to manage. This demand is forcing all the actors of the construction process to adapt themselves.

In the building industry there is a large discussion about sustainability of materials, products and technologies. There is however an essential sustainability of methodologies and process that aims to improve the quality of the design and of the decisions. The process is the key to the success of a strategic initiative on sustainable building and it must be regulated by rigorous governance procedures and implementation methods, and must be shared since it is widely participatory. Recourse to agencies able to carry out the commissioning process from the design stage to the delivery of the building to the owner would allow controlling the construction process and assuring that sustainable building goals are achieved.

The public bodies are working on promoting durable, energy efficient and water saving construction at a national level through economic incentives for renewable energy sources and, at a local level, through the issue of building regulations less rigorous in urban standards and promoting suitable technical solutions.

At present non-institutional investors are still not interested in building life cycles and not inclined to evaluate building costs over a longer period (primary costs plus operational costs). This is one of the most difficult obstacles to overcome, since no legislative rule can constrain private investors changing their attitude and 60 per cent of the new buildings are private, residential and non-residential.

The property market can effectively influence this trend only through the growth of user preferences towards first-rate building characterised by low operational cost. It has been experienced that extra-capital costs for a sustainable building (compared with the current non-sustainable building) are not so great to alter the property prices that are already high in themselves and that can fluctuate by a factor of the same magnitude because of short-term business trends.

As regards institutional investors, it is necessary to solve the problem of the building contracts, in which it is easy for the bidder to remove, during the phase of construction, those technical solutions that, at first sight, do not show favourable cost-benefit ratios. New terms of contract, promoting the actual achievement of sustainability goals through the demonstration of the results achieved by a post-occupancy evaluation, may solve this problem.

Finally, as stated before, a new mentality is needed in architects and building designers. This mentality concerns the propensity to work out an integrated project in a team of professionals characterised by the presence of different competencies aiming at working together from the concept design stage onwards, by a willingness to innovation and a consciousness of the consequences of choices taken time by time and by a skilfulness of drawing up a project that avoid a bad interpretation. Actors involved in major projects are certainly taking this direction. It seems important that the experience of an interdisciplinary design, once tested, is subsequently implemented even in smaller scale projects, as if this experience discloses a new way of making architecture and particularly a way of making a sustainable architecture.

NOTES

1   Agenzia Torino 2006 is a public body and was instituted by law in 2000; its status is that of a legal public body with organisational, administrative and accounting autonomy. Its role was to put into effect the operation and plans defined by the Organising Committee; it awarded all contracts for the necessary works and oversaw planning, contracting and realisation of most of the infrastructures for the Olympic event.

2   The *Guidelines* were drawn up under the scientific coordination of Marco Filippi and were published on behalf of TOROC in Autumn 2002 by the Environment Park – Scientific and Technological Park for Environment in Turin.

REFERENCES

Beccali, M., Cellura, M., Chimenti, S., Lascari, G., Rizzo, G. et al. (2007) I metodi a punteggio per la valutazione energetica e ambientale degli edifici. In M. Filippi and G. Rizzo (eds)

Certificazione energetica e verifica ambientale degli edifici. Palermo: Dario Flaccovio [Italian].

CRESME ([Italian] Building and Land Economic, Social and Market Research Centre) (2005) *Rapporto sul mercato dell'edilizia* [Italian].

CRESME ([Italian] Building and Land Economic, Social and Market Research Centre) (2006) *Il mercato delle costruzioni 2006* [Italian].

Filippi, M. (2006) Sustainability and the 2006 Olympics. *ASHRAE Journal* 48(9): 82–92.

Filippi, M. and Mellano, F. (2004) *Agenzia per lo svolgimento dei XX Giochi Olimpici Invernali Torino 2006 – Progetti*, Electa [Italian and English].

Filippi, M and Mellano, F. (2006) *Agenzia per lo svolgimento dei XX Giochi Olimpici Invernali Torino 2006 – Cantieri e Opere*, Electa [Italian and English].

Filippi, M., Ruggeri, B., Mana, F., Moro, S., Dotta, M. et al. (2002) Guidelines for sustainable Olympic Villages in Torino 2006. *Proceedings of the International Conference: Sustainable Building 2002*, Oslo.

Grumman, D.L. (2003) *ASHRAE GreenGuide*. Atlanta, GA: American Society of Heating, Refrigerating and Air-Conditioning Engineers (ASHRAE).

Hatfield Dodds, S. (2000) Pathways and paradigms for sustaining human communities. In R.J. Lawrence (ed.) *Sustaining Human Settlement: A Challenge for the New Millennium*. North Shields: Urban International Press.

Lantschner, N. (2006) *KlimaHaus. Casa Clima. Vivere nel più*. Raetia.

Lollini, R., Meroni, I. and Zampiero, P. (2006) Designing building environmental sustainability: Support tools and procedures. In A. Moro (ed.) *Proceedings of the International Conference: Architettura. Urgenza sostenibilità*. Turin.

Moro, A. (2005) ITACA: A GBC based environmental performance assessment tool for the public administration in Italy. *The World Sustainable Building Conference – SB05*. Tokyo, 27–29 September.

Moro, A. (ed.) (2006) *Proceedings of the International Conference 'Architettura. Urgenza sostenibilità'*. Turin.

Piccoli, G. (2007) Development of sustainable built certification system according to the sustainable building tool assessment system: Italian experience. In *Proceedings of the International Conference: Sustainable Building South Europe*. Turin, 7–8 June.

TOROC (Organising Committee of the Olympic Games of Turin) (2003) *Environmental Report 2001/02*. Turin [Italian and English].

TOROC (2004) *Sustainability Report 2003*. Turin [Italian and English].

TOROC (2005) *Sustainability Report 2004/05*. Turin [Italian and English].

Websites

www.itaca.org/
www.anab.it/SB100/
www.iisbeitalia.org/
web.bioarchitettura.it/
www.agenziacasaclima.it/
www.itc.cnr.it/
www.envipark.com/

12

Building Operations and Use
Robert Grimshaw

The role of the existing building stock in addressing sustainable development issues receives little attention. Yet with an annual replacement rate for buildings of around 1 per cent it remains the case that the majority of buildings that will contribute either positively or negatively to sustainable development in its widest sense in the next few years are already with us. As most of them were built when sustainability was not a design issue it can be safely assumed that at present their impact is negative – it is one of the major challenges of the property industry over the next 20 years to change that impact to positive. The built environment professions must play a leading role in this reversal.

In their introduction to this book Cooper and Symes discuss the emergence of a 'new professionalism' in the built environment in response to new challenges including sustainability. The 'profession' of facilities management (FM) that has emerged since the late 1980s is part of this phenomenon and a good exemplar of the wider issues involved. It has been recognised as a separate function since the late 1980s and has ambitions to become a globally recognised profession; in this respect it has made impressive strides. But it has also developed in parallel with recognition of sustainability as a global issue and it would be fair to assume that if any profession was to be shaped by sustainability issues and include these in its professional curriculum then it would be FM. This chapter examines the issues surrounding the development of FM and how the workplace, driven by technology, is changing the whole basis of how the professions support the emergent working environment.

PROFESSIONAL DEVELOPMENT OF FACILITIES MANAGEMENT

The development of any new profession raises issues for all professions about how they are defined and developed. Facilities management is becoming recognised as a professional function worldwide and it has developed largely nationally based professional structures that reflect the conventional national approach to professional recognition and regulation. Only the International Facilities Management Association (IFMA), the US-based association, has projected itself as a global body and its

Certificate of Facilities Management (CFM) qualification is available worldwide. In the UK FM has developed a traditional professional infrastructure. The British Institute of Facilities Management (BIFM), formed by the merger of two smaller associations in 1993, sees itself as the only dedicated professional gatekeeper for FM, and has established a rigorous professional qualification based on a set of core competences. Both the Royal Institution of Chartered Surveyors (RICS), with its Faculty of FM, and Chartered Institute of Building (CIOB) also see FM as a legitimate but not exclusive part of their professional activities.

So, in spite of being a 'new' profession, FM is following the lineage of professions in the modern era that can be traced from monastic origins; they still retain an ethos of the denial of self-interest and of social duty. The professions play an important role in advanced industrial society and there is an on going debate about their nature.

In this debate some concentrate on the vocational aspects of applying 'an understanding of the theoretical structure of some department of learning or science' (Cogan 1953). Lennertz (1991) has maintained that the essence of a profession above other complex social institutions is its synonymity with public purpose, intellectual tradition and a fiduciary relationship. This approach, with its idea of a profession holding important areas of policy and practice in trust for the public, is supported by Raelin (1991), who regards professions as an authoritative symbol of social responsibility. The picture however is not consistent and the view that the term 'profession' has been devalued by the proliferation of 'quasi-professions' is supported by Savan (1989) who defines professions as 'groups which apply special knowledge in the service of a client'. Collins and Schultz (1995) also argue that as most professions sell their services direct to clients then their allegiance should only be to the client and Briloff (1972) declares that it is the client's responsibility to worry about the public interest, not contracted professionals.

What is certain is that professions have a prestigious, powerful and trusted place in society (Frankel 1989) and both the public and the courts expect high standards of conduct, especially where society allows self-regulation. The transgression of professional standards by those claiming to be professionals is judged harshly and the issue of how professional conduct is monitored is always topical. The ethical element in professional conduct cannot be ignored and the need for professions to be aware of ethical issues in the way they conduct themselves is an important element of their recognition (Freidsen 1973).

The essence of a profession is special training around a specific body of knowledge leading to an exclusive area of practice, the ideal of being learned, and a duty of social responsibility in how its members carry out their work. So, in spite of the obvious market demand for facilities managers since the mid-1980s, for FM to be accepted as a profession it had to be able to demonstrate that its area of operation has a social dimension, that it had direct relevance to the public interest and that its general conduct took account of this public interest.

Yet the challenges facing FM did not meet with the traditional requirements of professional recognition. From its establishment in the early 1990s it has struggled to define itself. There are many aspects to this debate: is it a profession or an industry? Is it operational or strategic in nature? Should it focus on buildings or management? Is it a cost control function or can it contribute to adding value? Is it a people focused or a technology focused discipline? These debates are indicative of the organisational changes driven by ICT that caused demand for FM service to emerge in the first place. They pose a challenge to all built environment professions in the twenty-first century.

The demand for FM services, which can be characterised as managing change in the workplace, was market led as the need grew within large commercial organisations for a function that could deal with technologically driven change in office facilities. FM's academic supporters, especially Becker (1990), seized on this growth of a new function to develop the concept of a socially based strategic profession that could lead organisational change from the top based on the sociological principles of 'fit'; if workplace environments could be made to fit the needs of users better, then space would be better used and employees would be happier and more productive. But most of those who came into facilities management were operational and concerned with the technical aspects of the physical work environment. So there has always been a tension at the heart of FM and its 'language' has always reflected the interface of the three aspects of the workplace: organisational culture, employee needs in the workplace, and the technology of facilities provision. These inclusive social and managerial aspects of FM gave it the potential to be different from other established BE professions and gave it an exciting multidisciplinary aspect.

However, it grew as a coordinating function largely at operational level and attracted people with a range of 'specialisms' in design, maintenance and engineering and did not seem to have a specialist function in its own right. It was in danger of failing the first test of 'professionalisation' because of the difficulty in defining the boundaries of its own specialist knowledge, a precondition of ensuring that its members have sufficient expertise in that area of knowledge to be accredited. Three areas caused concern:

• Its knowledge base is very wide: the BIFM has 20 competences that cover a diverse range of social, managerial and technical skills.
• Many of the individual areas identified by BIFM, like property management or maintenance management, are specialist professional areas in their own right.

- The areas of knowledge are shifting all the time – the addition of sustainability and networking skills to FM are good examples of new substantial areas of knowledge that may be vital in the future.

But these are also indicative of the problems facing large organisations and the need for integrated professional support to manage rapid change.

Defining its knowledge base was not the only problem facing FM in its quest for professional recognition. It was clearly not addressing a nationally based problem as most of the large commercial organisations that employed facilities managers went global in the 1990s and needed employees who could operate across national boundaries (Chotipanich 2004; McLennan 2000). This was an early indicator of globalisation the full impact of which we are now feeling. The new global economy with the integration of China and India as described by Friedman (2005) and the growing centrality of both ICT and knowledge have further undermined the power of nation states to influence economic development. This new and growing global landscape of organisational need makes the national focus of the professions seem less and less tenable.

Nor could FM demonstrate the unity of practice that underpins professional status – its very breadth made it hard to define a set of core activities that were both specifically FM and manageable. Its coordinating function made it multidisciplinary in nature from the start. Its core competences included areas of expertise common to other BE professions and it was clear that FM was extremely wide in scope (Alexander 2003; Cairns 2003).

It is hardly surprising then that in 1993 the BIFM opted for a conventional professional structure that mirrored that of its closest competitor the RICS and other established BE professions. It put in place the traditional structure for an individual rigorous professional membership in order to demonstrate its professional credentials. This has had a mixed outcome. The BIFM is undoubtedly regarded as a credible institution and it participates fully in policy debates with government and industry. However, in spite of having a membership approaching 10,000, the number of professionally qualified facilities managers remains very small largely because the market does not demand 'professionally qualified' facilities managers. The BIFM's 20 Core Competences that drive its qualification process are also traditionally drafted, focusing on management in terms of the physical facility; the BIFM did not take a more generic approach that might have seen sustainability as one of its areas of expertise.

However, of all the defining characteristics of a profession discussed earlier (from any middle-class job to Schön's (1987) strict definition of a major profession being based on sound positivist science), the one that stands out as being the most endurable is the concept of social responsibility. A profession is one that can clearly demonstrate a social impact over and above the immediate contract between employee and client. This is a socially based rather than a task based definition and implies that the role has an ethical dimension. Under this definition it is easy to see that doctors and lawyers have and exercise such a duty but harder to see the social dimension of some BE professions. Grimshaw (2001) has argued that facilities management has a clear social responsibility as its practices affect millions of people in the workplace; this validates its claim for professional recognition but also imparts to FM a strong ethical dimension. Grimshaw (2001) identifies ethical issues relating to advocacy for user needs and the need to maintain healthy, sustainable working environments. He also argues that FM and its professional institutions should be leading the national and international debates on the sustainable workplace.

The issue of the workplace and commercial property is relevant to the general argument of the book in two respects. The first is that it has become the front line in the restructuring of organisations driven by technology. Second, while there may be arguments about the exact impact of the existing building stock there can be little doubt that it does make a significant contribution to the overall equation that is sustainable development. The next two sections examine the drivers and challenges.

TRADITIONAL WORKPLACE

Since the Industrial Revolution the workplace has been defined contractually in terms of space and time. The traditional workplace has been the arena both within which work was carried out and in which the work process was managed. Just as it was created by the industrial technology of the nineteenth century so it is being altered by twenty-first-century technology. The transformational impact of ICT is starting to be fully felt as computers and peripheral devices open up access to information, customers and new ways of conducting business. This combined with the high cost of corporate real estate (CRE) and the perennial problem of poor utilisation of space is increasing the pressure to justify why so much wasteful CRE is necessary (Becker 2003). The alteration in organisational structures towards flatter less hierarchical cultures also changes the needs and symbolism of workplace environments, especially the office.

These pressures that are changing the form and function of the workplace are highlighted in the MIT/Gartner report *The Agile Workplace* (Joroff et al. 2003) that examined the relationship between organisation and workplace in 22 US corporations. Their concluding predictions included the demise of the territorial office, the growing reliance on electronic links and web-based tools to manage a more distributed workforce, the integration of infrastructure support services including FM, human resources (HR), IT, CRE and finance: a multidisciplinary approach to workplace design.

Joroff et al. (2003) developed the concept of the 'Resilient Virtual Organisation'. This emphasised the need for organisations to be more people centric, more project focused and more flexible. The name reflects the shift away from the static office to a more flexible infrastructure model where the emphasis is on the organisation as a network. Underlying these changes is the shift from product to knowledge as the key to competitive advantage. The ability to create and apply new knowledge has long been promoted by organisational theorists like Drucker (1997) and Senge (1997) as the key to economic success and the world described by Friedman (2005) with the rapid export of both routine and high value jobs to India and China shows how far this is becoming a reality. The traditional discreet long-term work facility does not fit well into this world.

For the 'buildings in use' this shift towards flexibility raises questions about the relationship between cost and value in the conventional office facility. The development of FM has been plagued by a continuation by organisations of the 'Hawthorne' view that buildings are a necessary cost but that they are essentially passive and add little tangible value to the work process (Cairns and Beech 1999). The built environment professions have so far failed to make any quantitative headway on the claim that organisational buildings add value. In spite of much anecdotal evidence that well-designed workplaces improve productivity, the closest we have to a causal link is research on self-assessment by employees (Haynes and Price 2002). With many routine commercial jobs in the west becoming increasingly exportable and therefore cost sensitive, there is an urgency in demonstrating how the physical workplace adds value. If not, the cost of CRE has to be driven down.

The danger for so-called 'green offices' is that built-in measures to improve sustainability are seen as an additional and unnecessary cost. Even though sustainability and corporate social responsibility are at the top of the political agenda and green offices are seen to be the mark of a responsible organisation, there remain remarkably few examples of green offices and little evidence that they are more creative, innovative or productive than more conventional designs.

But underlying the whole issue of the traditional office is the increasing disconnect between high-cost inflexible fixed assets designed to last for a minimum of 60 years and the increasing short-termism of organisational planning. Even the growth of more flexible and shorter term leases is not the whole answer. For the first time since the Industrial Revolution we can raise the question of what exactly offices are for, because increasingly individual non-interactive office work can be carried out more cheaply elsewhere. FM and the other BE professions need to be part of a move to justify the value that fixed offices can add to an organisation and to assess which activities should be carried out there. Early indications are that offices should be designed to promote social interaction and that they retain their symbolic significance in organisational culture. But FM also needs to assess how it can support work away from the traditional office setting (Alexander 2003; Chotipanich 2004).

NEW INFRASTRUCTURES OF WORK: MOBILITY AND CONNECTION

In 2007 the magazine *Business Week* claimed that 'work is no longer a place you go but something you do'. It is the changes going on outwith the conventional office that pose the biggest problems for all building-based professions including FM. The growth of flexible working and new web-based organisational structures is rapidly undercutting the basic tenet of the whole property supply industry that work is a product of discreet physical facilities. The simple argument that we can improve the sustainability of business by improving the sustainability of the buildings they occupy is no longer tenable. There is strong evidence now that the flexible workplace in the network organisation is a reality. Organisations are altering the way they organise work in response to the possibilities of ICT and the challenges of globalisation. The trend is away from the traditional office and towards much more flexible general working arrangements both in terms of space and time (Grimshaw 2005).

Many organisations are now moving towards a more flexible approach to work process and Sun Microsystem's 'Open Work' system is a good example of where the organisation of work is heading. 'Open Work' is not just the introduction of more flexible working arrangements but a new concept of how the work process is organised and managed. Although it relies on a secure corporate intranet, its central feature is the choice that employees have about where and when they work. The system is designed to support work anywhere any time. Employees are categorised on their main work site – mainly office, mainly home or mainly mobile – and this category dictates their infrastructure support package. This has enabled a large reduction in traditional office work and the provision of office space. The claimed outcomes are a happier more flexible workforce and huge reductions in CRE costs. Sun claims to have reduced CRE costs by $300 million in five years. Sun's innovative credentials have been recognised by its winning of CoreNet's 'Global Innovation Award' (Grimshaw 2005; Joroff et al. 2003).

Other examples from the IT sector like BT, which claims to be saving £42 million per annum in CRE costs in the UK, are now common but examples now exist in both the public and retail sectors. Surrey County Council with its 'Workstyle' initiative has given much more flexibility to its employees, moved essential services closer to its customers and disposed of 40 council-owned buildings. Best Buy, a regional American electronics and electrical retailer, has introduced a system of flexible working called 'Results Only Work Environment' (ROWE) whereby office employees are judged not on attendance but purely on results. Where and when they carry out their work is entirely up to them. The policy not only applies to offices but also was rolled out in the company's 700 retail stores in February 2007. ROWE is not just a variation of flexible working but a complete revision of the concept of how work happens (Grimshaw 2006).

Any organisation can identify with a county council or an electronics retailer and many are sure to follow as the combined benefits of reduced CRE costs and improved employee flexibility become recognised. All the examples have been preceded by a radical shift in management culture that recognises the different approach needed for non-proxemic management. In these organisations the individual workplace has a reduced importance and takes second place to the network.

The key feature of all the above is the issue of connectivity and a change in management culture. It would be a mistake to think that this is just about the application of technology. It is a symptom of globalisation and the complex 'flattened' world described by Friedman (2005). This world is technologically driven but the consequences are being felt in all aspects of life. Technology has enabled the entry of India and China into the advanced world economy, transformed many industries and led to the emergence of powerful new kinds of organisation like Google, eBay and YouTube. In this global and highly competitive world the relationship between organisations and their physical space is very different (Puybaraud 2005; Puybaraud and Grimshaw 2003). These businesses have a different attitude towards property; it is not central to the way they operate. Amazon.com for example has a very different property requirement from its rivals like Borders, which use high quality facilities to sell the same product range.

The conceptual model here is the network. Castells (1996) has developed the idea of a networked world linked by technology. In this world, governed as it is by global flows of capital and information, workplaces might look physically the same but in reality they have become nodes within a wider organisational network. Networks are mathematically driven, in a way that few BE professionals yet appreciate and in a network it is the connections that are important not the individual nodes. Flexible working either temporally or spatially makes use of the network structure and its technical infrastructure. This poses questions about how work and employees are supported and how the organisational infrastructure is designed; yet these questions are barely on the screen of any BE-related profession.

FM needs to shift away from the management of discreet facilities to the provision of support for the whole infrastructure of work. This is closer to logistics than pure facilities and requires the integration of infrastructure services and the need to align network facilities strategy with business goals (Varcoe 2004). It breaks away from the roots of FM into territories requiring major new skill sets. It poses questions like how can FM support more flexible structures where many employees are not in an office, how to design a communication strategy and how to prevent social isolation; these are very different from the traditional FM skills. It also raises issues about the sustainability of network environments.

SUSTAINABILITY OF NETWORKED ORGANISATIONS

When two vaguely defined terms like sustainability and facilities management are combined, it is not surprising that the result is a little fuzzy. However, the above illustrates how far and how fast the ground is shifting and both areas must be able to respond. It is clear that just managing the carbon footprint of the workplace in an attempt to prove the green credentials of organisational premises is not enough – the immediate challenge is to develop and maintain a socially sustainable and healthy working environment how ever broadly that is defined. The concept of a 'distributed' or 'networked' sustainability that assesses the total impact of a networked organisation on the environment is needed. Both organisational sustainability and FM need the same reconceptualisation of their missions away from the individual building to an inclusive view of infrastructure support. Large organisations have global networks and global supply chains with many aspects both positive and negative that impact on sustainability.

The relationship may be symbiotic – how FM addresses sustainability and how sustainability makes itself relevant to FM are parts of the same process. It is an indication that sustainable concepts must be built into the fabric of every BE profession; the principles of sustainability must suffuse the whole philosophy and not just be another subject on the list of competences.

On an operational level too the issues are clearer. Flexible working and increased mobility have several conflicting aspects to contend with. People who work at home for all or part of the time reduce the pollution and carbon associated with commuting but will increase the use of their own central heating and electricity consumption potentially offsetting any gain. Socially the freedom of working away from the office may be offset by isolation and lack of visibility. Yet these negative aspects are not usually considered in the general approach taken to 'sustainable mobility', which tends to focus solely on the transport aspects of commuting and not the wider issues of a distributed workforce and where they actually work.

These trends also emphasise the need to re-examine the academic underpinning of the relationship between people time and space in the workplace. Both Urry et al. (2006) and Sennett (1998) have investigated the impact of mobility. They have demonstrated how radically different the social consequences of a networked world and the associated problems of lack of identity can be. They link back to a strong humanist body of work by social psychologist/ecologists. Barker's (1968) 'behaviour settings' and Gibson's 'affordances' (Greeno 1994) among others provide the tools to illuminate the concepts developed by Guy and Farmer (2000). They emphasise that this is a social issue not a technical problem and that the potential disjuncture between people and the psychological security of their work identity is serious (Beck 2000). FM and the other BE-related professions need to respond with innovative solutions to a responsive, agile and healthy work infrastructure, and address the fundamental issues this raise about their 'professional' credentials.

CONCLUSION

The issues facing the new profession of facilities management are indicative of the pressures on built environment professions to address both the contemporary challenges of a rapidly changing global economy and the need to be traditionally 'professional'. The common thread that makes them a 'profession' is the idea that, because of the nature of their work, they have a duty to society over and above the contractual responsibilities they owe to employers and clients. Sustainability is increasingly a part of this changing landscape and has become an ethical imperative; FM and other BE professions have a duty to be advocates of healthy working environments. Sustainability is part of the complex multidimensional global challenges that now face the professions. To meet these challenges requires them to be innovative and flexible, and not allow their traditional conservative structures to hamper them.

FM has a social role in advocating better working conditions for employees within organisations; a healthy sustainable working environment is part of that advocacy. In Guy and Farmer's terms the shift to web driven networked organisations shifts the emphasis from the 'eco-technical' to the 'eco-social' – the new concept of the networked infrastructure of work is the world of logistics not of discreet fixed facilities and the concept of place has shifted away from space towards the time dimension.

The concepts that drive the relationship between people and the physical environment in this new world of work have shifted fundamentally. The important elements in this brave new world are connectivity not proximity and an ability to get the maximum benefit from the networked environment. Organisational buildings are no longer the only physical setting for work and the idea of 'Buildings in Use' may no longer be useful. Perhaps it will be replaced by the term 'Sustainability of the Working Environment'.

REFERENCES

Alexander, K. (2003) A strategy for facilities management. *Facilities* 12(11): 6–10.

Barker, R. (1968) *Ecological Psychology: Concepts and Methods for Studying Human Behaviour*. Stanford, CA: Stanford University Press.

Beck, U. (2000) *The Brave New World of Work*. Cambridge: Polity.

Becker, F. (1990) *The Total Workplace*. New York: Van Nostrand Reinhold.

Becker, F. (2003) Integrated portfolio strategies for dynamic organizations. *Facilities* 21(11–12): 289–298.

Briloff, A.J. (1972) *Accountable Accounting*. New York: HarperCollins.

Cairns, G. (2003) Seeking a facilities management philosophy for a changing workplace. *Facilities* 21(5–6): 95–105.

Cairns, G. and Beech, N. (1999) Flexible working: Organisational liberation or individual straightjacket. *Facilities* 17(1–2): 18–23.

Castells, M. (1996) *The Rise of the Network Society*, 2nd edn. Oxford: Blackwell.

Chotipanich, S. (2004) Positioning facilities management. *Facilities* 22(13–14): 364–372.

Collins, A. and Schultz, J. (1995) A critical examination of the ACPIA Code of Professional Conduct. *Journal of Business Ethics* 14: 31–41.

Cogan, M.L. (1953) Towards a definition of a profession. *Harvard Educational Review* 23: 33–50.

Drucker, P.F. (1997) The future that has already happened. *Harvard Business Review* Sept–Oct: 20–24.

Frankel, M.S. (1989) Professional codes: Why how and with what impact? *Journal of Business Ethics* 8: 109–115.

Freidson, E. (1973) *The Professions and their Prospects*. London: Sage.

Friedman, T.L. (2005) *The World is Flat: A Brief History of the 21st Century*. New York: Farrar Straus Giroux.

Greeno, J.G. (1994) Gibson's affordances. *Psychological Review* 101(2): 336–342.

Grimshaw, R.W. (2001) Ethical issues and agendas. *Facilities* 19(1–2): 43–51.

Grimshaw, R.W. (2005) *Mobility: Indicators of Performance*. Facilities Innovation Knowledge Paper. London: Johnson Controls.

Grimshaw, R.W. (2006) Mobility and change management. In T.I. Haugen, A. Moum and J. Bröchner (eds) *Changing User Demands on Buildings*. Proceedings of CIB W70 International Symposium. Trondheim, Norway.

Guy, S. and Farmer, G. (2000) Contested constructions: The competing logics of green buildings. In W. Fox (ed.) *The Ethics of the Built Environment*. London: Routledge.

Haynes, B. and Price, I. (2002) Quantifying the complex adaptive workplace. In J. Hinks, D. Then and S. Buchanan (eds) *Applying and Extending the Global Knowledge Base. Proceedings of the CIB Working Commission 070 Facilities Management and Maintenance 2002 Global Symposium*. Glasgow.

Joroff, M., Porter, W., Feinberg, B. and Kukla, C. (2003) The agile workplace. *Journal of Corporate Real Estate* 5(4): 293–311.

Lennertz, J.E. (1991) Ethics and the professional responsibility of lawyers: A commentary. *Journal of Business Ethics* 10: 577–579.

McLennan, P. (2000) Intellectual capital: Future competitive advantage for facility management. *Facilities* 18(3–4): 168–172.

Puybaraud, M. (2005) *Annual Flexible Working Survey 2005*.

Puybaraud, M. and Grimshaw, R.W. (2003) *Annual Flexible Working Survey 2003*.

Raelin, J.A. (1991) *The Clash of Cultures: Managers Managing Professionals*. Cambridge, MA: Harvard Business School Press.

Savan, B. (1989) Beyond professional ethics: Issues and agendas. *Journal of Business Ethics* 8: 179–185.

Schön, D.A. (1987) *Educating the Reflective Practitioner*. San Francisco, CA: Jossey-Bass.

Senge, P. M. (1997) Communities of leaders and learners. *Harvard Business Review* Sept–Oct: 30–32.

Sennett, R. (1998) *Corrosion of Character: The Personal Consequences of Work in the New Capitalism*. New York: Norton.

Urry, J., Larsen, J. and Axhausen, K. (2006) *Mobilities, Geographies, Networks*. London: Ashgate.

Varcoe, B. (2004) The good to great challenge. Presentation to Corenet Global Summit, Budapest. RBS Group.

13

Conclusions
Ian Cooper and Martin Symes

This volume is the fourth in a series stimulated by the work of the BEQUEST Network, an international discussion group originally funded by the European Commission. The relationship of this volume to the trajectory defined by BEQUEST was set out in the Preface, as was a summary of the contents and findings of the first three volumes. This volume is focused on discussion of the 'sustainability transition' in the development of built environment, introducing and reporting on research findings from a number of studies of professional practice concerned with Sustainable Urban Development.

There are two main themes in the book:

- Information management is as much a social as a scientific process.
- Uncertainty in the definition of sustainable urban development has interacted with variations in institutional arrangements to produce quite different professional agenda for spatial planning, property development, design and construction processes in different parts of Europe.

The approach taken to selecting and ordering the individual chapters has been as follows:

- Although institutional issues affect all aspects of the new and changing development processes which are discussed, some studies are focused more strongly on process than on institutions.
- Because the book will have an international readership, the specific context for each of the case studies included is extensively described.
- Since elsewhere the problems of practice are so often discussed in terms of new construction, an effort has been made to give sufficient emphasis to the modification of existing built environments.

From the Introduction, which consisted of a literature review followed by a summary of the case-based chapters included, a single (albeit multi-part) question emerged:

Can the transition to a new form of *practice* be identified, and if so, how is it linked with new forms of *governance*?

The case-based chapters of the book were grouped in two parts: Part I (Chapters 2 to 6) dealt with the more general studies showing the adoption of new processes in professional practice, while Part II (Chapters 7 to 12) dealt with more detailed studies investigating the pressures on the institutions of governance.

In this Conclusion, we seek therefore to respond to the main question and a number of sub-questions by asking:

What evidence does the book provide for the emergence *in development processes* (for the urban built environment) of:

- new types of professional knowledge and practice?
- new relationships between planning, property development, and construction?
- new forms of integrated and collaborative teamwork?

And for the emergence *in the institutions of governance* (for spatial planning and construction) of:

- new links between public, private and lay organisations?
- new ideas about the longer term responsibility of project promoters, construction firms, design professions and building operators?
- new ways of working with and/or for the public (interest)?

In the Introduction, we also established an implied but more highly articulated set of questions for addressing the main issues, and their underlying problems. These questions are made explicit here as a way of framing evidence from the case study material, provided in the intervening chapters, which takes the reader some way towards answering these questions.

THE QUESTIONING FRAMEWORK

The processes of sustainable urban development

1   Is sustainable development still an exception to the rules and regulations that govern the planning, development, design and construction of projects – or is it becoming institutionalised as a new norm?
2   Is there any emerging consensus, expressed through demonstrable changes in professional practices, that sustainable development requires more than just adding a few extra criteria to an already extensive list of project requirements?

3   Have there been substantive changes in professional practices or culture in response to the new criteria and methodologies proposed for engaging with sustainable development?

4   For instance, are professionals giving more attention to the broader economic and social impacts of development on the wider community or do they remain primarily driven by meeting their economic clients' requirements?

5   Has the advent of sustainable development ushered in new professional identities or just added to the agendas of existing professional organisations?

6   Are the ways in which professionals are responding to pressure to make cities more sustainable differentiated by geography, history or culture?

7   How are the information and techniques required for designing more sustainably being absorbed into everyday practice?

The institutions of governance for sustainable urban development

8   Have attempts to implement sustainable urban development required new forms of governance?

9   Are new actors emerging, especially from the NGO and voluntary sectors?

10   Is there confusion surrounding the professional structures, and more particularly the professional behaviours, necessary for delivering a more sustainable built environment?

11   In practice, is the challenge presented by sustainability more a matter of project-specific interpretation than of setting universal or objective goals?

12   Is there an emerging consensus at the different international, national, regional, local or project scales about the interpretation of how to implement sustainable development?

Underlying problems

13   To what extent is any 'new professionalism' emerging in response to sustainable development universal or shaped by variations in the geography, history or culture of governance structures?

14   To what degree is there certainty or agreement about the 'science' required to underpin delivery of sustainable development?

15   Does the knowledge required for implementing sustainable development in practice remain contested?

TOWARDS A SET OF CONCLUSIONS

The following discussion aims to draw implications from the findings of chapters in both parts of the volume. As these chapters contain reports of a selection of recent, current and, in some cases, unfinished, research projects, these implications should be seen as interim rather than final conclusions. Nonetheless certain themes do emerge, and have allowed the editors to invite readers to focus:

- first, on the new types of knowledge and practice being adopted for sustainable urban development
- second, on political and procedural approaches linking the traditional professions with new actors and new forms of responsibility
- third, on the theory underlying our understanding of the changes observed by the authors of these eleven research chapters.

Types of knowledge, relationships between professions, the need for teamwork

Questions 1 and 2: New criteria and existing knowledge

The studies reported in this book show that the skills required for managing sustainable urban development are often defined quite narrowly, as being concerned with exerting control over a small number of impacts which urban development may have on the use of resources. In the Introduction (Chapter 1), this point is made about the UK government Stern Report of 2006, which defines its central concern as that of climate change brought about by excessive emissions of carbon dioxide, implying that the need for new knowledge be focused in this area. Rydin and Moore (Chapter 2) also suggest a narrow focus when they discuss sustainable construction and design, although they do admit that thinking about only materials, energy use and waste reduction may leave aside a 'complementary but practically disparate agenda' of cultural and behavioural adaptations. Later in the book, Cooper (Ian) (Chapter 5) gives case studies of sustainable construction and neighbourhood renewal as independent activities, controlled by different policy measures, although here too a link is seen. This is that improved practice could derive in both instances from more 'boundary crossing' (technological or political, as the case may be). Scheck et al. (Chapter 7) show what some may consider the 'best developed' and the 'least developed' examples of how the new agenda is interacting with existing – and historically very different – traditions of environmental development and design.

Questions 3 and 4: The professional structure and division of responsibility

Henry and Paris (Chapter 8) discuss the institutional changes leading to the introduction of evaluation guidelines in France and the UK (HQE and BREEAM respectively). They demonstrate the strength which can come from having clear criteria together with well-defined methodologies. But this chapter also indicates the importance of observers' understanding the context in which such specialisation occurs, by using the Netherlands as a third example: a country in which broader views on the need for integrating environmental policy have existed for many years. The argument in favour of introducing precise goals, even if only of limited aspects, is reinforced by Filippi and Fabrizio's report (Chapter 11) on their experience in Italy. Here projects in which the implementation of even limited evaluation tools is not fully supported by building owners and controllers are seen as highly compromised. A 'worst case scenario' arises when architects take a 'rhetorical' view of designing for sustainability, using concepts in publicity material which they are unable to implement in practice. More broadly, Ludlow (Chapter 3) argues that the new agenda raises fundamental difficulties for those concerned with coordinating response to a diversity of existing policy priorities.

Question 5: Professional identities

An influential, and positive, critique of this 'specialisation thesis' is foreshadowed by Cooper (Ian) (Chapter 5), when he introduces the notion that sustainable development 'is said to require integrated, whole systems thinking' and 'teamwork'. This point is made with considerable force by Roberts (Chapter 6), discussing the need for the skills of 'leadership, negotiation and influencing, financial and project-management, multidisciplinary working and project management'. These Roberts terms generic skills, explaining that they may be introduced in the training of all types of professional, as well as of the community leaders who may represent user interests in a development process. Roberts indicates that existing professional traditions ('silo thinking') often act as barriers to the introduction of cross-cutting interests. But the case is not altogether clear: indeed it may be one of the unresolved issues this book reveals, for there are examples in certain chapters of the very teamworking skills which Roberts considers generic, have themselves become specialisations! The growing 'new' profession of facilities management discussed by Grimshaw (Chapter 12) began as a 'coordinating' function but is now seen as having its own distinct, and adaptive, identity. The French 'new professions' AMO (assistant maître d'ouvrage) and conseil environnement shown by Henry and Paris (Chapter 8) and in the cross-channel case studies of Debizet and Symes (Chapter 9) have a quite specific role to advise on cross-team coordination in respect of sustainable construction.

Questions 6 and 7: Cultural differentiation and everyday practice

In most of the European countries mentioned in the chapters of this book, the architect used traditionally to be the leader of the development team. The future of this role is often being contested. Whether to become a specialist in design (for sustainable construction), or to allow oneself to be seen as a 'specialist on specialisations' (in design for sustainable construction), is a real issue for some of the architects interviewed by Abrial (Chapter 10) in her fascinating report on the personal dilemmas professionals now experience.

Links with the public, ideas about responsibility, concepts of the public interest

Questions 8 and 9: New actors and new decision-points

Authors of chapters in this volume adhere to the notion that professionals must be involved in sustainable construction, but most also argue that communications between professional groups and the general public must be opened up. The crucial problem is that of the need to transfer decision-making authority, since any new information conveyed by better communications can have few consequences for what is done if the authority to make decisions remains unchanged. Rydin and Moore (Chapter 2) show that although there are a number of levels of decision-making in which authority may be vested (European, national, regional and local), the system is not best thought of as hierarchical. In practice, coalitions of different actors will control decision-making, some international groups of professionals having little influence at lower levels, and the smallest organisations (endemic in construction) often having remarkable autonomy. Boyko and Cooper (Rachel) (Chapter 4) throw a valuable perspective on the wide distribution of authority common in construction projects by dividing those involved in decision-making into approvers, takers, shapers and influencers. Many of these may be strongly influential in practice but lack any legitimate position in the structure of authority. Filippi and Fabrizio (Chapter 11) in their Italian case study maintain, perhaps unsurprisingly, that private sector builders continue to work according to traditional methods and may have little idea of the priorities held by, for example, those working in the public sector. So they suggest new terms of contract in which responsibilities for different technical aspects are clearly allocated to different actors (e.g. building owners to take on assessment of long-term costs).

Questions 10, 11 and 12: Local challenges versus global consensus

The French and British cases reported by Debizet and Symes (Chapter 9) show that even in the public sector the situation has been confused by the introduction of new political priorities at intermediate stages in a project. Roberts (Chapter 6) and Cooper

(Ian) (Chapter 5) in different chapters argue that cooperation between both public and private sector actors and local community groups must be given greater priority but seem to fall short of saying that this may require radical political development. Abrial's interviews (Chapter 10) include the words of 'personalities' who say 'environmental concern stems from an ethical position' and who may be highly sceptical of attempts to incorporate their views in traditional political systems. Scheck et al. (Chapter 7) and Ludlow (Chapter 3) discuss, at different levels of generality, problems and opportunities arising from large-scale political changes.

When Henry and Paris (Chapter 8) discuss the French and Dutch professional structures, they appear to approve clear and precise moves to establish new regulations for sustainable construction projects which confer authority (and hence 'professional status') in various stages of a development process on specific groups of actors. But the counter-argument is also clear. Grimshaw (Chapter 12), outlining the history of the new FM profession, states it thus: 'Sustainability is part of the complex multidimensional global challenges that now face the professions. To meet these challenges requires them to be innovative and flexible, and not allow their traditional conservative structures to hamper them.'

Theory concerning the processes of change: a summary

Question 13: Gradual transition or revolutionary change

So the research results reported in this volume suggest that changing professional practice to achieve more sustainable urban development, in the European context, may depend predominantly upon the possibility of introducing new skills to a traditional structure of professions. The chapter authors vary in the degree to which they have been able to address this issue. Henry and Paris (Chapter 8) collected information about three different approaches in their studies of the Netherlands, France and Britain. In the first of these European Member States, a national tradition of creating consensus in planning has been harnessed to the control of resources in urban and building design; in the second, policy has focused on specific building projects and on achieving measurable goals on specific criteria in project management; in the third, a broader approach was identified, putting an emphasis on quality of life improvements. In the first case, it would seem that existing negotiating skills have facilitated change. In the second instance, precise new forms of knowledge have been added to existing professional portfolios. But in the third, existing business practice (tendering methods and forms of contract) has been unsympathetic to new or less familiar types of analysis. Grimshaw (Chapter 12) considers existing professional traditions a constraint on innovation in the exercise of skill: Cooper (Ian) (Chapter 5) shows how this can arise from defensive measures taken by professionals 'defending their turf'.

Debizet and Symes (Chapter 9) suggest that variations in approach can result from claims made by existing specialisms for unique expertise in particular parts of the construction industry, such as hospital building, or renovation of important monuments for a new use. Boyko and Cooper (Rachel) (Chapter 4) demonstrate the variation which can arise when ownership changes during the life of a project, as do Filippi and Fabrizio (Chapter 11) when authority over design decisions is deliberately left vague or normally contested.

Questions 14 and 15: The science – is it or should it be contested?

Is it to be expected that the specific skills available for sustainable planning and construction will always remain a local matter, or dependent on specific negotiated agreements, as in the cases noted by Ludlow (Chapter 3) and Scheck et al. (Chapter 7)? Or is there a possibility, as implied by Roberts (Chapter 6), that universal systems can be introduced?

The chapters in this volume suggest the predominance of particularity, albeit within some very general aims. The literature review in the Introduction (Chapter 1) showed that the definition of sustainability in development has long been contested, and our authors' research suggests that this looseness of intellectual boundaries is being translated into practice. Sustainable development is a global problem. But Fudge (Foreword) shows that even in the European Union (where aims are more widely agreed than in other parts of the global community), divergence of implementation has been the inevitable consequence of the methods of international cooperation adopted.

But particularity of this kind may also be desirable. As a late member of the BEQUEST 'extranet' warned:

> As governance (regulations, standards, codes, financial instruments, etc.) changes to become more international and pervasive, local practices may be sacrificed, even when the codes are based on performance. Regulations and other forms of governance will require close scrutiny to ensure they do accommodate local culture and do not homogenise the built environment.
>
> (Cook 2003: 362)

The case studies reported in this book suggest that such homogeneity has yet to arrive. Instead particularity, arising from variations in history, geography and culture, remains widespread. This opens up an interesting line of inquiry. To what extent does the professionalisation of sustainable urban development need to be universally homogeneous or locally specific in order to be effective. In practice, this may be a false antithesis since there are likely to be elements that should be universal alongside others that should be local. On the basis of the evidence presented in this book, it is not yet clear which elements are which.

At the front of this volume, the BEQUEST Network was reported as emphasising the idea that sustainable urban development is a process, rather than a final product. In this book, we have taken up the call from the European Expert Group, to see what is happening in the 'transition' towards sustainable urban development. It seems evident from the reports of chapter authors that this transition is incomplete, with uneven development across the European states examined despite pan-EU commitments to policy statements and positions. The pursuit of sustainable development is clearly being framed as a collective European journey. So does it matter that different states are travelling at different rates or even heading in slightly different directions? Should homogeneity be our goal? Or should particularity be defended, even cherished? In short, should we still be asking the normative question, where should we (individually and jointly) go from here?

Writing on why the European Union has been successful to date, Leonard (2005: 10) has suggested that the Union is itself a journey with no destination and that its lack of single vision is the key to its strength. Its genius, he argued, has been:

> To develop a 'European invisible hand' that allows an orderly European society to emerge from each country's national interest . . . leaving national institutions outwardly intact but inwardly transformed.
>
> (Leonard 2005: 13)

In this way, the European Union has not aimed to establish a single model of human progress. Instead, Leonard (2005: 17) claimed it is about allowing diverse and competing cultures to live together in peace. If Leonard is correct, then allowing sustainable development to unfold at different rates and in different directions within the framework of a shared set of European values would map on to both the Union's founding objectives and its subsequent modus operandi.

REFERENCES

Cook, J. (2003) Understanding delivery processes. In R.J. Cole and R. Lorch (eds) *Buildings, Culture and Environment: Informing Local and Global Practices*. Oxford: Blackwell.

Leonard, M. (2005) *Why Europe will Run the 21st Century*. London: Fourth Estate.

Index